Context and Cognition: Interpreting Complex Behavior

Gordon R. Foxall
Cardiff University

D1153616

CONTEXT PRESS

Reno, NV

iv

Context and Cognition: Interpreting Complex Behavior

Paperback   pp. 158

Library of Congress Cataloging-in-Publication Data

Foxall, G. R.
    Context and cognition : interpreting complex behavior / Gordon R.
Foxall.– 1st ed.
        p. cm.
Includes bibliographical references.
    ISBN 1-878978-46-2 (pbk.)
    1. Behaviorism (Psychology) I. Title.
BF199.F69 2004
150.19'43–dc22

                                        2003023282

© 2004 CONTEXT PRESS
933 Gear Street, Reno, NV   89503-2729

Printed in the United States of America

Context and Cognition: Interpreting Complex Behavior

Table of Contents

Preface

He who knows only his own side of the case knows little of that.

(John Stuart Mill, 1859)

The authority exercised by schools of thought within the social scientific disciplines often seems a counter-productive consequence of the compartmental-ization of knowledge, inimical to intellectual vision if only because every way of seeing is a way of not seeing. It is, nevertheless, what this essay celebrates. For, unlike religious and political ideologies which can be imposed by force upon their chosen adherents, scientific ideas naturally evoke their antitheses and do battle with them. Unless such an idea is powerfully stated, unless the evidence for it is articulated with vigor, it is unlikely to bring forth the combative reaction upon which intellectual progress depends. The view that methodologies come and go over time, replacing one another in a process of paradigmatic conflict and supersession, holds sway over many social scientists. It is a view reflected in the common but superficial understanding that behaviorism has given way to cognitivism in psychology and that there is no going back. However, to the contrary, intellectual progress in social science relies heavily on the clash of extant theories, paradigms, and methodologies as well as on the more linear accumulation of knowledge that takes place within each. The co-existence of competing frameworks of conceptualization and analysis, far from providing evidence that psychology is a pre-paradigmatic field of inquiry that is yet to attain the status of mature science, is vitally necessary to the growth of knowledge. (Cf. Feyerabend, 1975; Kuhn, 1970). Such growth requires, however, that the adherents of the rival approaches interact, consider their several positions and methods, and are sufficiently open-minded to appreciate the intellectual challenges posed by synthesis and integration as opposed to the cozy acceptance of this or that locally-established world-view. Such interaction aids the process in which one paradigm impinges on, but never replaces, another, producing new syntheses, innovative predictions, and more satisfying explanations, none of which would be forthcoming but for the initial clash.

But a clash of ideas is not a war. The intellectual is an arena in which no one need be hurt by friendly fire, and there need be no other kind. An essay is an attempt, neither a treatise nor a manifesto. In so designating what follows, I draw attention to the tentativeness of knowledge and argument. Holding our views tenaciously is essential to the fruitful interaction of our cherished theories with others', but it is not the point of the exercise. A hundred years from now even our devoutest disciples, if we had them, would smile at our present schemes: perhaps we have something to learn from them.

And so, to the point.

Whilst the general wisdom has it that behaviorism is dead, it not only survives but is intellectually active in areas such as psychological theory, the analysis of language and cognition, and behavioral economics. It is a successful, albeit limited, source of behavioral science. Its chief difficulty arises when its practitioners look out from their laboratory windows and attempt to explain the complexities of human behavior that will never be amenable to direct experimental investigation. Behavior analysis has failed to establish a methodology of interpretation to deal fully with such complexity. The message of this essay is that it cannot do so without embracing intentional explanation in the form of an interpretive overlay that plugs the gaps in its explanations of life beyond the lab.

The science of which behaviorism is the philosophy has produced not only a unique experimental analysis of behavior but also an array of applications to social and economic practice, and a basis of interpretation from which complex activities such as those involved in human economic behavior can be accurately predicted. It would be a travesty if the general wisdom prevailed to the extent of eclipsing these accomplishments. But the gaps remain: radical behaviorist interpretation is unable to deal with the personal level of explanation (at which an individual knows what pain is without being able to analyze it further, a level on which physiological accounts of pain cannot operate), or with the problem of why behavior persists in the absence of the immediate rewarding consequences that form the central plank in behaviorism's explanatory scheme, or with the need to delimit the range of consequences that can reliably account for complex behavior. The attribution to individuals of desires and beliefs ("intentional ascription") can perform these functions in the absence of which behavioral interpretation both founders and flounders. But the resulting methodology, which has the potential to unify aspects of behaviorism and cognitive psychology, is subtle and not without irony.

There seems on the surface little hope of compromise between psychologists who are willing to attribute mental functioning to both humans and nonhumans, and those for whom behavior is always the result of non-cognitive learning and environmental history. Nevertheless, despite the tendency of behaviorists and cognitivists to misunderstand and disparage one another when in truth neither of their systems of thought is complete without the other, it is possible to find a new resting place for the debate in which they currently assume opposing positions. The differences between their methodologies, which revolve around the meanings they attribute to the term *intentional behavior,* have also the potential to unite them. The paradox is that the brand of behaviorism which is the central theme of the book, Skinner's *radical* behaviorism, appears fundamentally antithetical to the approach which can rescue it, Dennett's "intentional stance."

To those behaviorists who define thinking, deciding, believing and other cognitive activities as behaviors, albeit private, that are ontologically similar and subject to the same causal factors as public behaviors, intentional behavior is no more or less than the behavior that these events constitute. Hence Skinner (1974) portrays thinking, knowing, believing, and the like simply as "covert behavior." This is of course an a priori assumption necessary to sustain a particular philosophy of psychology as it seeks to broaden its range of application from the experimental laboratory to the interpretation of everyday behavior, and it is not subject to direct empirical evaluation. The other meaning of *intentional behavior* is behavior that can be explained fully only in terms of the ascription of intentional content, particularly desiring and believing. It is not that this behavior is *caused by* cognitive events in some mechanistic fashion: rather that understanding and perhaps predicting the behavior requires the ascription to it of cognitive content or intentionality. In this vein, Dennett (1978, p. 271) defines an intentional system, which might be a person, an animal or a machine such as a chess-playing computer, as one "whose behavior can be (at least sometimes) explained and predicted by relying on ascriptions to the system of beliefs and desires (and other intentionally characterized features) – what I will call intentions here, meaning to include hopes, fears, intentions, perceptions, expectations, etc."

Whilst this essay is generally concerned to clarify the relationship between these understandings of intentional behavior, it is largely concerned with the authors mentioned and their explanatory systems: that is, with *radical* behaviorism, a philosophy of psychology that invokes the first definition, in relation to Dennett's intentionally-based approach which provides a basis for the currently far more dominant social cognitive psychology. Differentiating the meanings of these portrayals of intentional behavior and appreciating their place in diverse styles of scientific discourse is prerequisite to understanding the symbiotic association between behavior analysis and cognitivism. The methodology of Skinner's paradigm is constructed on what we may call the *contextual* stance, the view that *behavior is predictable in so far as it is assumed to be environmentally determined; specifically, in so far as it is under the control of a learning history that represents the reinforcing and punishing consequences of similar behavior previously enacted in settings similar to that currently encountered.* In evaluating the exploitation of this methodological perspective in practice, it is essential to recall that modern behavior analysis, no longer confined to the rat and pigeon psychology that prevailed during the heyday of behaviorism, nowadays treats subject areas that lie at the very heart of cognitive psychology, among them thinking, decision making and language. Its proponents claim that radical behaviorism is sufficient to deal with these phenomena, indeed with all human and animal behavior, on its own terms. That means without resort to "mentalistic" concepts such as beliefs, attitudes and intentions which are the very stuff of modern information processing views of behavioral causation. Such views, which predominate in contemporary cognitive psychology, encapsulate an altogether different, indeed incommensurable, stance. The *intentional* stance (Dennett, 1978, 1983, 1987a) claims that *the behavior of systems such as people and computers can be predicted from the desires and beliefs, and other intentional, idioms, that can be rationally attributed to them.*

We shall return to both stances. For now it is enough to state the major question raised in this essay: whether the conceptual independence of behavior analysis can be maintained without its practitioners' adopting the countervailing stance in order to predict and explain complex human behavior. This extends the success criterion of behavioral science beyond mere prediction and control/influence into the realm of explanation and understanding. Putting prediction on the pedestal goes too far. As the physicist, David Deutsch (1977, p. 6) puts it, "Prediction is not the purpose of science, it is part of the characteristic method of science." Prediction without understanding the nature of the world is in any case a highly limited goal of science and the elevation of prediction to occupy the sole position of importance in science may be antithetical to progress. As he further says, "Whereas an incorrect prediction automatically renders the underlying explanation unsatisfactory, a correct prediction says nothing at all about the underlying explanation. Shoddy explanations that yield correct predictions are two a penny..." (p. 65). A catholicity of vision that has not generally characterized behavior theory must become part of the scientific purview of its adherents. Recognition that the psychological theory it provides is unlikely to be of universal and exclusive application, that it has bounds that are defined by its competitors, and that the exploration of those bounds can expedite the growth of knowledge, is essential to intellectual progress.

I thank Dermot Barnes-Holmes, Dawn Burton, Jean Foxall, Michael Kirton, Leonard Minkes, Jorge Oliveira-Castro, and John O'Shaughnessy for their comments. The book has some of its origins in a presentation to the annual conference of the Association for Behavior Analysis in New Orleans in 2001. I am grateful for encouragement received on that occasion, particularly from Norman Somach. Of course, the usual disclaimer applies. The essay is critical, within the spirit of academic discourse, of several behaviorist approaches to the interpretation of complex human behavior. My criticism of these theories is solely for their not accomplishing that for which they were never intended: a level of behavioral explanation over and above description, prediction and control. Nor is my criticism in any way *ad hominem*: the authors of these theories are after all the proverbial giants on whose shoulders the rest of us stand, even if we necessarily see things a little differently from that viewpoint.

Gordon Foxall
Penarth
September 2003

Chapter 1

Intentional Behavior

In Wolfgang Köhler's classic experiment, a banana was suspended well above the head of a chimpanzee so that it was inaccessible. After a period of confusion, in which jumping toward the fruit was of no avail, the chimp dragged a box into position, stood on it and reached the banana (Köhler, 1925). For decades, this behavior was widely attributed to the animal's exercise of "insight": the single movement in which *Koko* the chimp manipulated the box and obtained the banana was hailed as problem solving through "the sudden appearance of novel behavior" (Chance, 1960) that could only be attributed to the ape's mental processes. After all, the sequence of behavior exhibited none of the so-called "trial-and-error" learning or "behavioral shaping" by which behaviorists liked to explain actions as responses to environmental stimulation. The behaviorists argued that an organism's history of learning could account for its problem solving behavior, but in the absence of direct experimental evidence, their accounts seemed weak and speculative interpretations rather than genuine explanations (Chance, 1999).

Animals may well learn novel behavior as a result of "insight," but the alternative possibility – that learning history plays the decisive part – received emphatic support only some six decades after Köhler's work had been published. It came in the report of an experiment by Epstein, Kirshnit, Lanza and Rubin that appeared in *Nature* in 1984. These authors argued that if animals needed to have had specific experiences in order to show novel behavior – the basic behaviorist line – they would have to have acquired two skills: moving objects to specific targets, and climbing on those objects to reach other objects. Pigeons usually do neither and thus presented a model opportunity to assess how prior learning might influence problem solving: in this experiment, pushing and climbing on a box in order to peck a facsimile of a banana. The training histories of the birds were varied in the course of the experiment, the results of which indicated that, if insight were necessary for novel learning, it was highly dependent on experience. Just those birds that had learned both skills succeeded: those which had only learned to climb on to a box and to peck did not solve the problem, but those that had in addition learned to push a box toward a goal, randomly placed in the floor of the experimental chamber in the absence of the banana, did manage to do so. The behavior in question was certainly novel since the pigeons had not encountered the banana until the trial on which they used the box to get at it. But where was "insight"? As Chance (1999, p. 162) points out, "the appearance of a novel solution was shown to be the product of specific learning experiences – to physical, not mental, events."

Between these two pieces of research is suspended an intense debate among cognitive and behaviorist psychologists over the thought processes not of chimpanzees and pigeons but of human beings. It is a debate at the center of the philosophy of psychology between behaviorists and cognitivists who present a bewildering array of perspectives.

It's Only Words...

Indeed, there are so many behaviorisms, so many cognitivisms, that it is natural to inquire what definitively separates one from the rest. What are their boundaries? Perhaps most important of all, how are they related and what are the implications of one for another? My focus in this essay is *radical* behaviorism, "the area of philosophy, research and application that encompasses the experimental analysis of behavior, applied behavior analysis, operant psychology, operant conditioning, behaviorism, and Skinnerian psychology" (Vaughan, 1989, p. 97). Its essential methodology is to explicate behavior in terms of its contingent relationships with the consequences it produces, and associated environmental stimuli. Thus, "A behavioral contingency consists of a stimulus, a response, and the outcome the response produces in the presence of that stimulus" (Malott, 1986, p. 208). We can summarize the basic paradigm of behavior analysis, the "three-term contingency," as $S^D: R \rightarrow S^{R+}$ where S^D is a cue or *discriminative stimulus*, R is a response, and S^R is a reward or *reinforcing stimulus*. As Moore (1999, p. 48) points out, "This notation suggests that a discriminative stimulus (S^D) sets the occasion (:) for a response (R) to produce ($\rightarrow$) a reinforcing consequence (S^{R+})." (For a recent review, see Staddon & Cerutti, 2003).

The reasoning behind this paradigm need not be circular: Some behavior *operates* on the environment to produce consequences which govern its future rate of emission, predicting its frequency and providing means for its control. The explanation of this "operant" behavior lies in the contingencies of reinforcement and punishment, that is, the relationships among the behavior, its consequences, and stimuli in the presence of which the behavior is emitted. These discriminative stimuli do not elicit the behavior as in classical conditioning but set the occasion for its performance by signaling the consequences it is likely to have. Reinforcing consequences are those which increase the likelihood of the behavior's being emitted again; punishing consequences, those which reduce this probability. A behavioral response, the discriminative stimulus which sets the occasion for it, and its reinforcing and/or punishing outcomes comprise the three-term contingency. The essay explores whether this basic device is sufficient to account for all behavior, whether it is possible to make over all of psychology in its likeness, or whether it has boundaries beyond which alternative modes of prediction and explanation must be sought. The bounds of behaviorism are verbal: they can be set only by comparing the locutions employed by radical behaviorists with those utilized by proponents of alternative psychologies. An inevitable consequence of pursuing the bounds of behaviorism is that those of cognitivism will become clearer too since their frontiers are necessarily shared. In order to elaborate my thesis at this stage I must anticipate much of the case with which the remainder of the book is concerned even to the point of employing some terminology which may become clear to some readers only as the argument progresses. But a preliminary statement of what I am asserting and what I am not may nonetheless be useful. In pointing out that the bounds of behaviorism are verbal I wish only to argue that by employing particular locutions we may invite modes of explanation that appear distinct from that with which we started. However, if such a locution and explanatory mode makes no (or minimal) ontological demands and either aids predictive accuracy or fills gaps in our explanations of behavior we might choose to embrace it. At the very least we should be aware of them and the linguistic usages from which they arise. If however we find that we are unable to convey the theories and findings of one explanatory system other then by borrowing the locutions that belong to or imply another, we should give thought to the possibility that our original philosophy of science stands in need of some modification.

Radical behaviorism has sought to differentiate itself from other neobehaviorisms and from cognitive psychology by avoiding locutions that embrace intentionality. This has worked well in its attempts to build an extensional science of behavior based on an experimental analysis. An experimental analysis is almost by definition concerned with behavior occurring in a relatively closed setting. The exclusion of non-operant explanation of such behavior is favored by the small range of variables that can be shown to control simple responding in such circumstances. The kinds of behavior to which radical behaviorists have sought to apply an interpretation based on the principles gained in the laboratory are again almost by definition subject to a large range of influences from which it is much more difficult to abstract those that are particularly salient in predicting, controlling and explaining the behavior in question. In moving from the confines of the laboratory to the task of explaining such complexity in operant terms, radical behaviorists have extended the locutions they employ to make possible (not inevitable) an intentionalistic mode of explanation. They have necessarily had to include private events, thoughts and feelings, in their accounts and the forms of language in which these events are described involve *aboutness* which is the hallmark of the intentional. We do not simply think and feel: we think and feel *about* something. Recognition of this can make available a new dimension to the interpretation of behavior. Whilst it is antithetical to radical behaviorism on one level it can also complement it in a way that plugs the gaps in its interpretations.

It is open to radical behaviorists to maintain that thoughts and feelings are simply part of the stimulus setting within which behavior occurs – discriminative stimuli, establishing operations or derived stimuli – that influence interpreted behavior just as these stimuli control responses in the laboratory. I have no argument with this and would not wish to discourage the research programs which stem from these views. But I would point out that an intentional interpretation can be just as feasible and permissible once we admit thinking and feeling to our account of behavior. And it may prove useful in generating some kinds of radical behaviorist interpretation which at present lack conviction. Such adoption of the intentional is a linguistic phenomenon, one which behaviorist philosophers such as Quine have simply sought to ignore on the grounds that it cannot be fitted into an extensional understanding of the logic of science. But it is a legitimate one nonetheless for those who can take on board the intensional nature of sentences of a particular form. I wish to show some of the implications of doing this in the context of radical behaviorist interpretation and shall argue that by embracing the intentional behavior analysts may secure a more adequate explanation of complex behavior without making ontological concessions to cognitive explanation. Behavior analysis can furnish an extensional science of behavior based on the experimental analysis of behavior in the laboratory. It can also inspire and produce a variety of sources of operant interpretation which retain the extensional stance each with its own sources of substantiation whether based on experimental or nonexperimental method. But its interpretations, as opposed to its predictions, will not I believe be as comprehensive as they might be without recognition of the implications of an intentionalistic overlay added to the findings and theories of its extensionally based investigations.

I have elsewhere sought to establish the conceptual bounds of behaviorism as opposed to cognitive psychology by means of a comparison of the underlying philosophical and methodological stances on which they respectively rely (Foxall, 1999). The current work again explores the methodological bounds of radical behaviorism in contradistinction to cognitive psychology. It argues further that the eschewal of propositional content is the defining characteristic of radical behaviorism and that this distinction demarcates radical behaviorism from the alternative neo-behaviorisms of Tolman and Hull as well as from cognitivism. This delineation differs from the more usual assertion that it is the avoidance of mediating events and processes that demarcates radical behaviorism. Whereas that paper explored the conceptual bounds of radical behaviorism as the means of discriminating this system from cognitive accounts, the present analysis is concerned primarily with the methodological bounds of behaviorism. The earlier analysis gave rise to the possibility of two psychologies, each providing an inescapable and essential approach to explanation. The present analysis suggests that each of these methodologies is intrinsically contingent on the other, and that a psychology of social complexity requires both.

The End from the Beginning

Although there are many cognitivisms, many behaviorisms, and although the stories of all their relationships and connections will prove fascinating when they come to be written, I concentrate here on one example of each: those which need each other the most. Even so, in presenting each as a *sine qua* non of the other's explanatory completeness, I am critical where necessary of deficiencies that inhere in each. In synopsis, the argument proceeds as follows. "Intentional behavior" can mean two things. To Skinnerians, it is the behavior constituted by thinking, feeling, intending, believing, hoping, etc., for radical behaviorism understands these things as behaviors. For Denettians, it is behavior that can be predicted by the use of the intentional stance. Between these alternatives lies a spectrum of varying possibilities for the philosophy and methodology of the behavioral and social sciences. It is the difference between an approach to behavior based on the contextual stance which in its turn is founded upon an extensional understanding of science and one based on the intentional stance in which a heuristic interpretation is used to overlay extensional findings and theories in order to produce an account of human behavior at the personal level. Radical behaviorism's capacity to generate an extensional experimental science of behavior in is not in doubt: it is when radical behaviorism attempts to provide an account of behavior that is not amenable to an experimental analysis that questions of its explanatory adequacy arise. In particular the status of private events, the inclusion of which provides the explicit definition of radical as opposed to other behaviorisms, calls for careful examination. The delimitation of scientific schools is a matter of identifying the verbal usages unique to each. Cognitive explanation requires intentional explanation in order to delineate the mental which is its peculiar preserve, the recognition that mental terms have the characteristic of aboutness. Dennett proposes that extensional science provides a necessary but insufficient basis for psychology: psychology requires that a personal level of analysis be made available in addition to the subpersonal level provided by physiology. This is done by adding a heuristic level of interpretation to the theories and findings of extensional physiological science. The definitional essence of radical behaviorism which has not been made explicit by its exponents is its avoidance of intentional explanation, of intentional idioms as part of its locutions, of propositional attitudes. This demarcates it from cognitivism and also from the neobehaviorisms of Hull and Tolman. It does not rule out mediating events as part of its interpretations: indeed as the practice of radical behaviorists who have engaged in interpretation indicates such theoretical terms are in fact unavoidable.

Central to my thesis is that these stances cannot operate independently: at some level each makes use of the other. I argue that social cognitive psychology employs the contextual stance as a prelude to its ascription of intentional content. Hence, the user of the intentional stance faces the problem on what basis the ascription of intentional content should be based. Webb argues that in humans it must be based at least in part on the verbal behavior of those whose behavior is being predicted. Second, and connectedly, the manner in which attitude theorists and researchers have resolved the problem of a lack of empirically demonstrable attitudinal–behavioral consistency is to solicit verbal responses from those whose behavior they wish to predict which reflects their learning histories and the stimulus settings they currently face. From these responses they infer their subjects' attitudes and intentions and other cognitive precursors of action. I argue that radical behaviorist interpretation contains explanatory gaps that can be filled only by intentional ascription. Behaviorism's lack of a personal level of analysis leaves gaps in its explanations (though it does not affect its capacity to predict behavior, which is generally on a par with that of intentionalistic psychology). The gaps are (1) the lack of a personal level of explanation itself which leads to an undue reliance on an empirically unavailable learning history as a basis of interpretation of current behavior, (2) an inability to account for the continuity of behavior, and (3) an inability to delimit the reinforcement context of radical behaviorist interpretations by circumscribing the problem of equifinality. Not to acknowledge the gap, or to blithely assume that it will someday be bridged by the findings of physiological research, seems to me to evince not a scientific attitude but a dogma. Equally, to jump to the conclusion that a cognitive theory or any particular information processing model fills the gap in some ultimate sense betrays the same assertive stance. The conclusion that has been drawn is, as all knowledge must be, tentative, but it seems the best hypothesis to advance in order first to acknowledge the gap left by behavior analysis, to promote research which will help fill it with extensional scientific findings, and to promote the cause of radical behaviorist interpretation. All of this can be accomplished without making unwarranted ontological assumptions about the nature of the gap and whatever can conceivably fill it. It is the essence of intentional behaviorism.

A rapprochement between the intentional and contextual stances can be accomplished by applying Dennett's logic for arriving at a personal level of analysis but substituting the super-personal level of analysis provided by extensional behavioral science for physiology. Adding an intentional overlay to the findings and theories of operant psychology leads to a more comprehensive explanation of behavior than either radical behaviorism or Dennett's "physiological psychology" can provide. The incorporation of sub-, personal and super-personal levels into a single scheme of behavioral explanation makes possible a complete personal level psychology of social behavior. Hence, an extensional radical behaviorist interpretation is perfectly feasible in addition to the social behavioral science proposed here for purposes of prediction, but not as a comprehensive explanation. The resulting social behavioral science is a-ontological: no conclusions are drawn with respect to the veracity of any particular cognitive theory or as Dennett calls them sub-personal cognitive psychologies. By adopting the intentional stance in this way radical behaviorist interpretation does not commit itself to a cognitive ontology: it merely acknowledges that its explanations are incomplete in the absence of the personal level of explanation which an intentionalistic heuristic overly makes possible. The result is a new model for radical behaviorist interpretation: *intentional behaviorism*, which combines the contextual stance of behavior analysis with the heuristic overlay of the intentional.

Radical Behaviorism and Intentionality

Radical behaviorists usually claim, following Skinner (1945) that what distinguishes *radical* behaviorism is its incorporation of private events, thoughts and feelings. This certainly sets it apart from Watsonian behaviorism and the neobehaviorisms of Tolman and Hull. However, more important in distinguishing radical behaviorism is its attempt to base psychology on an extensional approach to science, something that sets it apart not only from those neobehaviorisms but also from any cognitive approach that embraces intentional explanation (Smith, 1994). Two concerns arise. The first is whether the inclusion of private events into the operant account of human behavior sufficiently compensates for its attempted omission of the intentionalistic inner states (whatever the ontological basis on which they rest) that are found in cognitivism and neobehaviorisms. This is to ask: what is the status of a science of human behavior that treats thoughts and feelings as nonmental private events, collateral responses under the same external contingency control as public behaviors? The second is whether a purely extensional approach, i.e., one which excludes from proper scientific discourse terms such as desiring and believing, is sufficient to form the basis of a psychology of human behavior that deals not only with publicly available responses but responses that are observable only by the person to whom they are occurring – that is, private events again. This is to ask: can intentionality be avoided in a science of psychology that takes private experience as part of its subject matter?

In seeking the bounds of behaviorism and its relationship to intentionalistic psychology, it is impossible to ignore the contribution of Daniel Dennett whose work suggests indirectly a rapprochement between cognitivism and behaviorism which he fails to take up directly. Dennett has argued that by attributing propositional content to the findings of an extensional science, namely physiology, it is possible to account more comprehensively for behaviors (such as pain) than is possible within the confines of physiology alone. Yet, despite the fact that such an enterprise is implicit in his criticism of behaviorism to the effect that it is incapable of an adequate explanation of behavior without accepting the intentional idioms into its system, he does not pursue the possibility that behavior analysis can provide an extensional basis for a social cognitive psychology that proceeds by overlaying intentional content on the findings of that science of behavior. Rather, he argues that behaviorism cannot provide a basis for psychology since it has failed as a predictive behavioral science. There is a missed opportunity here. A more critical and systematic approach to the nature and methodology of radical behaviorist interpretation would have revealed to behaviorists and intentionalists alike its shortcomings and its potential as the purported emanation of a fully-fledged extensional science. The missed opportunity has not only stymied the development of radical behaviorist interpretation, leaving it open to the ridicule of non-behaviorists who have drawn attention to its open-ended identification of stimuli and responses as they are required to support the behaviorist account of complexity: it has also had deleterious repercussions for the development of psychology as a whole. For, not only has behaviorism not failed as a method of prediction, at least within the experimental space where its scientific credentials are worthy of respect, but its methodology may be the sole way in which psychology can deal with intentionality.

Dennett's *intentional stance* proposes that an organism's behavior is predictable from the beliefs and desires it ought to have by virtue of its rationality and its current position. The use of this stance in, for instance, the realm of cognitive ethology (Dennett, 1983, 1987b, 1988; cf. Allen & Bekoff, 1997; Seyfarth & Cheney, 2002; Shettleworth, 1998) can proceed only by making assumptions – based on observation or deduction – about the organism's learning history and the opportunities presented by its current behavior setting, and this requires the prior exploitation of either the observed temporal and spatial context in which the organism has existed/ exists and/or the *contextual stance*, a philosophical position based on the scientific analysis of environmentally-determined behavior. The methodology of the intentional stance requires the prior application of the findings of extensional behavioral science. This is moreover precisely the way in which social cognitive psychology proceeds as witness contemporary attitude theory and research. The increased capacity demonstrated over the last three decades of attitude measures to predict behavior is attributable to their authors' incorporation into their models of variables relating to respondents' learning histories and the social and physical settings in which their behavior takes place. This reliance of intentionalistic psychology upon a *contextual stance* suggests a resolution of how the intentional and extensional approaches are related in the context of the psychology of social cognition. The implication for cognitive psychology is that it is logically and methodologically founded upon the ascription of content to the findings of extensional behavioral science. But what are the implications for behaviorism, notably the radical behaviorism that uniquely incorporates private events into its explanatory mode?

Three possibilities arise. First, that radical behaviorism is a necessary but insufficient basis for a psychology of complex behavior; second, that *private events* raise many problems of psychological explanation that they are helpless to solve; and, third, that the social cognitive approach (that is, the attribution of content to the findings of extensional behavioral science) is essential to the production and evaluation of plausible interpretations based on the findings of behavior analysis. I argue for all three.

Interdependencies

The bounds of behaviorism are drawn in three ways, each of which reveals the dependency of radical behaviorist interpretation on the intentional stance. The first is defined by the level of analysis which a radical behaviorist interpretation based directly upon the findings and theories of an unreconstructed behavior analysis is capable of generating. The second is determined by the inability of behavior analysis to account for the continuity of behavior on its own terms. Behavior analysis, an approach to psychology that is staunchly founded upon the contextual stance, cannot in practice do without the intentional stance if its interpretations are to be valid. The third is required in order to delimit the context within which the causes of behavior are located in such an interpretation. Taken together, these means of delineating the nature and the scope of radical behaviorist interpretation help define the relationship between behavioral and cognitive psychology and also promote unity among psychologists who for too long have described themselves exclusively as "behaviorists" or "cognitivists" and in doing so have overlooked the interdependencies of these two perspectives. Those interdependencies arise also from the recent development of social cognitive psychology. The traditional approach has been for social psychologists to seek the explanation of behavior entirely in the mental, in the attitudes and intentions and other cognitive processes that are deemed to prefigure overt action. But, since context is always relevant to explaining behavior, why has it been so often ignored? Is it that psychologists have sought to emulate the "physics that never was" by searching for universal laws which, by definition, are true regardless of context, for example, "when metals are heated, they expand"? There are no such "laws" in social science simply because context always is important. This, after all, is why the economist is constantly having to speak of "other things being equal." Yet there has been a subtle change in social psychology that has recognized, albeit not always explicitly, the influence of context.

Although there is a traditional tendency for cognitive psychologists to seek asituational determinants of behavior in intrapersonal mental states and events, social cognitivists who have studied for instance the relationship among attitudes, intentions and behavior have increasingly adopted the contextual stance, prior to the application of the intentional stance, in order to ensure the accuracy of their behavioral predictions. Just as radical behaviorism is unable to generate interpretations of complex human behavior at the required personal level or to delineate the role of contextual influences on behavior without invoking the intentional stance, so social cognitivism cannot ascertain the appropriate desires and beliefs of the human systems it seeks to predict in the absence of prior knowledge of their learning histories and the stimulus contexts of their current behavior settings. The relationship between behaviorism and cognitivism is of course many-faceted. Any book-length treatment necessarily delimits its subject matter and I have explicitly confined my terms of reference. Whilst they are inadequate frameworks to discuss and debate cognitive behavior in all its manifestations, they are sufficient to illustrate the implications of an extensional science of behaviorism for cognitive explanation and, more controversially, those of mental ascription for behaviorist explanation. In the process of making explicit the reliance of social cognitivists on the prior exercise of the contextual stance, the analysis draws more clearly the bounds of behaviorism and in the process delineates the cognitive task more sharply.

Modus Operandi

Malcolm (1977, p. 85) writes that "... [T]he dispute over the place of behaviorism in psychology is fundamentally a philosophical issue," and although that view is not contested, this book is written from the viewpoint of the psychologist. Moreover, the location of behaviorism in psychology must, for the sake of the theoretical development of psychology as a science, be treated first and foremost as a psychological issue, one related to the methodological sophistication of psychology. There sometimes remains a style of analysis that frequently marks the writings of philosophers especially when addressing theoretically what others approach in a predominantly empirical way. The "manner of philosophers" – as acquaintance with the history of philosophy confirms – is to break down each system of thought into its most basic form and then to render a devastating critique of it such that it can no longer apparently stand. And so on to the next system, and the next, until the author comes to his or her own favored philosophy which is presented as the answer to all philosophical questions. But, of course, no so-treated philosophy lies down for long, since for every competent intellectual destroyer there is at least one equally competent supporter. Nor does each favored philosophy itself stand longer than it takes another proficient purveyor of the manner of philosophers to attack it.

That I do not adopt this strategy in regard to Dennett's philosophy of intentionality does not imply that I am unaware of the criticisms that have been leveled at it, nor that I am not sensible of the alternative portrayals in the philosophy of mind of intentionality, nor yet that I do not know at least some of the many other approaches to the explanation of behavior. (I draw attention to a number of them but do not here pursue any at length.) It is simply that like many others I find virtue in Dennett's approach and believe that it is capable of contributing to a problem in psychology that I find particularly important and apparently intractable: how to present an acceptable interpretation of "complex" behavior, that which is not susceptible to an experimental analysis, according to the principles derived by behavior analysts from their laboratory-based studies of simpler behavioral systems.

The approach to the growth of knowledge assumed here is explicitly in consonance with the methodological pluralism advocated by Feyerabend (1975) while stopping short of his "anything goes" dictum. Against the popular view that scientific progress is the straightforward result of the continual accumulation of facts within a given framework of conception and analysis, Kuhn hypothesizes that "mature" sciences, notably physics, develop by means of dramatic paradigmatic supersession. The revolutionary replacement of a previously productive paradigm has profound implications for the concepts that are deemed relevant, the canons of theoretical judgment which are applicable and the appropriate practical methods of data collection, techniques of analysis and procedures of interpretation. The paradigm which provides the current framework for "normal science" tends to become a fiercely-protected and restrictive superstructure to which the scientific community compels obedience. By contrast, Feyerabend (1970) argues that competing theories proliferate not intermittently, during the periods of crisis that precede the revolutionary overthrow of one paradigm by another, but all the time as a constant feature of scientific investigation and discovery. Hence, he writes that "Science as we know it is not a temporal succession of normal periods and periods of proliferation; it is their juxtaposition. Science has its normal and proliferative modes but their relationship is accurately described as one of simultaneity and interaction" (p. 209). The deliberate proliferation of competing theories produces an active interplay of various tenaciously held views which is necessary to progress, at least in the sense of the growth of knowledge (Feyerabend, 1975). This method has three components (Valentine, 1992, pp. 98–9): *counter-inductivism* (the evidence required to test one theory may be adduced only through the agency of a competing, even incompatible, theory), *the principle of proliferation* (it is important to provide a critical counterpoint from which theories can be evaluated in order that they may be developed and refined), and *a pluralistic methodology* (the growth of knowledge depends on innovativeness in the development of theoretical and technical approaches). Feyerabend (1962) shows that only the advent of the kinetic theory revealed the inadequacies of classical thermodynamics, for instance. Brown (2001, p. 89) points out that "No amount of direct testing [of the kind proposed by Popper] would have sufficed to make its problems manifest." Hence,

> *Theory testing is comparative.* We do not take a theory directly to nature to test its correctness. Instead we test a theory comparatively in the sense that we look to both nature and its rivals. A phenomenon becomes evidentially relevant to some theory when a rival theory can account for it (*ibid.*; italics in original.)

Whilst, as Brown notes, the "epistemological anarchy" that Feyerabend came to advocate contains elements of trivialization of what scientists do, his principle of pluralism is valuable and it is within this approach to the growth of knowledge that the present argument proceeds.

Among the attacks on behaviorism that have proliferated over the last century, there have been a handful of thoughtful rebuttals, among which that of Zuriff (1985) stands out. However, there is little to be gained by rehearsing the standard philosophical arguments for and against intentionalism and behaviorism for their own sake. More important is to concentrate on the practical difficulties of conducting a radical behaviorist interpretation of complex behavior without invoking the intentional stance. In the course of doing this, it will become apparent that intentionalists are forced to use the contextual stance in order to carry out their scientific progress. Hence, the symbiosis which is the inevitable relationship between these philosophies of explanation.

Rationale

Resolving the contradiction that behaviorist and intentionalist standpoints present might still seem a matter of empirical science alone, especially as both behaviorism as presented by Skinner and intentionalism as presented by Dennett are pragmatic approaches that rest on the accurate prediction of behavior. It might be argued that the theoretical stance that gives rise to the more accurate predictions and the more effective means of controlling behavior ought to be judged the more acceptable approach to explanation. Why, then, if the ultimate criterion is empirical science, should behavior analysts and cognitive psychologists get involved in the philosophical bases of these methodologies? There are five reasons that seem particularly apposite to the present investigation.

The first is that radical behaviorism rests upon a distinctive explanatory basis, and this has implications for theoretical and empirical work in both behavior analysis and cognitive psychology. It is valuable for researchers within both frameworks to appreciate what radical behaviorism uniquely entails (if only to comprehend fully its implications for the interpretation of their findings). This is what is meant by "delineating radical behaviorism." But it cannot be done in a vacuum. Because scientific explanation is verbal behavior, the bounds of behaviorism are necessarily linguistic. But our own verbalizations are insufficient to the task. Because psychological science is competitive, radical behaviorism contends with alternative explanatory systems to provide a plausible and comprehensive account of a subject matter to which many other than ourselves also lay claim. Any analysis of scientists' verbal behavior which attempts to delimit one of the available approaches must, therefore, take the form of a comparative examination of the locutions of practitioners from rival schools.

Second, this unique explanatory stance is the source of a profound philosophical disagreement between radical behaviorism and cognitive science. The intentional stance which underpins cognitivism claims, in essence, that the behavior of intentional systems can be predicted based on the desires and beliefs that can be rationally attributed to them. This is a mentalistic philosophy of science that seeks to understand and predict the behavior of individuals and other systems by attributing to them interpersonal states and events. By contrast, the contextual stance on which radical behaviorism is founded is based on the understanding that behavior is predictable in so far as it is shown to be environmentally determined. Behavior is to be understood and predicted in terms of the stimulus conditions that are consequent upon it and which signal its likelihood. In spite of claims that little if anything nowadays separates radical behaviorist and cognitive psychologies (e.g., Overskeid, 1995), there are fundamental differences in the ways in which these philosophies approach the explanation of behavior which render them incommensurable (Foxall, 1999). The difference is verbal. Intentional explanation deals in sentences that are *about* something else, sentences that say that the subject believes *that* something is the case, or thinks *about* our vacation, and so on. The philosophical meaning of intentionality with which we are concerned here is that it refers to this *aboutness* of our verbal expressions. Hence, sentences based on the intentional idiom typically take the form: "Mary believes *that* the man at the desk is Neil Armstrong." Such intentional sentences are said to be referentially opaque meaning that a term that is equivalent to "Neil Armstrong" may not be substitutable for this name in the sentence. We cannot say, having heard the sentence about what Mary believes, that "Mary believes *that* the man at the desk is the first man to step on the moon," for Mary may not know that Neil Armstrong was the first man on the moon. However, sentences within the extensional idiom that marks the contextual stance display referential transparency: "That planet is the fourth from the sun" can be consistently substituted for "That planet is Mars." This linguistic difference has given rise to a dichotomy between the mental and the physical that is often used to differentiate the realm of natural science from that of psychology including the science of behavior. We shall return to this distinction in the context of Dennett's work but this overview is sufficient for the present. (Among highly accessible introductions to these ideas are those of Dennett (1996), Heil (1998), and Symons (2002). For broader discussion, see Rosenberg (1988). For contrary positions to Dennett's, see, again among several, Dretske (1988), Stich (1983), and Searle (1999).)

As a result, behaviorists and cognitivists happily talk past each other, and the necessary rapprochement between them is as elusive as ever. Scheerer (1996, p. 171) writes that: "…[B]ehavior analysis needs "inner processes" if it wants to realize its own program, that is, the functional analysis of behavior aimed at prediction and control. I accept Skinner's basic premise that private behavior, of both a conscious (i.e., rule-based) and an unconscious (i.e., contingency-shaped) nature, arises as the result of differential reinforcement by the verbal community. Once acquired, however, "mental" processes take on a degree of autonomy that qualifies them as causes of behavior. Skinner's basic fault consists in conflating the (correct) thesis that inner processes are ultimately derived from overt behavior and interaction with the environment with the (incorrect) thesis that they do not play any causal role whatsoever. If behavior analysis is to survive at all, then it *must* turn cognitive."

But there is no indication of how this might be accomplished, no indication of how this epistemological turn might be performed.

Third, it is widely and persuasively argued that an extensional science of behavior is infeasible, that psychology is necessarily intentional. Admittedly, the claim that a science of behavior resting on the philosophical terms proposed by radical behaviorists is logically and methodologically impossible comes predominantly from cognitivists. But, except in behavior analytic circles, the cognitive argument is winning the battle. As Schnaitter (1999) intimates, part of the reason for that is behavior analysts' disdain for philosophical involvement. The issue of intentionality reveals the tendency of behaviorists to show either flight or fight reactions to the philosophical question it raises rather than to assert their unique explanatory position, the *contextual* stance. Faced with making sense of intentional explanation, some behaviorists tend either to dismiss the whole question as beneath their consideration, a meaningless intellectual escapade of cognitivists, or to attempt to meet the intentional position head on by trying to refute it. Sometimes they simply get on with the job of showing by experimental means that a non-intentional approach to behavioral science can work, leaving philosophy to those who have the time.

The challenge to behavior analysts is to demonstrate the capacity of radical behaviorism, as a philosophy of psychology, to show how an empirical behavioral science can predict its subject matter without resort to the propositional attitudes that are the stock in trade of intentionalism. If it can go further, by demonstrating (rather than merely asserting) that the contextual strategy is methodologically prior to the intentional strategy that underlies cognitive psychology, it will have begun to redress the philosophical balance that is undoubtedly tilted at present in favor of intentional explanation. Moreover, the resolution of this issue has implications for the procedure of radical behaviorist interpretation which behavior analysts cannot ignore if their science is to have significance beyond the walls of the laboratory. The challenge to cognitivists, as contenders for the prevailing paradigm, is to appreciate that they can similarly benefit from understanding the role of the contextual stance in their empirical and theoretical work. Unfortunately, exponents of the normal science component of knowledge are not so pressed as other contenders to underpin their paradigm philosophically. By rubbishing behaviorism rather than appreciating and meeting its arguments and the content of the science it produces, cognitive psychologists are in danger of missing the contextual basis of their endeavors. Most critics of behaviorism from a cognitivist viewpoint base their understanding of behavior analysis on a pre-1960s version of "Skinnerism" that is confined to the analysis of contingency-shaped behavior including Skinner's (1957) extrapolation from the animal laboratory to the complexities of human verbal behavior. It is rare for critics to have any awareness of Skinner's (1969b) conceptualization of rule-governed behavior, let alone knowledge of recent empirical and theoretical work on verbal behavior as symbolism such as is contained in the stimulus equivalence (Sidman, 1994), relational frame theory (Hayes, 1994), or naming (Horne & Lowe, 1996, 1997) paradigms. The number of scholars who speak of "Watson and Skinner's radical behaviorism" and otherwise show no understanding of the role of private events in the definition of radical behaviorism is dispiriting to say the least. (An example that has today fallen across my desk is Baars, 2003, but it is perhaps invidious to single out an author of this widespread ignorance).

Fourth, through non-involvement, behavior analysts are losing by default a debate to which they have much to contribute and from which they may gain substantially; equally, cognitivists are presenting a view of behavior which leaves it unsituated when both their empirical methodology and their required theoretical contribution require that behavior be appropriately contextualized. The level of debate, and hence of understanding, on both sides is often unsophisticated and uninformed. So, Skinner says of Dennett, "The underlying terms in Dennett's statements… are apparently offered as referring to cognitive and intentional states or acts. They can all be interpreted as referring to consequences." (Skinner, 1983, p. 378) As it stands, this is no more than an assertion that is unsupported by detailed argument, as is what Dennett says of Skinner: "Skinner's experimental design is supposed to eliminate the intentional, but it merely masks it." (Dennett, 1978, p. 15) The difference is that cognitivists can afford not to take behaviorists seriously because cognitivism now provides the normal science component of psychological science. But it is not in the interests of behaviorists to ignore the debate. This requires a more philosophically engaged approach than has usually been the case. As Schnaitter, 1999, p. 239) puts it: "At the very least behaviorists should consider the problem of intentionality to be a most interesting case of verbal behavior, not to be dismissed but to be explored and understood. The standard behavioristic line that the mental is the fictional is just not good enough."

Finally, there is the goal of intellectual diversity and the intellectual progress that is the result of the active interplay of competing theories (Feyerabend, 1975). There are times when behavior analysis and intentionalistic psychology reach the same conclusion (e.g., with respect to third-person accounts). It is important to understand how each system reaches this conclusion in its own way if we are to appreciate the differences in logical reasoning and methodology that each employs. It is also important to recognize that mutual agreement with respect to a conclusion does not necessarily mean that the conclusion should not be further examined. Philosophers and psychologists who belong to neither the cognitive nor the behaviorist camps may have a third take on the material that led to that conclusion and may conclude differently. We should know why. If they are wrong, we shall have strengthened our reasons for adopting and maintaining our own perspective; if they are right we have much to gain by knowing why and, if warranted, by incorporating their reasoning. Moreover, if one system of interpretation produces a particular state of affairs, perhaps a limitation of its capacity to explain some aspect or other of complex behavior, we may simply put that down to the inadequacies of that specific theoretical system. However, if more than one methodology is limited in this way, we have an opportunity to learn more about either methodology in general (and, perhaps, how it can be improved) or about the subject matter of which we are concerned to make sense. Our scientific integrity and our intellectual credentials demand the plurality of methodologies implicated in our quest.

The urgency of our addressing these themes is apparent from even brief consideration of the likely state of affairs should we fail to do so. The problem is not so much that intentionalists and contextualists have ignored one another but that they have avoided intellectual engagement of the kind necessary to resolve issues. The question of the relationships between the intentional and the contextual stances, for example, is important because the principal exponents of each position appear to think that their own approach is so inherently superior as to automatically refute the other without detailed consideration of its basis and ramifications. Hence, commenting on Dennett's (1983) intentional stance, Skinner (1983, p. 378) offers neither argument nor analysis but counter-assertion: "The underlying terms in Dennett's statements... are apparently offered as referring to cognitive and intentional states or acts. They can all be interpreted as referring to consequences." But where is the interpretation, where the examination of how cognitivists actually use intentional idioms, where the delineation of the crucial underlying differences in the philosophies of psychology offered by each school that recognizes that we come to know our own thesis only by knowing its antithesis? It is assertion of this kind that brings inquiry prematurely to an end. Dennett often offers little more than counter-assertion, too; he claims, for instance, without extensive argument, that establishing *what has happened?* or *what is the history of reinforcement?* is impossible "with a 'pure' (utterly non-interpretivist) investigation, without, that is to say, a healthy helping of adaptionist (or intentionalist) assumptions. This is because without answers to 'why' questions, we cannot begin to categorize *what has happened* into the right sort of parts" (Dennett, 1987a, p. 278). This is not an unimportant point, but it is a stance-laden remark unlikely to impress the implacable contextualist who can assert differently from the standpoint of the contextual stance. But elsewhere

Dennett's attack rests less upon straight assertion, more on a line of argument that cannot be answered by mere counter-assertion.

The intentional and contextual stances carry within themselves ontological and methodological assumptions that determine to a degree what is observed and how it is interpreted. It is not necessary to adopt the entire philosophical paraphernalia that accompanies the idea of the theory-ladenness of observation to appreciate that scientific behavior is somewhat influenced by *a priori* reasoning. The act of translation inherent in moving between a data language that describes observed phenomena and a theoretical language that renders them intelligible in a broader framework of analysis necessarily relies upon the guiding role of some philosophy of science or other. Only by making explicit the philosophical foundations of our work and by being aware of their alternatives can we rest assured that our interpretations are sensible. As we do so, the interdependencies of the intentional and the contextual are revealed: the way forward is not by battle and conflict alone but by mutual understanding and cooperation.

Chapter 2

Radical Behaviorist Interpretation[1]

The explicit distinguishing feature of radical behaviorism is its admission of thoughts and feelings ("private events") into its explanatory system, albeit as responses attracting an operant explanation rather than as causes of behavior (Skinner, 1945). Whereas the *methodological* behaviorism of John Watson (1913) placed such phenomena beyond the scope of scientific investigation, Skinner's system refuses to admit that private events differ ontologically or methodologically from those overt stimuli and responses that are open to communal corroboration (Smith, 1986). Private events have nevertheless been of little relevance to the experimental analysis of behavior. Behavior analysts, who have traditionally been involved in laboratory experiments with rats, pigeons and other nonhuman animals, have had little need of the concept, which has received minimal elaboration in behavioral science even when the explanation of human behavior in non-laboratory situations has been the objective. The success of radical behaviorism depends, nonetheless, on its ability to make the transition from laboratory to life, and Skinner's answer is neither extrapolation nor theory but "interpretation."

He argues that areas of human behavior that lie beyond the rigor of experimental procedure are amenable to an account based on the extension thereto of scientific laws derived from the analysis of simpler behavior patterns observed in the laboratory (Skinner, 1969a, p. 100). In the study of complex actions, such as everyday verbal behavior, it is usually impossible to ascertain the contingencies that control response rate with the accuracy and precision available to the scientist who can assiduously control and monitor both dependent and independent variables. But it is possible to present a "plausible account" of such complex actions (Skinner, 1957, p. 11) which is essentially "an interpretation, not an explanation... merely useful, neither true nor false" (Skinner 1988e, p. 364). The behavior analytic interpretation, like those that deal with the evolution of life or the geophysics of the earth's core, is unprovable, but preferable nonetheless to those which cannot be supported by knowledge of simpler systems gained from carefully executed experiments (Skinner 1969a, p. 100; 1974, pp. 226–7; 1988c, p. 208). "When phenomena are out of reach in time or space, or too large or small to be directly manipulated, we must talk about them with less than a complete account of relevant conditions. What has been learned under more favorable conditions is then invaluable" (Skinner 1973, p. 261). Would that it were so straightforward. In terms of methodology, "plausible" is an amazingly weak word to employ here. There is never any problem in rationalizing a plausible interpretation, especially if its main function is to satisfy those who already accept the principles of behavior to which it makes reference, as opposed to an account that is warranted or defensible given the evidence. Skinner seems to have no inkling that what Dewey refers to as a "warrant of assertibility" is required if radical behaviorist interpretation is to have any epistemological merit. The modus operandi of this extension of radical behaviorist explanation beyond the laboratory into the everyday world requires close delineation since it opens up new vistas of theoretical and methodological concern. Moreover, formulating an appropriate strategy of interpretation brings radical behaviorism inescapably into contact with its borders, notably the interpretive stance inherent in social cognitive psychology. (The problem of interpreting behavior in natural environments in terms of principles gained through experimentation is familiar to ethologists; see, for instance, Kacelnic, 1993; Shettleworth, 1998). The difficulty is that while sentiments such as Skinner's have promoted the proliferation of somewhat ad hoc and extrapolative interpretations of complex human activity (for example, Skinner, 1953, 1957, 1971, 1974), radical behaviorists have done little to formulate a *methodology* of interpretation. Although the essential feature of such interpretations is clear – the identification of discriminative antecedents to responses and their relationship of both to the reinforcing and punishing consequences of behaving – no systematic procedure has been evolved which leads plausibly to the unambiguous discernment of these elements of the "three-term contingency". Issues of validity and reliability scarcely arise in so deterministic a system. This neglect gives rise to the criticism that radical behaviorist interpretation consists largely in the "vague analogical guesses" attributed by Chomsky (1959) to Skinner's operant account of verbal behavior (Skinner, 1957). Interpretation cannot be based on an arbitrary procedure but must be capable of judgment based on the criteria to which any scientific hypotheses would be subjected.

The absence of criteria by which to pursue and evaluate "plausible" interpretations leads to dogmatic assertion that environmental element x is or is not an operant response, a discriminative stimulus, or a reinforcer/punisher. This is apparent even to some radical behaviorists, those who refuse to entertain the view that the private events which are not amenable to an experimental analysis are deserving of their scientific acknowledgement. Further, the radical behaviorist principle that discriminative stimulus, operant response and reinforcer are separate events comes under criticism from those who see a single event as capable of constituting all three (Bandura, 1986.) The use of these necessarily theoretical terms requires not ontological dogma but a methodology of interpretation and the setting of limits within which the results of applying that methodology can be safely entertained. A more formal construal of radical behaviorism is essential to the appreciation of where experimental science and interpretive system diverge.

Radical behaviorism is an amalgam of positivism, descriptivism, operationism and pragmatism directed toward the prediction and control of behavior (Delprato & Midgley, 1992; Foxall, 1996; Moore, 1999; Ringen, 1999; Smith, 1986; Smith & Woodward, 1996; Thyer, 19999; Zuriff, 1985.) It seeks to explain its subject matter, observed behavior, by relating operant responses to the environmental conditions which have selected and preserved them. Internal events, states and processes, whether mental, neural or hypothetical, even if real, are not usually admitted as causes of behavior, though later Skinnerian thought considered them proximal or "non-initiating" causes thereof (Skinner, 1988c; cf. Foxall, 1990). The ultimate causes of behavior nevertheless reside always in the environment. (Skinner, 1977)

Science and Interpretation

Despite Skinner's (1974) view that part of the environment is enclosed within the skin and that the skin is but an arbitrary barrier, here he appears to be thinking of an extra-personal environment. An alternative view of private events is that the relevant environment is that of the behavior rather than the organism. Similarly, radical behaviorists differ in how far they adopt private events in the interpretation of observed behavior, how far they confine their accounts of complex behavior within the scope of experimental science or are willing to speculate about the influence of covert actions. Radical behaviorism does not deny the existence of "private events" such as thoughts and feelings – indeed, we have noted that its essential distinction from methodological behaviorism inheres in its acceptance of such events as part of its subject matter – but any proximal control exercised by these covert entities over overt behavior will endure only in so far as it is consistent with the environmental consequences of the overt responding. This is consistent with empirical findings on instructed behavior (Catania, Matthews & Shimoff, 1982; Hayes, Brownstein, Haas, & Greenway, 1986, Horne & Lowe, 1993). Public or private, events are ontologically identical. Nevertheless, the inclusion of private events in *interpretations* of complex behavior complicates this simple account considerably. In the paper that marks his first use of the term *radical* behaviorism, Skinner (1945, p. 275) writes:

> The response "My tooth aches" is partly under the control of a state of affairs to which the speaker alone is able to react, since no one else can establish the required connection with the tooth in question. There is nothing mysterious or metaphysical about this; the simple fact is that each speaker possesses a small but important private world of stimuli. So far as we know, responses to that world are like responses to external events. Nevertheless, the privacy gives rise to two problems. The first difficulty is that we cannot, as in the case of public stimuli, account for the verbal response by pointing to a controlling stimulus. Our practice is to *infer* the private event, but this is opposed to the direction of inquiry in a science of behavior in which we are to predict a response through, among other things, an independent knowledge of the stimulus. It is often supposed that a solution is to be found in improved physiological techniques. Whenever it becomes possible to say what conditions within the organism control the response 'I am depressed,' for example, and to produce these conditions at will, a

degree of control and prediction characteristic of responses to external stimuli will be made possible. Meanwhile, we must be content with reasonable evidence for the belief that responses to public and private stimuli are equally lawful and alike in kind.

But are we justified in being so content? Since Skinner's preference was always for radical over methodological behaviorism, his system has since its inception required a dual approach to accounting for human behavior. This duality has become sharper with the passage of time and the extension of radical behaviorist explication from simple animal behavior in the operant chamber to the complexities of human social, economic, political, verbal and cultural practices. The *experimental analysis of behavior* entails relating simple responses in closely regulated laboratory settings to the environmental events (discriminative, reinforcing and punishing stimuli) that control them. The success criterion of this inductive behavior science is pragmatic rather than realist (Mackenzie, 1977). This stance derives essentially from the brand of positivism on which it is based – not the logical positivism of the Vienna Circle but Machian positivism founded upon biological expediency (Smith, 1986).

In this philosophy of science to describe is to explain in detail. Science is thus part of the human species' effort to adapt to its environment through predicting and controlling nature. Whatever works in this sense is true; in Skinner's terms, whatever reinforces behavior that ensures the survival of effective cultural norms is "right." Science is not, therefore, neutral: the operant chamber leads inexorably to *Walden Two* (Skinner, 1948) and the design of cultures (Skinner, 1971). The dimensions of science, the operational rigor of its conceptual definitions, the pragmatic outcomes of its program to predict and control are more than Enlightenment ideals; they are the means to the good life (Flanagan, 1991). Though the link may be inexorable, it is not direct. Beyond the confines of the operant laboratory, radical behaviorism's accounts of complexity, notably human behavior, consist in *interpretation*, "an orderly arrangement of behavior derived from an experimental analysis of a more rigorous sort" (Skinner, 1957, p. 11). Principles of behavior gained from the observation of responses in laboratory contexts can be applied to complex behaviors that are not amenable to an experimental analysis in the same way that astrophysicists interpret inaccessible solar events by reference to physical knowledge derived from a more feasible analysis. The success criterion of such behavioral interpretations is as we have seen not their pragmatic contribution to the prediction and control of behavior but their "plausibility" (Skinner, 1969, 1974, 1988a).

The many experimentalists who became behavior analysts in order to investigate the behavior of organisms in the tightly-controlled circumstances of the laboratory have made an immense contribution to the derivation of behavior principles by means of which not only the conduct of their experimental subjects may be explained but by which the behavior of both human and nonhuman animals might be investigated and explained beyond the confines of the laboratory. Many experimenters are content with that and do not seek to extend their scientific analysis outside the experimental space. For them, the experimental analysis of behavior has become an end in itself, a means of exploring and explaining animal behavior in closely regulated situations. Others, however, have been drawn to behavior analysis because they sought explanations in terms of behavior–environmental interactions for patterns of non-laboratory behavior with which they were familiar by virtue of analysis within other disciplines – economics, sociology, consumer science, or whatever. Some of our interest has expressed itself in experimental or quasi-experimental work but by the very nature of its grounding in human behavior beyond the laboratory such interest has also found expression in what Skinner called "interpretation", the application of behavior principles gained in the analysis of simpler systems to environments not amenable to an experimental examination. Looking through the laboratory window at the world of affairs, it is easy to see notional "three-term contingencies" at every turn. Moving from the laboratory to life requires that we modify our conceptual and methodological framework in order to show within what bounds our imported explanations carry conviction. Psychologists of other theoretical persuasions have long sought *rules of correspondence* by which to relate their unobservable explanatory terms to the data language in which they describe their observations. Such rules are not what we seek here but, analogously at least, we require rules of interpretation, means of transcending the expanse between accounts of experimental findings in terms of behavioral–environmental contingencies and operant explications of complex behaviors that are more than merely plausible.

Whilst there had once been a hope – even expectation – that the analysis of the actions of rats, pigeons and other nonhumans would permit the uncomplicated interspecies generalization of results, the analysis of verbal behavior eventually indicated that extrapolation would be an insufficient means of accounting for the complex interactions of human beings. Between the extrapolative attempts of Skinner's (1957) *Verbal Behavior* and his conceptually-innovative account of the rule-governance of much human behavior (1969b) lies at least an implicit recognition of this. *Verbal Behavior* attracted the criticism that it made "vague analogic guesses" in its attempt to find equivalences in the complex world of the discriminative stimuli, responses and reinforcers and punishers so readily identified in the laboratory (Chomsky, 1959; see also Broadbent, 1961, Schwartz & Lacey, 1982). The vast interspecies differences between the animals that had typically been studied in the laboratory and those capable of verbal behavior were finally taken into consideration in Skinner's second major contribution to this study, the paper of 1969 in which he dealt with decision-making.

By this time, when the "cognitive revolution" was well under way, it was clear that human behavior could not be comprehensively accounted for in terms of the contingency-shaping that provided a plausible explanation of the behavior of infrahumans at least in the laboratory. Some human behavior undoubtedly is explicable in such terms but the vast majority of its instances are rendered intelligible in operant terms only if they are portrayed as rule-governed, that is subject to the verbal stimuli provided by the actor and, especially, by others in the form of rules, advice, instructions, admonitions, and so on. The complexities of human behavior occurring outside the closed setting of the laboratory experiment, especially when conducted with nonhuman subjects, could not be accommodated within the framework of conceptualization and analysis that had served so well for the explication of simpler patterns of conduct. New explanatory devices were required that were not predictable from the analysis of nonhuman or perhaps even human behavior in the experimental setting. Hence the origin of rule-governance, a mode of explanation that has resulted in a great deal of empirical and theoretical research that continues to this day and which has taken the analysis of verbal behavior far beyond the (often invaluable, but limited) insights of *Verbal Behavior*.

Whilst verbal behavior is frequently amenable to an experimental analysis, however, this is not always the case. Human interaction in naturalistic settings is often incapable of a reduction to laboratory analogues and experimental analysis: it is at best open only to an interpretation in operant terms. We can seek simple plausibility in such interpretations, in which case we shall undoubtedly succeed. But this is a strategy that from the beginning sees interpretation as a secondary activity compared with experimentation. Alternatively, we can look beyond such simplicity toward the establishment of a system of operant analysis of complexity that rests on a reasoned epistemological foundation.

Interpretive Stances

Interpretation consists in the adoption and application of an analogic stance by which complex behavior, the causes of which are inaccessible to experimental science, is described in terms provided by a causal system which has achieved plausibility when rigorously applied to a simpler behavior system. A stance is, first, an *assertion*. The contextual stance *asserts* that the variables of which behavior is a function can be extensionally characterized (that is, without recourse to propositional attitudes or other intentional idioms). Second, a stance is a *pre-empirical* position. This does not imply that it is pre-scientific, of course: the adoption of a stance is part of the scientific process. Rather, it permits a basis for behavioral prediction to be advanced without prior ontological assumption. Note, however, that as an ideological position that engenders research, a stance is neither true nor false: it gives direction to research by indicating where answers may be found, but it does not guarantee the veracity, usefulness or superiority of the results to which it leads. However, formulating our strategy by reference to its underlying stance forces us to make explicit the ascriptions and suppositions on which we are basing it. Third, a stance is a *philosophical position*. Dennett continually criticizes behaviorism as a psychology. His remarks about radical behaviorism's *masking* the intentional stance are couched solely in terms of what behaviorism is as a psychological method. It does not recognize that behaviorism is founded on a philosophical stance as surely as cognitivism is. This stance is a means of prediction (and partial explanation). It can be compared with the intentional stance only if it is itself construed as having stance-like qualities. Finally, a stance is *universal of application*. One way of dividing the intellectual landscape would be to claim that the intentional stance applies to open settings (those in which the individual has several to many choices open to him or her so that his or her behavior is difficult to predict), the contextual stance to closed settings (those in which all but one or two behaviors are proscribed by the kinds of consequences they will attract). But our *assertion* is that the contextual stance applies as surely to behavior in open settings as to that in closed.

The rationale for the adoption of such a stance and for its continued application to the complexity in question must be externally derived. In the case of radical behaviorist interpretation, our success criterion must be initially that of prediction and control imposed by the experimental science on which it is based. "Understanding", "explanation", the provision of a "plausible operant account" are far too vague for a rigorous test. In order to clarify the nature and scope of radical behaviorist interpretation, it is first necessary to delineate radical behaviorism itself as a philosophy of psychology, to understand what sets it apart. Once this has been done, it is possible to explore the relationship between the explanatory basis of radical behaviorism and that which underlies cognitive psychology, the strongest alternative contender as explicator of complex human behavior. Dennett's approach to intentionality (for example, Dennett 1969, 1987a, b, 1996) provides a reference point since it is not only generally available, current and persuasive, but engages with behaviorism at a number of points. In this way it is possible both to facilitate a comparative analysis of Dennett's *intentional strategy* and the *contextual strategy* that is the foundation of the behaviorist enterprise, and to explore the manner by which an operant interpretation of complex human behavior, that is, behavior not amenable to laboratory experimentation, can be accomplished.

The selection of these exemplars of cognitive and behaviorist philosophies of science is not arbitrary. Most cognitive theories, especially those that render pre-behavioral events in terms of information processing, rest on the intentional idiom, while the extensional approach that underlies the contextual stance is a necessary component of a genuine behavioristic approach. The endeavor to delineate the bounds of radical behaviorism, in light of the competing explanations of behavior offered by cognitive psychology, makes necessary the critical comparison of these stances.

The intentionalism encapsulated in Dennett's *intentional stance* is basic to psychological explanations predicated upon information processing. Commenting on the relationship between cognitive accounts, such as Dennett's, which employ propositional attitudes, and those such as the social cognition models, Bechtel (1988, p. 75) challenges "those working on processing accounts to attend to the intentional perspective, in which the behavior of a cognitive system is characterized in terms of its beliefs and desires about the environment. It is this intentional perspective that identifies what aspects of the behavior of a system need to be explained by the processing account." The argument, central to Dennett's entire enterprise, that the intentional stance elucidates cognitive ethology (Dennett, 1983) rests, after all, on the claim that it identifies the mental qualities and capacities of organisms and species. The intentional strategy, by identifying the propositional attitudes necessary for the organism's adaptation to its environment, provides social cognitivism, the dominant paradigm within cognitive psychology (Ostrom, 1994), with a rationale for its research program.

The relevance of the comparison to radical behaviorism is equally compelling. For, *contra* Skinner, the central fact in the delineation of radical behaviorism is its conceptual avoidance of propositional content. This eschewal of the *intentional stance* sets it apart not only from cognitivism but from neo-behaviorisms such as those of Tolman and Hull. Indeed, the defining characteristic of radical behaviorism is not that it avoids mediating processes *per se* but that it accounts for behavior without recourse to propositional attitudes. Based on the *contextual stance*, it provides accounts of contingency-shaped, rule-governed, verbal and private behaviors which are entirely non-intentional. Its capacity to do so is independent of any prior assumption of intentionality: it is therefore methodologically autonomous. Cognitive explanation by contrast requires the prior application of the contextual stance before its propositions can be translated into an intentionalistic explanation. These ideas are explored on the basis of an examination of recent advances in attitude theory and research, as an exemplar, but there are grounds for believing it to be a universal characteristic of the social-cognitive school of psychology. The import of this is that a social-cognitive psychology can be constructed by ascribing intentional content to the findings and theories of extensional behavioral science. Although this does not affect the pursuit of extensional behavior analysis as a largely experimental enterprise, it has profound implications for the nature of radical behaviorist interpretation. Consideration is given to whether operant accounts of complex human behavior (that which is not amenable to an experimental analysis) can proceed most effectively through such a combination of the intentional and contextual stances or through a reconstruction of intentional idioms in extensional language.

Beyond the Experimental Space

Scientific explanation is verbal activity and the boundaries of a particular school of thought are set by the locutions of its practitioners (Skinner, 1945, 1956, 1957). When rival scientific communities lay claim to a common subject matter, as is the case for psychology, delineating any one approach begs consideration of the verbal behaviors of its competitors. Specifically, therefore, this essay compares the linguistic bounds set respectively by Dennett (for example, 1983) and Skinner (for example, 1945) for the *intentional stance* which claims that mentalistic sentences are distinguished by the referential opacity of their terms, and the *contextual stance* which claims to underpin an extensional science of behavior by virtue of the referential transparency of its statements (Foxall, 1999). Skinner's radical behaviorism uniquely represents the non-intentional approach to psychology and provides the foundation for such a science. Indeed, I shall argue that the defining characteristic of radical behaviorism is the avoidance of propositional attitudes – ascribed intrapersonal events and states that are regarded as causes or predictors of behavior by virtue of their intentionality, their being intrinsically *about* other entities. As a consequence, radical behaviorism avoids a distinction between the mental and the physical that is usually traced to Brentano (1995/1874). That approach reaches an apogee in Chisholm's (1957, 1960) sophisticated treatment which distinguishes not mental from physical substances but mentalistic from physicalistic sentences. The distinction between verbal expressions that are referentially opaque and those that are referentially transparent is a distinction between two apparently incommensurable philosophical approaches to behavioral science (Dennett, 1969).

For those who are principally interested in the experimental analysis of behavior, this may have limited relevance. Private events are not amenable to experimental analysis; nor are they essential to a scientific system that is confined to the animal laboratory; they may enter into the interpretation of results obtained in the human operant laboratory but their role can be only peripheral. Even the phenomena of rule-governance are usually fairly simply dealt with in these circumstances. Those whose principal interest in behavior analysis is the interpretation of complex human behavior, defined as that which is not amenable to a direct experimental analysis, are heavily dependent on private events and on the attribution of rules if they wish to keep their interpretations within the bounds of an extensional behavioral science. The difficulty of the interpretive task is made clearer by considering not only that complex behavior is not subject to a direct experimental analysis, but that the contingencies of reinforcement that are assumed to operate on the behavior are not specifiable in advance of observation, nor can they be manipulated to isolate their influence. Even the behavior itself may be determined only after observation. Moreover, a comprehensive learning history is not available for the target individual and his/her target behavior (Lee, 1988).

There is within behavior analysis a natural understanding that knowledge must at some time be derived from or tested by experiment. Even though agreeing with the idea that complex behavior such as verbal behavior cannot itself be subjected to an experimental analysis, Burgos and Donahoe (2000) argue that scientific interpretation can take place only on the basis of principles gained from experimentation. Their citing verbal behavior is interesting because even the theoretical analysis of rule-governance that Skinner (1969) offered was as we have seen the result of a conceptual advance that went beyond the mere extrapolation of learning principles derived from the experimental study of animal behavior. More recent empirical work on verbal behavior (e.g., Hayes, 1989) has also required an a priori conceptual development of the verbal behavior of the listener for instance that is not the result of experimentation but of pre-experimental observation and analysis. Undoubtedly as they point out experimental analysis has the great advantage of revealing how few variables of the many that might influence a response are actually implicated in its performance: I should be the last to argue against the method *per se*. But there are no grounds for going as far as claiming that our interpretations of complex phenomena can be considered scientific only if they are directly based on principles derived from an experimental analysis of simpler phenomena. Whilst such principles are a sine qua non of the interpretation of complexity no theoretical enterprise can be confined to terms derived in this way. Moreover, much of the behavior that requires an interpretive analysis leads to explanations that cannot be subjected ex post to an experimental analysis but which require alternative means of substantiation (Foxall, 1998). Even when this has been done, there will be theoretical terms that simply cannot be so subjected to empirical verification but which are essential nonetheless in order to fill the conceptual gaps that will be inescapably left by any body of empirical data.

Recognition that such interpretation is an essential component of behavior analysis has not led to the formulation of any systematic approach to understanding complex behavior in operant terms. Whatever the status of our observations of behavior under experimental analysis, as soon as we leave the laboratory to observe and interpret the behavior of our fellow humans engaged in the everyday business of life, we are plunged into the epistemological problems of establishing the validity and reliability of our interpretations (subsumed by Skinner under the label of "plausibility"). The establishment of the grounds of genuine plausibility depends on our knowing what radical behaviorist explanation is and how it is delineated from alternative approaches. That is, it entails an exploration of the bounds of behaviorism. And the irony of that is that it requires first an appreciation of the nature and implications of intentionalism psychology, the very underpinning of cognitive psychology.

Chapter 3

The Intentional Stance

Cognitive explanation begins with the "poverty of the stimulus," the view that only by positing unobservable mental events can psychologists account for the richness of the repertoire of response outputs available to humans given the parsimony of the stimulus inputs that behaviorists insist are sufficient to explain behavior (Fodor, 1983). The argument is familiar to those who know Chomsky's (1959) review of Skinner's (1957) *Verbal Behavior*: surely only some kind of inner processing, transformation, computation can possibly account for this stimulus–response discrepancy (Plotkin, 1997; see also Pinker, 1997; cf. Fodor, 2000). Behavior analysts also have ready a counterargument. They point out the poverty of cognitivists' understanding of modern behaviorism – Plotkin's idea that "behaviorists believed that psychological explanation reduced entirely to a rather fancy theory of reflexes" (pp. 130–1), for instance – and contrast this with the sophisticated treatments of private events, internal states, rule-governance and stimulus equivalence that now characterize behaviorists' assault on whole areas of behavior that are no longer ceded *faute de mieux* to cognitive psychologists (e.g., Hayes & Ghezzi, 1997; Hayes, Barnes-Holmes & Roche, 2001; Sidman, 1994; Staddon, 2001a, b).

Stated thus, however, both arguments lack a clear understanding of what demarcates cognitive from behaviorist explanation and how the two approaches are related in practice. Moreover, some of the more elaborate behaviorist explanations of complex behavior appeal to ("private") events taking place within the skin, be they behavioral or physiological. However well behavior analysts may think they have handled the cognitivist onslaught, non-behaviorist psychologists can argue eloquently that little if anything nowadays separates radical behaviorist and cognitive psychologies. That the message has not got through is due in part to some behavior analysts' deliberate avoidance of the philosophical basis of the two psychologies (Schnaitter, 1999) and partly to a laxity in the use of words such as "attitudes," "intentions," and "beliefs" by some behavior analysts whose work extends into applied fields. Words like these as they are used in cognitive psychology as well as everyday discourse carry within themselves a whole universe of explanation that is as essential to cognitive science as it is antithetical to orthodox behavior analysis.

Defining that essence and its antithesis is not a simple task. In contrast to the intentional stance which underpins cognitive psychology, a contextual stance can be identified which is the concomitant foundation of radical behaviorism (Foxall, 1999). To appreciate the role and implications of that contextual stance, we must first delve more deeply into the role and implications of intentionality. As previously noted the intentional stance maintains that *the behavior of systems such as people and computers can be predicted from the desires and beliefs that can be rationally attributed to them* (Dennett, 1987a). It is useful to understand how Dennett arrives at this stance. He in fact distinguishes three stances by which we may seek to make systems intelligible. The *design* stance is used to "make predictions solely from knowledge or assumptions about the system's functional design, irrespective of the physical constitution or condition of the innards of the particular object" (Dennett, 1978, p. 4). The information provided by this stance leads us to define what an object will do, what its function must minimally be, regardless of its form.

From the *physical* stance we make predictions on the basis of the physical state or conditions of the system; it depends on knowledge we have in the form of laws of nature. Predicting that when the bough breaks the baby will fall involves using the physical stance, as does forecasting that the atmospheric conditions that are about to bring rain will also bring on my lumbago. It is through the recognition that the best chess playing computers now defy prediction by either of these stances that Dennett arrives at the third: the *intentional* stance. In using it, "…[O]ne assumes not only (1) that the machine will function as designed, but (2) that the design is optimal as well, that the computer will 'choose' the most rational move" (Dennett, 1978, p. 5). Note that rationality here means optimal design relative to goal, and that prediction is relative to the nature and extent of the information the system has about the field of endeavor. "One predicts behavior… by ascribing to the system *the possession of certain information* and supposing it to be *directed by certain goals*, and then by working out the most reasonable or appropriate action on the basis of these ascriptions and suppositions. It is a small step to calling the information possessed the computer's *beliefs*, its goals and subgoals its *desires*." (Dennett, 1978, p. 6) "Lingering doubts about whether the chess-playing computer *really* has beliefs and desires are misplaced; for the definition of intentional systems does not say that intentional systems *really* have beliefs and desires, but that one can explain and predict their behavior by *ascribing* beliefs and desires to them…" (p. 6). "The decision to adopt the strategy is pragmatic, and is not intrinsically right or wrong" (I). This is reminiscent of Skinner's claim that using the radical behaviorist interpretive stance is "neither right nor wrong, merely useful." It shows that in each case we are using an interpretive stance that is founded on ascriptions and suppositions. The statement of the contextual stance makes these explicit.

Hence as we also have noted the contextual stance maintains that *behavior is predictable in so far as it is assumed to be environmentally determined; specifically, in so far as it is under the control of a learning history that represents the reinforcing and punishing consequences of similar behavior previously enacted in settings similar to that currently encountered* (Foxall, 1999). While the intentional stance proceeds by the attribution of propositional attitudes to a system that is assumed to be rational in order to reveal the intensionality of its behavior, the contextual stance is methodologically extensionalistic, seeking to explain behavior exclusively by reference to its environmental determinants.

Intentional Explanation

In elucidating the nature of intentionality my account is largely limited to Dennett's exposition of content which he covers principally but by no means exclusively in the first part of *Content and Consciousness* (1969) and in *The Intentional Stance* (1987a).[2] We have already covered the basic idea but it will be useful having briefly restated it to elaborate upon its meaning in preparation for the ensuing argument. The "intentions" which Dennett urges we ascribe to systems in order to predict them are words portraying actions which are *about* something else. A person does not simply hope or fear or decide but hopes *something*, fears *something*, decides *something*: Mary hopes *that* the bus will come soon, fears *that* the age of miracles is past, decides *that* she will learn to drive, searches *for* a driving school, and so on. Sentences containing these intentional idioms are said to contain propositions or propositional content and the mentalistic terms preceding those propositions such as *hopes* and *fears* and *decides* and *searches* are known as propositional attitudes.

The intentional stance, or something much like it, underlies our everyday experience in which we try to make the behavior of other people (animals, things) intelligible and predictable. Folk psychology of this kind is resilient. The argument can be made, moreover, that the intentional stance is fundamental to cognitive science including cognitive psychology. As Dennett further points out, (1998, p. 313) "[I]ntentional systems theory is an attempt to provide what Chomsky, no behaviorist, calls a competence model, in contrast to a performance model. Before we ask ourselves how mechanisms are designed, we must get clear about what the mechanisms are supposed to (be able to) do." Central as intentionality is to so much psychological explication, however, we must be constantly aware that intentionality in this philosophical sense carries a special connotation. It refers not to behavior but to sentences or statements *about* behavior. Moreover, the distinction between physical sentences and mental or intentional sentences has implications for strategies of scientific research and explanation. Some sentences refer simply to physical matters – for example, "That planet is Mars" – while others appear to refer to a mental reality – "John believes that the woman at the podium is the Queen of England". The two kinds of sentence have quite different properties.

Brentano distinguished the intentional by pointing to the *inexistence* of the object to which mental states referred: the objects to which they refer may not exist, as in "I believe that the golden mountain is in Spain". The crux of Brentano's argument is that mental statements' uniquely exhibiting intentional inexistence points to the means of demarcating physical and mental phenomena. The problem of speaking of inexistent objects raises ontological difficulties, however. Later philosophers like Chisholm made the distinction on the basis not of objects but of the linguistic difference between transparent and opaque statements. Chisholm's view was that in speaking of the physical, there is no need to use intentional language: we can say all we need to say about it without resorting to intentional language. But in order to speak of the mental/psychological (including thinking) we need to use intentional language. (Chisholm, 1957, 111–112; cf. Bechtel, 1988, p.

46). The advance here is that Chisholm does not speak of the ontological status of the objects of thoughts, etc. but makes the distinction entirely in terms of language. Like Dennett after him, he argues that the two kinds of sentence differ fundamentally: physical sentences are *referentially transparent* in the sense that, in the sentence we have already considered, a term equivalent to "Mars" can be substituted for it without altering the truth of the statement. We can as easily say "That planet is the fourth from the sun" as "The planet is Mars". "Mars" and "the fourth planet from the sun" are said to have the same *extension* since they name the same red planet. Hence the substitutability of the terms. But, as we briefly noted above, so-called mental sentences are *referentially opaque* insofar as equivalent terms may not be substitutable. John may well believe that a particular woman is the Queen of England, for instance, but not that she is Elizabeth II: he may simply not know that Elizabeth II is the Queen of England. Hence, whilst we would be justified in saying, "John believes that that woman is the Queen of England," we could not assert that he knew that she was Elizabeth II. The linguistic approach to defining intentionality, such as Chisholm introduced, may throw up an anomaly of language rather than tell us anything about the nature of intentionality itself, as Searle (1981) points out. But the alternative may be to go back to Brentano's problematic position. Russell (1940) used the term "propositional attitudes" to refer to sentences like *John wants to use his new washing machine this afternoon* in which the verb is followed by "that" and a proposition. Bechtel points out that an advantage of this approach is that it allows us two degrees of freedom in characterizing mental states, based first on the verb or attitude and second on the proposition. We can believe that John will get to use his washing machine this afternoon but desire that he does not. This suggests a course of action: doing something to prevent his use of the washing machine.

A strong argument against the intentional approach is taken by Quine (1960, 1969) who assumes the opposite view of intentionality from Brentano. Whilst Brentano argues that the intentional has special significance on account of its different status from the physical – the implication is the "indispensability of intentional idioms and the importance of an independent science of intentionality" – Quine contends that it merely shows the "baselessness of intentional idioms and the emptiness of a science of intention" (1960, p. 221). The result is a behavioristic approach to behavior which has purged the intentional idioms from its language of explanation. Quine's logic has not carried the day where many philosophers, of widely differing orientations, are concerned, however. Bechtel (1978) and Chomsky (1969), for instance, are of the opinion that despite difficulties with intentional explanation, its merit consists in its ability to facilitate explanation of behavior: if it does so it belongs in a scientific purview. We have some distance to travel yet before we can endorse this pragmatic solution.

Nevertheless these fundamental considerations allow us to restate and refine several terms that will be central to the argument. The *extension* of a term or predicate of a sentence is the thing or set of things to which the term refers, whereas the *intension* of that term or language is the particular way in which this thing or set of things is picked out or determined. "Queen of England" and "Elizabeth II" name the same person, the current British monarch, and so have the same extension. But they delineate this entity in different ways and thereby have different intensions or meanings. Referential transparency means freedom to substitute terms that have the same extension. Referential opacity arises out of the different intensions of terms; it occurs in sentences that take propositions as their predicates. Hence terms and predicates that are identical in an extensional sense may not be substitutable because of their differing intentions.[3] We are now ready to consider in detail Dennett's argument against extensional behavioral science.

"Intentional Phenomena are Real"

The import of Dennett's restatement of what he calls "the ontological status of mind" (1969, Ch. 1) is that it transforms Brentano's thesis that the intentional denotes a separate, non-extensional reality or ontology into the view that the correct distinction is *solely* one between sentences. "Intentionality is not a mark that divides phenomena from phenomena, but sentences from sentences" (Dennett 1969, p. 27; cf. Viger 2000). And the import of this transformation in the present context stems from the inference Dennett draws to the effect that there can be no extensional science of psychology, a claim that he employs to fashion a powerful critique of the behavioristic enterprise. Dennett's logical progression in reaching this conclusion requires elaboration. He initially admits that the logic of science is generally said to be "blind to intensional distinctions; the intersubstitution of coextensive terms, regardless of their intensions, does not affect the truth value (truth or falsity) of the enclosing sentences" (p. 29–30; otherwise unidentified page numbers are henceforth to Dennett, 1969). He argues that *intensional phenomena nonetheless exist*. The evidence he adduces for this claim appears unusual to those who have imbibed the traditional canons of (extensional) scientific judgment. "Our evidence that 'there really are' Intentional phenomena", he writes, "coincides with our evidence that in our ordinary language we speak as if there were, and if a science of behavior could be successfully adumbrated without speaking as if there were these 'things', the insistence that there really are Intentional phenomena would take on a hollow ring" (p. 33).[4]

It is difficult at first to get a fix on Dennett's philosophical position because he denies or redefines labels attributed to him such as instrumentalist and realist. He seems to be simultaneously accepting these labels and repudiating them (much as he seems, albeit reluctantly, to invite being described as a "behaviorist" and at the same time abhorring the designation.) The claim that he is an *instrumentalist* derives from his maintaining that no system we predict by means of the intentional stance, including ourselves, actually contains intentional content. Nevertheless, he claims to be a *realist* of sorts because he maintains that the patterns of behavior which the intentional stance predicts are real. Moreover, the intentional entities he posits (actually which are posited by folk psychology) are real in the sense that "dints" and "sakes," "miles" and "voices," "centers of gravity" and "electrons" are real. None of these terms refers to objects in the sense that the language of science would identify them but each is useful nonetheless in navigating our way around the world. It is a mistake to ask, for instance, whether "sakes" really exist: they exist in the sense that our ordinary language treats them as though they exist. Similarly with "minds" and other mentalistic terms. No-one believes that centers of gravity exist physically, and yet their usefulness in predicting the behavior of physical entities lends a reality to them that is generally accepted even by physicists. (See, inter alia, Dennett, 1981, 1991a). They do not exist in the way that trains and boats and planes exist but the reality of such physical artifacts is not the only mode of reality. Only by positing the intentional stance can we obtain certain kinds of useful knowledge – knowledge useful for the prediction and partial explanation of real behavior, that is – and this makes the ascribed entities real. "Realist," however, is another label which Dennett is reluctant to accept. For his ascription of intentionality to systems in order to predict them is not dependent on the intrinsic structure of those systems but on external, environmental things, the system's context. He is then not so much opposed to the idea that the ascribed intentions are real but to the idea that they are real internal states of the system. Beliefs are objective phenomena but not objective *internal* phenomena. They are ascribed on the basis of the relationship of behavior to its environment. (Bechtel, 1988, p. 72). Bechtel finds Dennett's instrumentalism a problem which he attempts to overcome by treating intentional states "realistically," i.e., as "states of the system that are adaptable to features of the system's environment." (p. 78)

Also of interest is Dennett's positioning of behaviorism within this configuration. "Behaviorism would attempt to discover the extensional laws governing the occurrence of events (animal – including human – motion) that are *initially* given extensional, non-intentional characterizations. If a truly predictive science of animal and human behavior (specified in pure 'motion' terms and including all human verbal behavior) could be produced, then the existence of Intentional idioms could be safely explained away as a peculiarity of natural languages, perhaps on a par with noun genders and onomatopoeia. Allowing working science to serve as ontological arbiter, one could claim that there really aren't any Intentional phenomena, and hence no science of Intentional phenomena is needed." (p. 33)

By way of commentary, it is necessary to make four points. First, we must note that in saying that intentional phenomena exist, Dennett is merely making an observation on our linguistic usage. The intentional–extensional distinction is a verbal one; it is about sentences, not things, and we *do* use sentences in a way that can be construed as invoking the intentional idiom; moreover the delineation of any system is a verbal matter. Second, *contra* Dennett's insistence that behaviorism is about S–R relationships, we must emphasize first that *radical* behaviorism invokes the R–S contingency in which the repetition of *emitted* behavior is determined by its consequences; in addition, its orientation tends toward the molar rather than the molecular. Thirdly, it is necessary to emphasize that behaviorism's starting point is the *functional* consequences of words in sentences, terms, predicates: not their intentions or meanings but their effects or functions. This provides the basis of an extensional science of behavior that is not derivative of the intentionalistic, that does not translate, interpret or paraphrase it but which proceeds independently of it. Finally but most significantly, the assertion that behaviorism has failed in its predictive objective may be true of the Hullian endeavor which was collapsing as Dennett wrote but fails to do justice to the capacity of behavior analysis based on radical behaviorism to predict and control behavior at least in the closed setting of the laboratory and the relatively closed settings of hospital, prison and therapeutic community. The claim that an extensional explanation of psychological phenomena in the absence of intentional input is necessarily incomplete is as I hope to show more defensible; meantime, Dennett's assertion as it stands is mystifying to anyone able to read the journals.

Irreducibility

Dennett sharply dichotomizes the intensional and the extensional and argues that statements in the former idiom cannot be reduced to statements of the latter kind. This "irreducibility thesis" goes back at least to Brentano. "Intentional sentences do not follow the rules of extensional, truth-functional logic, and hence they are intensional." Moreover, and this is the central claim of intentionalism, "Intentional phenomena are absolutely irreducible to physical phenomena ... [that is,] Intentional sentences cannot be reduced to or paraphrased into extensional sentences about the physical world." This rules out the possibility of an extensional account of intensional phenomena. "The claim goes beyond the obvious fact that Intentional sentences are intensional, and hence cannot be, as they stand, extensional – to the more remarkable claim that no sentence or sentences can be found which adequately reproduce the information of an Intentional sentence and still conform to the extensional logic" (1969, p. 30). "The Intentionalist claim is that no extensional sentence – or longer paraphrase – could reproduce the sense of an Intentional sentence." (pp. 30–31). Intentional phenomena are absolutely irreducible. "If so overt an activity as saying that something is the case is not subject to behavioral, extensional paraphrase, what hope is there for such hidden, private phenomena as believing and imagining?" (p. 31) Note that this absolute pronouncement derives not from empirical observation but from the underlying stance that Dennett has adopted. As he admits, the irreducibility thesis is impossible to demonstrate since this would require a demonstration that intentional idioms could *always* or never be reduced to extensional idioms and this is impossible; all one can do is contend strongly that this is the case.

Dennett's thesis does not go unopposed in philosophical circles: analytical behaviorists argue that it is feasible to paraphrase intentional language in extensional terms (e.g., Ryle, 1949). Let us nevertheless accept the irreducibility thesis for the sake of argument. This is not to argue *contra* Dennett that such translation is possible or legitimate. It is, as I shall contend, that while making strong claims about the predictive use of the intentional stance requiring knowledge of the environment within which behavior occurs, he hints at but fails to develop a vital level of analysis. That level is the extensionalistic analysis of behavior (which supplies a super-personal level of understanding of behavior) coupled with an intentionalistic interpretive overlay. Thereby he stymies the development of a comprehensive social psychology of human action. Whilst he sometimes implies that the understanding of environment–behavior relationships is an inevitable part of even an intentionalistic psychology, he fails to elaborate this thesis, partly because he is of the opinion that behaviorism has failed, partly because he seems to misunderstand some vital components of modern behaviorism.

"Behaviorism has Failed"

We have already noted Dennett's insistence that behaviorism has failed. Contrary to the aim of a science of behavior, "so far the attempts to produce such an austere Stimulus–Response science have been notably unsuccessful. While behavioristic research on animals and men over the last several decades has been undeniably fruitful from the point of view of crucial data obtained, these gains have been achieved independently of – and, in many instances, in spite of – the theories the experimenters were intended to confirm or disconfirm. One could even make a case for the claim that the value of experimental results has been in inverse proportion to the extent to which the shibboleths of orthodox behaviorism have been honored." (p. 33) This claim is repeated, without evidence, by Dennett and Haugeland (1987, p. 385): "Dispensing with intentional theories is not an attractive option, ... for the abstemious behaviorisms and physiological theories so far proposed have signally failed to exhibit the predictive and explanatory power needed to account for the intelligent activities of human beings and other animals. A close examination [which is not presented] of the most powerful of these theories reveals intentional idioms inexorably creeping in – for instance in the definition of a stimulus as the 'perceived' stimulus and the response as the 'intended' effect, or in the reliance on the imputation of 'information-bearing' properties to physiological constructs. Moreover, the apparent soundness of information-processing theories, [for which no evidence is adduced] and their utility in practice has strengthened the conviction that somehow we *must* be able to make sense of the ineliminable intentional formulations they contain without compromising thoroughgoing materialism" (emphasis in original). Moreover, whilst Dennett's argument here may apply to the deductive systems of Tolman and Hull, it misrepresents research in Skinner's radical behaviorist tradition, which has been stolidly inductive, seeking theories only after the accumulation of many results and then only in the form of empirical regularities (Skinner, 1950).

Dennett shifts tack at this point de-emphasizing prediction and raising a question of explanation: "The difficulty the behaviorist has encountered is basically this: while it is clear that an experimenter can predict rate of learning, for example, from the initial conditions of his mazes and experience history of his animals, how does he specify just *what* is learned?" (pp. 33–4). "What [the animal in the maze] learns, of course, is *where the food is*, but how is this to be characterized non-Intentionally? There is no room for 'know' or 'believe' or 'hunt for' in the officially circumscribed language of behaviorism; so the behaviorist cannot say that the rat knows or believes that his food is at x, or that the rat is hunting for a route to x." (p. 34) He still fails to appreciate the essential contribution of extensional behavioral science to a comprehensive psychology of complex behavior. Based on its empirical research behaviorism can tell a story about behavior that is both successful and independent of the physiologists' story about behavior. Both the behavioristic account and the physiological are extensional, they may deal more with what Dennett calls motion than with action, and they may need an intensionalistic overlay in order to encompass some human experiences. But that is not the same as saying that behaviorism has failed, unless behaviorists insist that their approach is sufficient to account convincingly for all human behavior, private as well as public.

"Psychology must be intentionalistic, but..."

Dennett agues that intentional science is the only game in town. Now begins his real assault on behaviorism: his view that psychology *must* be based on the Intentional and that an extensional psychology is impossible. He is tentative, but there is no doubt where his argument is leading: "This strongly suggests, but does not prove, of course, that psychological phenomena *must* be characterized Intentionally if they are to be explained and predicted, that no science of behavior can get along without the Intentional idioms" (p. 34). His rejection of an extensional science of behavior is getting stronger, though he is actually talking about the difficulties of an Intentional science. In moving toward a position where an Intentional approach must somehow deal with and use the extensional, he evinces the attitude that de facto rejects extensionalism when it derives from behavioral science though not when its origins are in physiology.

However, he notes that a *purely* Intentional psychology is also impossible, since it cannot specify its causal variables (beliefs, etc.) in ways that are conceptually independent of the behavior it seeks to explain or predict. "It follows directly from the Intentionalist's irreducibility hypothesis that no independent characterization of an Intentionally characterized antecedent is ever possible" (p. 35). Hume's second approach to causality cannot be fulfilled, therefore. So Dennett rejects the phenomenological approach to explanation as surely as he rejects behaviorism. In sum, unbounded Intentionalism cannot provide the basis of a scientific theory of behavior because its Intentional characterization cannot have an independent referent/specification/characterization; however, this line of reasoning has come about because of the impossibility of the Intentional being reducible to the extensional and extensional has been understood as referring to the external. But what if an *internal* basis of extensional characterization were possible that could be shown to have *content* and thus be specifiable in Intentional terms? The obvious candidate is physiology and the route to its understanding is brain evolution. Dennett's claim is that it is reasonable to postulate intelligent mental processes as long as an evolutionary explanation can be provided of how and why the mind acquired them (Bechtel, 1988, p. 74).

Realism Revisited

Before turning to how he accomplishes the task of intentional ascription, it may be useful to summarize here the implications to this point of Dennett's thought for radical behaviorist interpretation. Dennett does not ask the traditional ontological questions about mind such as what beliefs are, where they reside or what they are made of. The formalization of his approach to intentionality in the intentional stance justifies the attribution of intentional idioms such as desires and beliefs to any entity whose behavior can more easily be predicted by virtue of that strategy. Such intentions are said to be real in the sense that they are bound up in the behavior so predicted. This strategy is invaluable to behavior analysts whose interpretations require the assumption of intentionality in order to the overcome the problems of purely extensional accounts of complex behavior. There is no need to ask the standard questions of cognitive ethology which are concerned with another, stronger, kind of realism, which by their very form alienate behaviorists, and which may in any case be incapable of answer. Shettleworth (1998, p. 477) summarizes the issues raised by Griffin's path-breaking book *The Question of Animal Awareness* (1976) as follows:

(1) Do animals show behavior that can be taken as evidence of intentions, beliefs, deception, and the like? (2) If they do, do they have subjective states of awareness like those a person would experience while engaging in functionally similar behavior?

There is no need to become entangled in essentially philosophical problems about the ontology of intentionality if one simply adopts the strategy of rationally predicting and partially explaining behavior via the ascription of an interpretive layer that not only fulfills these functions but, with particular regard to the present argument, permits the gaps left by other systems of explanation to be filled – not by the kind of premature physiology that is based on blind faith in a particular sphere of scientific endeavor but by current intentionalism.

Extensional Science and Intentional Ascription

Dennett explores physiology as a candidate extensionalistic science to which propositional content might be added. The search for an extensional physiology that can be said to have content and therefore be understood Intentionally, begins with the claim that "[n]o creature could exhibit Intentional behavior unless it had the capacity to store information." (1969, p. 45). It is the intelligent storage of information that is required of such a system, that is the capacity of the entity to *use* information for its own ends. "...the information stored can be *used* by the system that stores it, from which it follows that the system must have some capacity for activity other than the mere regurgitation of what is stored" (p. 45). Noting that many definitions of information storage fall short of specifying information use, he quotes MacKay (1956): "any modification of state due to information received and capable of influencing later activity, for however short a time." Dennett's definition emphasizes *intelligent* information storage: "We should reserve the term "intelligent storage" for storage of information that is *for* the system itself and not merely *for* the system's users or creators." (p. 46) Evolution plays a central role in this argument. "The useful brain is the one that produces environmentally appropriate behavior, and if this appropriateness is not utterly fortuitous, the production of the behavior must be based somehow on the brain's ability to discriminate its input according to its environmental *significance*" (p. 47, emphasis in original). This means the brain must respond differentially to stimuli, distinguishing stimuli inputs on the basis of their appropriateness to the environment that they "herald"; else "it will not serve the organism at all". The capacity of the brain to do this does not depend on its size or physical structure. Rather, it is the brain's capacity to make appropriate linkages between its afferent (input) and efferent (output) functions that matters, that is, "to discriminate its input according to its environmental *significance*." (p. 47).

But environmental significance is "not an intrinsic physical characteristic." The brain cannot use physical tests to sort its inputs. (p. 48) Therefore, the only remaining hypothesis is that it does so by chance: "if such fortuitous linkages could in some way be generated, recognized and preserved by the brain, the organism could acquire a capacity for generally appropriate behavior". The sorting of physical structures must be done by an analogue of natural selection, though this cannot operate via a principle of physical fitness. What Dennett calls an excursion into elementary hypothetical evolutionary history helps. The upshot of this that the organism makes blind responses to stimulation but "the response that *happens* to be appropriate is endorsed through the survival of the species that has this response built in" (p. 49). "As the evolutionary process continues, the organisms that survive will be those that happen to react differently to different stimuli – to discriminate." Although discriminatory behavior is "only blind, dumb-luck behavior; that is, it is the fortuitous and unreasoned result of mutation, the appropriateness of which is revealed by the survival of the strain" (p. 50) it is through this process that "a variety of simple afferent-efferent connections can be genetically established, and once they are firmly 'wired in' the afferent stimuli can be said to acquire *de facto* significance of sorts in virtue of the effects they happen to have, as stimuli-to-withdraw from and stimuli-to-remain-in-contact-with." (p. 50) This is of course a "just-so" story, though probably typical of adaptionist evolutionary thinking – it ought to be acceptable on that basis to radical behaviorists who often subscribe to such interpretations of natural selection (Skinner, 1981). On the other hand, it ought not to be acceptable as a kind of behavioral science to radical behaviorists, who reject such physiologizing when it is done by Hullians, for example. Dennett traces how this brain processing of stimuli might be carried out via neural firings. The remainder of his chapter is given over to an account of Goal Directed Behavior.

The Ascription of Content

It is one thing to propose that a psychological theory requires the assertion of content to a pre-existing extensional theory such as that provided by physiology, quite a trickier endeavor to justify the proposed level of analysis in psychologically-relevant terms, lay down procedures for the process of ascription, and specify the relationship between the two. So Dennett finally explores the manner in which content might be ascribed to physiological systems. This is the crux of his argument against behaviorism and for a psychology that proceeds by ascribing content to the extensional facts of physiology. The personal level of explanation which is Dennett's focus here and which he contrasts with the subpersonal level at which physiology operates, is that of "people and their sensations and activities" rather than that of "brains and events in the nervous system" (p. 93). The subpersonal level provides mechanistic explanations but these are not appropriate to the explanation of socalled mental entities such as pain. While there is a good understanding of the neurological basis of pain, Dennett raises the question whether the presumed evolutionarily-appropriate afferent-efferent networks underlying this understanding are sufficient (they are certainly necessary) to account for the "phenomena of pain". This resolves itself into the question whether pain is an entity that exists in addition to the physical questions that constitute this network (p. 91).

There are no events or processes in the brain that "exhibit the characteristics of the putative 'mental phenomena' of pain" that are apparent when we speak in everyday terms about pain or pains. Such verbalizations are non-mechanical, while brain events and processes are mechanical. It is unclear for instance how an individual distinguishes a sensation of pain from a nonpainful sensation. The only distinguishing feature of pain sensations is "painfulness" which is an unanalyzable quality that allows of only circular definition. But people can do this and the personal level is the level at which pains are discriminated, not the subpersonal. Neurons and brains have no sensation of pains and do not discriminate them. Pains, like other mental phenomena, do not refer: our speaking of them does not pick out *any thing*; pain is simply a personal-level phenomenon that has, nevertheless, some corresponding states, events or processes at the subpersonal, physiological level. This is not an identity theory: Dennett does not identify the experience of pain with some physical happening; he maintains two separate levels of explanation: one in which the experience of pain, while felt, does not refer, and one in which the descriptions of neural occurrences refer to actual neural structures, events and states in which the extensionally-characterized science deals.

The task now becomes that of ascribing content to the internal states and events. The first stage is straightforward: since intentional theory assumes that the structures and events they seek to explain are appropriate to their purpose, an important link in this ascription is provided by hypotheses drawn from the natural selection not only of species but, as we have seen, of brains and the nervous system. A system which through evolution has the capacity to produce appropriate efferent responses to the afferent stimulation it encounters, clearly has the ability to discriminate among the repertoire of efferent responses it might conceivably make. Its ability so to discriminate and respond to the stimulus characteristics of its complex environment means that it must be "capable of interpreting its peripheral stimulation", to engender inner states or events that co-occur with the phenomena that arise in its perceptual field. In order for us to be justified in calling the process intelligent, something must be added to this afferent analysis: the capacity to associate the outcomes of the afferent analysis with structures on the efferent portion of the brain.

For instance, in order to detect the presence of a substance *as food*, an organism must have the capacity not only to detect the substance but thereafter to stop seeking and start eating; without this capacity to associate afferent stimulation and efferent response, the organism could not be said to have detected the presence of the substance *as* that of food. Dennett uses this point to criticize behaviorists for having no answer to the question how the organism selects the appropriate response. There is a need to invest the animal which has discriminated a stimulus with the capacity to "know" what its appropriate response should be. (In fact, behaviorists have ducked this problem by designating it a part of the physiologist's assignment and drawing the conclusion that the behavioral scientists need be concerned with it no longer. The conventional behaviorist wisdom over the kind of cognitive ascription to which Dennett refers is that it amounts to no more than "premature physiology".)

The content of a neural state, event or structure relies on its stimulation *and* the appropriate efferent effects to which it give rise, and in order to delineate these it is necessary to transcend the extensional description of stimulus and response. It is necessary to relate the content to the environmental conditions as perceived by the organism's sense organs in order that it can be given reference to the real-world phenomena that produced the stimulation. And it is equally important to specify what the organism "does with" the event or state so produced in order to determine what that event or state "means to" the organism. An aversive stimulus has not only to be identified along with the neural changes it engenders to signify that it means danger to the animal; in addition, the animal has to respond appropriately to the stimulus, for example, by moving away. Failure on its part to do so would mean that we were not justified in ascribing such content to the physiological processes occurring as a result of the stimulation. If we are to designate the animal's activities as "intelligent decision making" then this behavioral link must be apparent. Only events in the brain that appear appropriately linked in this way can be ascribed content, described in intentional idioms.

How are the intentional ascription and the extensionally descriptions related then? This ascribed content is not an additional characteristic of the event, state or structure to which it is allocated, some intrinsic part of it discovered within it, as its extensionally-characterized features are discovered by the physiologist. They are a matter of *additional interpretation*. The features of neural systems, extensionally-characterized in terms of physiology or physics, are describable and predictable in those terms without intentional ascription which makes reference to meaning or content. Such a scientific story, consisting in an account of behavior confined to talk of the structure and functions of neural cells and so on, is entirely extensional in character. But such an extensional story could not, according to Dennett, provide us with an understanding of *what the organism is doing*. Only an intentional account can accomplish this, "but it is not a story about features of the world *in addition to* features of the extensional story; it just describes what happens in a different way".

Such an extensional theory would be confined to the description/explanation of the *motions* of the organism rather than of its *actions*.

Physiologists in practice, do not seem able to get along in their account of the function of the central nervous system without viewing neural operations as signals, reports or messages (for modern corroboration, see, for a typical textbook treatment: Gazzaniga, Ivry & Mangun, 1998; and *inter alia* for direct research evidence: Angulo, Staiger, Rossier & Audinat, 1999; Kandel, 2001). As Dennett (1969, p. 79) puts it, "Were the physiologist to ban all Intentional coloration from his account of brain functioning, his story *at best* would have the form: functional structure A has the function of stimulating functional structure B whenever it is stimulated by either C or D... No amount of this sort of story will ever answer questions like why rat A knows which way to go for his food. If one does ascribe content to events, the system of ascription in no way interferes with whatever physical theory of function one has at the extensional level, and in this respect endowing events with content is like giving an interpretation to a formal mathematical calculus or axiom system, a move which does not affect its functions or implications but may improve intuitive understanding of the system." The required ascriptions of content would thus not comprise intervening variables within a physiological theory but a "heuristic overlay" on the extensional account. Such a centralist theory would have two components: "the extensional account of the interaction of functional structures, and an Intentional characterization of these structures, the events occurring within them, and states of the structures resulting from these. The implicit link between each bit of Intentional interpretation and its extensional foundation is a hypothesis or series of hypotheses describing the evolutionary source of the fortuitously propitious arrangement in virtue of which the system's operation in this instance makes sense." The ascription of content to afferent and efferent operations is necessarily imprecise since it depends on the inexact locutions we use in everyday life.

Prelude to Ascription

Dennett's (1983) intentional stance is the attribution of prebehavioral mental events to human and non-human animals in order to predict their behavior. Dennett claims that ascribing beliefs, attitudes and other mentalistic thought processes to individuals is a legitimate scientific endeavor as long as it results in more accurate predictions of overt behavior than would otherwise be possible. The intentionality of which he speaks is that of the philosopher and merely indicates that these processes are "about" something. The intentional stance may thus facilitate a richer understanding of behavior since it is possible to speculate what the individual is thinking about and, in the case of more than one person, to conjecture the inter-personal cognitive contingencies made possible by people's thinking about each other thinking about each other (Dennett, 1987a, pp. 239–40.)

The distinctiveness of Dennett's theory can be more clearly understood in terms of its contradistinction to physicalist theories of the mind-brain relationship. He contrasts it with *type identity theory* on the one hand and what he calls *Turing machine functionalism* on the other. Identity theory relates (identifies) each mental event to a physical brain event and claims that individuals who share a mental event (say, believing that grass is green) also share a physical brain event. The brain events in question are it is claimed "physically characterizable *types* of brain events" (Dennett, 1978, pp. xiv–xv.) The claim that mental events are identical with brain events retains its credibility, Dennett argues: it amounts only to the non-dualistic view that there is no need for a category of non-physical things to account for mentality. But the notion that there are types of physical brain event that account for the commonality of mental events is no longer tenable: it proposes too strong a view of the mind-brain relationship. What physical things have in common is not commonality of physical components or design (compare the manual, gasoline-driven and electric forms of lawnmower, for example) but their function or purpose.

Turing machine functionalism conserves the idea of mind-brain identity but has a novel take on the question of commonality. In it, the physical predicate corresponding to a mental predicate must abstractly specify functions and functional relationships. The language by which computers and programs are described fits this requirement. Software can be functionally described in the abstract, that is, independently of the description of the physical hardware that constitutes the computer. There is no need to argue that two organisms, both of which believe that grass is green, must be physically similar, but they must share a 'functional' condition or state (or, more accurately, be specifiable as such in functional language) (Dennett, 1978, p. xvi). This is still too "strong" for Dennett who argues that the notion that it is highly speculative to claim that individuals who share a common mental state could ever be described such that they would be in "the same logical state whenever they shared a mental epithet" (Dennett, 1978, p. xvi; see also Dennett, 1978, Chapter 2).

Dennett's answer is *token functionalism*: two people who share a belief in the color of grass have in common simply that they can be "predictively attributed" this belief, that is, their behavior can be more accurately predicted if this belief is ascribed to them. He avoids the charge of epiphenomenalism by retaining the assumption that every mental event is a physical event. The role of intentional systems is to legitimize (at least in part) mental predicates. Dennett avoids the view that our speaking ordinarily of mental events such as beliefs and desires picks out real corresponding entities. We can speak of *fatigues* for instance without there being any corresponding entities – this is much as he pointed out in the opening chapter of *Content and Consciousness* that "voices" and "sakes" do not refer. "For me, as for many recent authors, intentionality is primarily a feature of linguistic entities – idioms, contexts – and for my purposes here we can be satisfied that an idiom is intentional if substitution of codesignative terms do not preserve truth…" (Dennett, 1978, p. 4)

More specifically, the attribution of intentionality to organisms assumes that they are rational and that their behavior can be explained on some level in terms of what their mental processing is *about* (Dennett, 1987a, pp. 240–2). Dennett proposes several orders of intentional system, applied in his illustration, to the behavior of vervet monkeys. The assumption having been made that the behavior of the vervet can be better understood/predicted by attributing to it prebehavioral beliefs, desires and other mentalistic constructs, the question is *which* of these notions should be attributed? Given that the animal is assumed rational, the following hierarchy can be employed. *First order intention* simply incorporates beliefs, desires etc.: "*x* believes that *p*". If, however, *p* itself contains an intentional idiom, that is, beliefs about beliefs, the elaboration of the intentional system is increased: "*x wants y* to *believe* that *x* is hungry" is a *second order* intentional system. And so on: in principle, humans could presumably cope with a level of sophistication approaching infinity, but reaching beyond a handful of levels is probably impracticable. (Dennett, 1987a, p. 243).

What is even more interesting is that Dennett contrasts these levels of intentionality with *zero order*, "the killjoy bottom of the barrel: an account that attributes no mentality, no intelligence, no communication, no intentionality at all to the vervet" (Dennett, 1987a, p. 246a). Dennett's strategy is to argue against the anti-adaptionism of evolutionary biologists such as Lewontin and Gould, but in the process he ascribes to behaviorism this fundamental position in the classification of explanations. So why proceed beyond the zero-order level? An entirely descriptive psychology would presumably devote itself to providing reports of observed behavior, unelaborated by unobservables invented for the purpose of giving a more anthropomorphic account. Dennett's answer implies that the search for a more elaborate interpretation is motivated by a desire for enhanced predictiveness: "Lloyd Morgan's canon of parsimony enjoins us to settle on the most killjoy, least romantic hypothesis that will account systematically for the observed and observable behavior, and for a long time the behaviorist creed that the curves could be made to fit the data well at the lowest level prevented the exploration of the case that can be made for higher-order, higher-level systematizations of the behavior of such animals. The claim that *in principle* a lowest-order story can always be told of any animal behavior (an entirely physiological story, or even an abstemiously behavioristic story of unimaginable complexity) is no longer interesting. It is like claiming that in principle the concept of food can be ignored by biologists – or the concept of the gene or the cell for that matter – or like claiming that in principle a purely electronic-level story can be told of any computer behavior. Today we are interested in asking what gains in perspicuity, in predictive power, in generalization, might accrue if we adopt a higher-level hypothesis that takes a risky step into intentional characterization." (Dennett, 1987a, pp. 246–7)

Dennett proposes that the intentional stance invokes the intentional strategy by which it may be put into operation (Dennett, 1987a, p. 17): First, treat the object whose behavior is to be predicted as a rational agent; second, figure out what beliefs that agent should have given its place in the world and its purpose; do the same for its desires; third, predict how it will act to further its goals in the light of its beliefs. The use of the intentional strategy is a deductive process: it proceeds from the *a priori* ascription of rationality to the system whose behavior is to be explained. There is one application of this stance that could revolutionize behavioral science. I proposed earlier possibility that the extensional science developed by behavior analysts could form the basis of a social behavioral psychology through the ascription to its findings and theories of propositional content, much as Dennett proposes a physiological psychology in which content is ascribed to the findings and theories of neuroscience. Dennett's poor view of behaviorism leads him not to consider this possibility, but it is in fact both feasible and currently practiced – by social cognitive psychologists. Before this, however, it is necessary to establish whether behavior analysis can provide the extensional science of behavior, including human behavior, that would be required for such a venture. This brings us to the discussion of the nature of radical behaviorism.

According to Dennett, an extensional science of psychology is infeasible. That is, an extensional science could not deal with intensional phenomena – no paraphrase or translation is possible that captures the intentional idiom in extensional language – rather than that an extensional science can have no existence at all. But he obviously sees intensionality as the very heart of psychology. Extensional behavioral science just is not psychology. It is, however, entirely possible to show that an extensional science is feasible, and that the contextual stance on which it rests is the antithesis of the intentional stance on which intensional behavioral science (cognitive psychology) is based; that this extensional science of behavior uniquely inheres in radical behaviorism: other neo-behaviorisms do not qualify on account of their incorporation of intentionalistic explanations; that the extensional behavioral science can handle verbal behavior that cognitivists interpret, on the basis of Brentano's thesis, as intentional.

Chapter 4

The Contextual Stance

Despite Dennett's refusal to consider that behaviorism can provide other than uninteresting, killjoy, bottom of the barrel interpretations of behavior, radical behaviorism is able, via its inclusion of private events and rule-governed behavior, to embrace a hierarchy of behavioral complexity within its explanatory purview. There is no need to exclude thoughts and feelings, language and calculation, or the generation of novel behavior from its range of interpretation, nor to confine its accounts to simple responses in uncomplicated environments. The contextual stance is capable of accounting for the interpretation of human behavior in ways which make for its prediction and/or its at-least-plausible interpretation on an operant basis, as long as the intersection of the individual's learning history and the stimuli composing the current behavior setting remain the building blocks of its explication.

The operant interpretation looks to increasingly complex contingencies to explain increasingly complex behavior. Nor is such science confined to three-term contingencies. Sidman (1994) proposes that n-term contingences can be invoked to explain increasingly complex behavior. In the three-term contingency, R the basic $R \rightarrow S^R$ relationship ("performing a response, R, produces consequence S^R" which makes future enactment of R more likely) comes under the control of a discriminative stimulus, S^D such that S^R follows R only when S^D is present. If the presentation of an S^D sets the scene for reinforcement contingent upon the performance of R, then S^R will be produced only when S^D is present and R is enacted. The enactment of a response other than R (i.e., not-R) will not produce S^R even when S^D is present. When the prebehavioral stimulus is other than S^D (i.e., not-S^D) neither R nor not-R will produce S^R. The four-term contingency places this whole relationship under the control of a further stimulus. The discriminative stimulus, S^D, now controls the relationship between the response, R, and the reinforcing consequence, S^R, only when a further antecedent stimulus, A, is present. The presence of any other antecedent stimulus (not-A) means that neither R nor not-R will produce S^R. In the presence of A, R will produce S^R only when S^D is also present.

All of this may strike Dennett as little higher than the bargain basement level but when it is applied to verbal behavior its capacity to illumine a considerable range of human behavior that behaviorists have long ceded to cognitive psychologists becomes apparent. The n-term contingency does not have to be discussed within the confines of verbal behavior but some of its most significant implications for human behavior arise in this context. The fourth term, A or antecedent stimulus, in the four-term contingency may be considered what Michael (1982, 1993) calls an *establishing operation* (EO). An EO is a "function-altering stimulus," one, that is, which causes another stimulus to take on reinforcing functions. An advertisement for an anti-perspirant might make claims that using this product will reduce or eliminate sweating; in other words, it presents a rule for action based on the three-term contingency: the product becomes the discriminative stimulus, the proposed response repertoire involves buying and using it, and the promised consequences are a lower rate of perspiration and less social embarrassment. If the product is an entirely new brand, of which consumers will not have heard, they cannot by definition have established responding appropriately to these contingencies. Given the competitive nature of the anti-perspirant market, there is no reason for thinking that this product will work any better than those currently in use and thus no special reason why the rule presented in the ad should be motivating. If, however, the message is presented by a famous sports personality, his or her presence may become an establishing operation, changing the words into a motivating message by turning the rule into an augmental. The presence of this antecedent stimulus means that the rule has a greater likelihood of being acted upon.

The four-term contingency also gives rise to the analysis of *equivalence classes* and *stimulus equivalence* (Sidman, 1994). Nonhumans have proved capable of learning complex relationships if they are appropriately reinforced, but generally do not innovate by initiating relationships they have not been explicitly taught (Sidman, 1994). By contrast, even young humans display the emergent behavior of relating A to C having been trained that A is related to B and that A is related to C (that is, their selection of the appropriate response has been reinforced.) This capacity for transitivity is one of three criteria used to establish *stimulus equivalence*, a phenomenon which appears peculiar to human animals. The other criteria are symmetry (matching A to A), and reflexivity (matching B to A having learned that A relates to B.) The implication is that these stimuli (A, B and C) belong to the same *stimulus class*, since they evoke the identical response: for instance, a picture of a car (A), the written word "car" (B), and the written word "auto" (C) are all likely to evoke the oral response "car." The role of stimulus equivalence in radical behaviorist interpretation is particularly interesting as it participates in relational frame theory.

According to Sidman (1994) stimulus equivalence is a basic or primitive (that is, unanalyzable) occurrence, the result of the contingencies of survival encountered in the course of phylogenic evolution rather than something acquired by learning. In this it resembles the phenomena of reinforcement and discrimination: we are just "built that way" (Sidman, 1994, p. 389.)

However, relational frame theory (Hayes & Hayes, 1989; Hayes, Barnes-Holmes & Roche, 2000) seeks to extend the analysis inherent in the study of stimulus equivalence. It emphasizes that the functions of a stimulus can be transferred to other stimuli, indeed that such a function can be understood only in terms of its relationships with other stimuli. A stimulus may come to reinforce behavior depending on whether it is greater than, less than or equal to another stimulus that has already received the capacity to reinforce via a training procedure.

Language can be understood in this way as a symbolic process in which the functions of one stimulus are transferred to another which comes to stand for it. Because of the ubiquity of such transfers, the problem of the "poverty of the stimulus" is overcome: depending on the context, a pairing of stimuli can acquire numerous meanings and functions. An immensely wide range of linguistic abilities can thus be acquired. Relational responding of this kind is portrayed in relational frame theory as operant behavior, an overarching response class. Relational frames such as "equal to" or "fatter than" are defined in terms of three properties which partially overlap with those Sidman employed to define stimulus equivalence. The three properties that are peculiar to relational frames are (1) mutual entailment, (2) combinatorial entailment, and (3) the transformation of functions. (For an accessible introduction to relational frame theory, see Hayes, Strosahl & Wilson, 1999).

Mutual entailment is the symmetry of stimulus equivalence: the derived bidirectionality of stimulus relations. The relationship $A \rightarrow B$ entails the relationship $B \rightarrow A$. *Combinatorial entailment* is the transitivity and the equivalence of stimulus equivalence: when in a particular context $A \rightarrow B$ and $B \rightarrow C$, and also a relation is entailed between A and C and another between C and A. E.g., if A is harder than B and B is harder than C, then a harder-than relation is entailed between A and C and a softer-than relation between C and A. *A transformation of stimulus functions* occurs when the function of one stimulus is transferred to another stimulus which is a co-member of a relational network. If we have enjoyed a play by a particular author and are told that she has written a sequel, we are more likely to show marked approach behavior toward the new play: reading reviews, checking out where it is on stage, going to see it, and so on. If one hears that a scholar who has produced interesting research on the behavior analysis of environmental spoliation and conservation is now doing work on verbal behavior one is more likely to show similar attention to the later work. As these examples show, the transfer of function is highly situation- or context-specific, depending on how concepts such as "play," and "sequel," "environmental conservation," and "verbal behavior" participate in various relational frames that have become part of one's operant repertoire. In everyday discourse, we would say that the likelihood that one would exhibit the approach behaviors in question depends on one's interests and aspirations.

The Contextual Strategy

The contextual strategy, which follows from the contextual stance, is inductive: it makes no *a priori* assumption about the rationality of the system that is to be predicted but assumes that its behavior is environmentally determined. The environment is the agent. The procedure in which this strategy consists is as follows: first, treat the behavior to be predicted as environmentally determined; second, figure out the past contingencies that have shaped that behavior; third, predict how present and future contingencies will influence the continuity of that behavior. Steps 2 and 3 require figuring out the system's learning history, including the capacity of its behavior to be contingency-shaped and rule-governed. Step 3 predicts the susceptibility of future enactments of the behavior to rules and contingencies, and thereby requires an assessment of the motivating or inhibiting nature of the behavior setting.

This strategy results in levels of explication ranging well beyond the purely descriptive and, as the literature of behavior analysis makes evident having empirical justification that goes beyond that which Dennett would expect to adduce for his post-killjoy levels of analysis. The zero order level of analysis would be well illustrated by basic empirical regularities. It is purely descriptive and makes no demands on higher level constructs to explain it. Even from a radical behavioristic viewpoint however it is incomplete: it fails either to explain observed behavior by relating it to the environmental conditions that shape and maintain it, or even to interpret it in these terms. Even a radical behaviorist analysis requires a first-order level of explanation which achieves this. An operant psychology would need to relate observed individual behaviors systematically to the patterns of reinforcement and punishment by which they can be explained and to the discriminative stimuli under whose control they might come. But our analysis can go further still. Radical behaviorism has long proceeded beyond the analysis of contingency-shaped behavior (its first order level) by considering the (causal) role of private stimuli and the rule-governance of most if not all human behavior. Although in both cases the contingencies themselves have been held to provide ultimate control of human behavior, the interpretation of complex human behavior has in fact increasingly relied upon theoretical entities located within the individual. In contrast to the primitive radical behaviorism cited by Dennett (cf. Dennett, 1995), recent formulations deny that any but the simplest human behaviors can be considered entirely contingency-shaped – tapping one's fingers absentmindedly, for instance. The unlikelihood of operant conditioning occurring in humans without conscious awareness has long been noted (Brewer, 1974), casting doubt on whether the word "conditioning" is justified or useful. Most if not all human behavior is influenced by rules that specify setting-response-outcome contingencies which, at the most basic level, arise from the verbal behavior of others.

When the individual lacks a relevant learning history and therefore rules for performing a given behavior, decision making is required. In the cognitive depictions of this, behavior is said to be preceded by "deliberative processing" or "systematic processing" or the "central route to persuasion". In a radical behaviorist interpretation, such behavior is governed by "other-rules" embodying social pressures. Lacking a learning history, the individual uses other rules as a surrogate. As he or she develops experience, a history of reinforcement and punishment prompts the generation of self-rules which take the place of others' formulations of the situation. Finally, this person's behavior is characterized by apparent spontaneity as the discriminative stimuli that compose the behavior setting evoke self-rule-governed responses. The higher-levels of operant analysis which the contextual strategy makes possible apparently undermine Dennett's insistence that behaviorism cannot handle post-descriptive accounts of human choice.

An individual faced with a situation that is new to her has no specific learning history with respect to the behavior that is socially appropriate to such circumstances. However, in proportion to her having a learning history for rule-following, she is likely to seek out and act on "other-rules," those made available by members of her verbal community. As a result of her consequent actions, she acquires a learning history. Thereafter, reasoning with respect to her newly-acquired behavioral experience will lead to the formation of "self-rules," those she formulates by reasoning about the situation and her performance within it and these rules will henceforth guide action without constant deliberation. The initial lack of a relevant learning history prompted a search for other-rules; the acquisition of such a history means that self-rules can be extracted from experience. This account is entirely consistent with radical behaviorism. However, once we acknowledge the individual's capacity to make self-rules, her behavior cannot be predicted (let alone controlled) by someone whose knowledge of her is confined to the contingencies of reinforcement in operation. Her capacity to think beyond the contingencies, to create her own history of reinforcement, even her own fantasies that bear no relation to her actual learning history, renders the behaviorist program of predicting and controlling behavior unfeasible (Garrett 1996).

More generally, people have the capacity to create learning histories for themselves, to misrecall the past, and to act as though the resulting imaginings were true. People can reinterpret their past (and present) and act upon their deliberations even though (a) this is against their learning history and what it would lead one to predict they would do, or (b) it is not the only course of conduct open to them. People join religious sects for instance having convinced themselves that their entire lives were leading up to this moment of conversion (rather than to running the gangland empire they seemed to have been moving toward since age 14, or becoming the professor of art history their post-doctoral studies had seemed to be preparing them for). This does not mean cognitive processes are autonomous since, except in cases of psychosis, the imagined history or potential course of behavior must come from somewhere, must have been described by others, for instance. However, such "mental simulation" or "personal rule formation and following" means that behavior is not necessarily the result of learning history. If we recognize that behavior can result from rules or descriptions of contingencies never encountered then we are justified, in the absence of a known learning history, in ascribing intentionality in order to try to predict behavior more accurately.

The standard radical behaviorist response to this is twofold.

First, these imaginings, if real, are caused – and caused by external contingencies. But can this be empirically demonstrated? It would be necessary to demonstrate a one-to-one correspondence in order to do this. In fact, we have no access to an adult's learning history which would be necessary to make such a demonstration, nor to her imaginings since they are, by definition, covert events. Second, the real contingencies will take over control of behavior once the individual is exposed to them. Again, can this be demonstrated empirically rather than asserted as an act of faith? What are the "real" contingencies? In the animal lab we know what they are. In the real world, the complexity of different environmental impingements on an individual, the fact that her behavior is "multiply determined" even in the behaviorists' terms, that several schedules of reinforcement may have brought her here, etc. makes it impossible to know what the actual contingencies are with any greater accuracy than we can determine what the imagined contingencies are. Chomsky's review put paid to the idea that the precision available in the laboratory is equally available to the interpretive operant psychologist.

A system like radical behaviorism which posits prediction and control as the criteria for scientific success falls short as a comprehensive explanatory system if it can be shown that its subject matter cannot be predicted. The above argument implies not simply that, given the present state of knowledge and investigative technique, particular behaviors cannot be predicted, but that a certain class of behavior is inherently unpredictable. Rule-governed behavior often cannot be predicted: this is so whenever the individual acts upon covert rules which are not based on simple cost-benefit analysis and are not therefore directly amenable to others who are faced solely with the cost-benefit facts (Garrett, 1996; Prelec & Herrnstein, 1991).

The Stances Compared

While the intentional strategy thus provides a logical basis for understanding the philosophical underpinnings of cognitive psychology, radical behaviorism is a natural starting point for delineating the contextual strategy (Foxall, 1999). The equation of the contextual idiom that underlies radical behaviorism with its portrayal of psychology as non-intentionalistic is not always precisely what is meant by "contextualism", though Pepper's (1942) account of contextualism provides a philosophical treatment that is clearly contiguous with the present exposition of the contextual stance. Pepper (1942, p. 232–3) points out, for instance, that the contextualist is not interested in past events per se but in "the event live in its present. What we ordinarily mean by history, he says, is an attempt to *re-present* events, to make them in some way alive again... It is not an act conceived as alone or cut off that we mean; it is an act in and with its setting, an act in its context." The-act-in-context is the *root metaphor*, as Pepper puts it, of contextualism; we should, today, more likely call it a *global paradigm*. (For detailed discussion of contextualism, see Hayes, Hayes, Reese & Sarbin, 1993). There is no conflict here, but presenting contextualism as a philosophical *stance* (in parallel with the intentional *stance*) makes possible some emphases that are not explicit in Pepper's account. It also facilitates direct comparison with the intentional stance. However, there are certain advantages in presenting the argument from contextuality in terms of a *stance*, especially since the present aim is to compare this position with that which arises from the argument from intentionality.

Like the intentional stance, the contextual stance is a pre-empirical philosophy of science, a means of conceptualizing how the world may work prior to directly investigating it. It states that *behavior is predictable in so far as it is assumed to be environmentally determined; specifically, in so far as it is under the control of a learning history that represents the reinforcing and punishing consequences of similar behavior previously enacted in settings similar to that currently encountered.* It is the prediction and explanation of behavior in terms of the interaction of the current behavior setting and the individual's learning history that is at the heart of the contextual stance. Behavior setting and learning history intersect to define the *situation* which is the immediate determinant of the probability of responding. By prefiguring the likely positive and aversive consequences of behavior, the situation promotes or facilitates the kinds of response that the individual has previously enacted in similar settings.

Dennett's *intentional stance*, as we have noted, predicts behavior by attributing suitable desires (goals) and beliefs (information) to "intentional systems," those entities including humans and nonhumans, and computers, that are amenable to second-guessing of this kind. The contextual stance, by contrast, predicts and explains behavior by attributing it to its environmental effects, the rewards and sanctions it tends to produce. The intentional strategy, by identifying the propositional attitudes necessary for the organism's adaptation to its environment, provides social cognitivism, the dominant paradigm, with a rationale for its research program. The contextual stance, by contrast, proposes that the behavior of a system can be predicted from knowledge of its current *behavior setting* – that is the opportunities open to it to behave and the consequences of so behaving; and its *learning history* which gives salience to some elements of the behavior setting by permitting the individual to value/evaluate those consequences (that is, by comparing the *costs* of performing the behavior with its *rewards*). Hence, it is closely associated with radical behaviorism and provides a vehicle through which the nature of radical behaviorist interpretation can be explored.

The intentional strategy predicts the behavior of a *rational* system (Dennett, 1987a, p. 17) by, *first*, treating the object whose behavior is to be predicted as a rational agent; *second*, figuring out what beliefs that agent should have, given its place in the world and its purpose; do the same for its desires; *third*, predicting how it will act to further its goals in the light of its beliefs. The contextual strategy makes no *a priori* ascription of rationality to the system but predicts its environmentally determined behavior. The test of this strategy rests on its capacity to elucidate learning history and hence reveal the vulnerability of the individual's behavior to the setting variables to which it is exposed. Both strategies entail objective, third-person stances. Dennett (1978, pp. 3–4) states that "... a particular thing is an intentional system only in relation to the strategies of someone who is trying to explain and predict its behavior". There is no assumption in the intentional stance that the system *really* has beliefs and desires - only that its behavior is better predicted if these are ascribed to it. Hence, "The decision to adopt the strategy is pragmatic, and is not intrinsically right or wrong" (Dennett, 1987a, p. 7), words that echo Skinner's claim, already quoted, that the truth criterion of radical behaviorist interpretation inheres in its usefulness (1988e, p. 364). The contextual stance, by contrast, works not by ascribing internal mental operations to a system but by observing external environment-environment regularities. The sources of information on these regularities is three-fold: 1. by observation/inference of contingency-shaping; 2. by observation/inference of rules expressed by other persons to the system in question, or articulated by the system in question; 3. by inference from the regularities of context-in-context observed of the system.

These inferences and observations are never of "what is going on in the system's mind;" nor are they intentional ascriptions. They are observations or inferences of n-term contingencies (Sidman, 1994), of which the "three-term contingency" is the most familiar explanatory device within this paradigm. The difference between teleology and contingency is further clarified by consideration of the former's assumption of rationality on the part of the agent whose behavior is to be predicted or explained. Dennett (1978, pp. 6–7) states that an intentional system is rational in that it *optimally* achieves its designated/ascribed goals. Hence, "one predicts behavior ... by ascribing to the system *the possession of certain information* and supposing it to be *directed by certain goals*, and then working out the most reasonable or appropriate action on the basis of these ascriptions and suppositions" (p. 6). "It is a small step to calling the information possessed the computer's *beliefs*, its goals and subgoals its *desires*" (ibid.) The behavior of a contextual system is contingent upon the prior environmental consequences produced by its behavior; it is contingent, not necessarily rational in the sense of optimizing, though it may be rationalized in the sensed of reasoned out where "reasoning out" is understood to be a behavior (Skinner, 1974).

The intentional system is not autonomous – otherwise it would not be predictable. Indeed, Dennett (1987a, p, 49) claims that "A system's beliefs are those it *ought to have* given its perceptual capacities, its epistemic needs and its biography". "A system's desires are those it *ought to have*, given its biological needs and the most practicable means of satisfying them. Thus intentional systems desire survival and procreation, and hence desire food, security, health, sex, wealth, power, influence..." "A system's behavior will consist of those acts that it *would be rational* for an agent with those beliefs and desires to perform". The use of the intentional stance therefore depends on teleological reasoning by one intentional system about the needs, beliefs, desires, epistemology, biology and circumstances of what it takes to be another such system. This depends on common ground between the systems: the predicting system may generalize from its own needs, beliefs and desires to those of the target system. It may also rely on observation and reasoning. But the key component is the assumption that the target system is rational in the pursuit of its desires. Not that Dennett claims that intentional systems are fully rational at all times; but they are "marvelously rational" (1988, p. 52), rational enough that is for this to be a reasonable assumption for this stance. The contextual stance does not rule out rationality but understands it as a special case of contingent behavior. The focus in the contextual stance is on the actual control of behavior by its environmental consequences. There is no *a priori* reason to expect that this will accord with optimization; however, the empirical behavior analysis involving the matching law indicates that it usually will in practice (Herrnstein, 1997.) It is now possible to consider at greater length the special nature of radical behaviorism.

Extensional Behavioral Science

It is usual to portray the defining characteristic of radical behaviorism as its avoidance of mediational terms, be they intervening variables or hypothetical constructs (Moore, 1998; cf. Amsel, 1989). This is not an isolated opinion: Staddon (2001b, p. 148) states unequivocally that "for radical behaviorism as well as for the earlier Watsonian variety, 'internal states' are a no-no." The argument is that since the explanatory ideal of radical behaviorism is to account for behavior exclusively by reference to its contingent environmental consequences and their associated observable stimuli, the contingencies at its heart neither require nor permit mediation by cognitive, neural or hypothetical states, events or constructs (Skinner, 1963). Radical behaviorism is said moreover to be unique in its avoidance of terms that mediate stimuli and response: on this basis radical behaviorism can be delineated not only from contemporary cognitivism but equally from the neo-behaviorist approaches of Tolman and Hull. Skinner's oft-quoted statement in favor of the kind of theory that consists in empirical generalizations and avoids "theoretical terms" sums up the position. His objection to *theory* is an objection to "any explanation of an observed fact which appeals to events taking place somewhere else, at some other level of observation, described in different terms, and measured, if at all, in different dimensions." (Skinner, 1950, pp. 193–4). For Skinner, the practice of science consists in "a search for order, for uniformities, for lawful relations among the events in nature. It begins ... by observing single episodes, but it quickly passes on to the general rule, to scientific law" (1953, p.13). Such a descriptive science is not anti-theoretical, though its theoretical concentration is on the establishment of empirical regularities rather than on explanations that employ unobservables (such as attitudes, intentions and traits of personality) which are alleged to exist at some other level than the observed data (Skinner, 1950).

The suggestion has been made that radical behaviorism does not in practice avoid mediational terms and that its "private events" are simply theoretically under-developed mediational constructs (Staats, 1996). If this were accepted, it would be difficult to avoid the conclusion that radical, Tolmanian and Hullian systems differ only in degree rather than kind and that they have similar implications for the relationship between behaviorism and cognitivism and, indeed, for the origins of cognitive psychology. This issue is important at least in its implications for the relationship between behaviorism and cognitivism. For the argument has been made that cognitivism has its origins in the mediationism of both Tolman and Hull (e.g., Leahey, 1987, p.390; Schnaitter, 1999, p. 217): while cognitivism is cast as a natural successor to the mediational systems of both of these men, Skinner's radical behaviorism is portrayed as the natural offspring of the behaviorist ideal (e.g., Lee, 1988).

My argument that the avoidance of intentionalistic explanation rather than the avoidance of mediational processes is the hallmark of radical behaviorism has two components. First, radical behaviorism does indeed employ mediating events and that they are moreover essential to its conception of private events. Second, it is in this respect distinct from the neo-behaviorisms of Tolman and Hull which do employ propositional content. Definitively support for either of these arguments would require an exhaustive analysis of the entire output of Skinner: if such an analysis revealed a single instance in which he employed propositional attitudes, the thesis would fail. The argument, therefore, takes the following form. First comes the proposition that radical behaviorism has demonstrated that it can explain behavior without recourse to propositional content, thereby demonstrating the logical independence of the contextual stance as it manifests in radical behaviorism. Second, it is argued that radical behaviorism, nevertheless, employs mediating variables in order to achieve its explanations. Third, the neo-behaviorisms of Tolman and Hull are shown not only to employ mediating events but mediating events that are propositional in nature.

The first proposition concerns the logical independence of the contextual stance. Skinner's assertion that there can be an independent science of behavior rests upon the capacity of behaviorism to demonstrate that it can deal non-intentionally with the phenomena usually attributed to "mind". The claim of the contextual stance, as a philosophical basis of behavioral science, is that radical behaviorism can indeed cope with all the phenomena that fall within its purview without recourse to intentional idioms. That is, it can describe them extensionally, without resorting to propositional attitudes or opacity of reference. This is true of contingency-shaped behavior, the verbal behavior of the speaker, and that of the listener. As the following analysis shows, the language describing each of these is referentially transparent.

Behavior analysis is an extensional science that does not rely on the attribution of propositional content to any of the elements of the three-term contingency. It describes both contingency-shaped and rule-governed behaviors in terms of "a system of functional relationships between the organism and the environment" (Smith, 1994, pp. 127–8). Hence, an *operant response* "is not simply a response that the organism thinks will have a certain effect, it does have that effect". Further, a *reinforcer* "is not simply a stimulus that the organism desires to occur. It is a stimulus that will alter the rate of behavior upon which its occurrence is contingent". And a *discriminative stimulus* "is not simply a stimulus that has been correlated with a certain contingency in the organism's experience. It is one that successfully alters the organism's operant behavior with respect to that contingency". Descriptions of contingent behavior do not take propositions as their object; rather their object is relationships between an organism's behavior, its environmental consequences, and the elements that set the occasion for those contingent consequences. So behavior analysis does not attribute propositional content to any of the elements of the three-term contingency. "Instead of accepting a proposition as its object, the concept of reinforcement accepts an event or a state of affairs - such as access to pellets - as its object" (p. 128). Mentalistic description: "The animal desires that a pellet should become available". The behavior analytic description is not "The animal's lever presses are reinforced that a pellet becomes available". It is: "The animal's lever presses are reinforced by access to pellets". A discriminative stimulus would not be described as a signal *that* something will happen but simply that a contingency exists. "It attributes an effect to the stimulus, but not a content". Whereas the substitutability of identicals fails in mentalistic statements (such statements are said to be logically opaque), behavioral categories are logically transparent, suggesting that "behavioral categories are not a subspecies of mentalistic categories" (p. 129).

Neither is the proposition that "reinforcer" merely denotes "desire" feasible: desires are not equivalent to reinforcers, nor reinforcers to desires. Common-sense notions imply that if a stimulus is (positively) reinforcing it is desired, and if it is desired it is because it is a (positive) reinforcer but in fact neither holds. Objects of desire may not be attainable (the fountain of youth, perpetual motion) and so cannot be (linked to) reinforcers. Nor are reinforcers necessarily desired: on FI schedules, electric shock maintains responding for monkeys, pigeons and rats. The shocks are easily avoidable, but are not avoided. They cannot be "desired," yet they reinforce behavior. Nor yet do functional units of the speaker's verbal behavior such as mands and tacts (Skinner, 1957) have propositional content. They are simply statements of contingencies that account for an individual's behavior in the absence of his or her direct exposure to those contingencies. A mand is "a verbal response that specifies its reinforcer" (Catania, 1992, p. 382): for example, "Give me a drink" plus the unspoken, "You owe me a favor" or "Else I shall ignore your requests in future". Even if this is expressed as "I desire that you give me a drink...," it is actually no more than a description of contingencies. A tact is "a verbal discriminative response... in the presence of or shortly after a stimulus" (Catania, 1992 p. 399): "Here is the bank". Even if this were expressed as, "I want you to see the bank", its function would be confined to establishing the stimulus control of the word "bank", as when the listener replies, "Oh, yes, the bank." More technically, the *mand* denotes the consequences contingent upon following the instructions of the speaker or of imitating his or her example. Much advertising consists of mands – "Buy three and get one free!" "Don't forget the fruit gums, mum" – which indicate contingencies that are under the control of the speaker. *Tacts* present a con*tact* with part of the environment and, depending on learning history, a potential for behavior on the part of the recipient. A trade mark or logo may be followed by making a purchase or entering a store. The definitive source is Skinner's *Verbal Behavior* (1957).

The functional units of the listener's verbal behavior, as proposed by Zettle & Hayes (1982) similarly describe contingencies rather than express propositional content. Pliance, for instance, is the behavior of the listener who complies with a verbal request or instruction: hence, "Pliance is rule-governed behavior under the control of apparent socially mediated consequences for a correspondence between the rule and relevant behavior" (Hayes, Zettle & Rosenfarb, 1989, p. 201). Pliance is thus simply the behavior involved in responding positively to a mand. Tracking is "rule-governed behavior under the control of the apparent correspondence between the rule and the way the world is arranged" (Hayes, et al., 1989, p. 206). It involves tracking the physical environment as when following instructions how to get to the supermarket. Once again, its form – for example, "Turn left at the traffic light" plus the unspoken "And you'll get to Sainsbury's" – is a basic description of contingencies rather than an expression of propositional attitudes. Precisely as Smith has concluded with respect to contingency-shaped behavior, we may conclude with respect to rule-governance: "Beliefs and desires have propositional content. ... Designations of discriminative stimuli and reinforcing stimuli, by contrast, do not accept *that*-clauses." (Smith, 1994, p, 128) A third functional unit of listener behavior has no corresponding unit for the speaker: the *augmental* (Zettle & Hayes 1982) is a highly motivating rule that states emphatically how a particular behavior will be reinforced or avoid punishment. "Just one more packet top and I can claim my watch!"

Nor does radical behaviorism attribute propositional content to the "inner world we subjectively observe" (Smith, 1994, p. 138). This is interpreted as a "world of events". "Beliefs, desires, intentions, etc., have propositional content but are not the objects of subjective awareness, whereas inner speech, feelings, images, etc., are objects of inner awareness but do not have propositional content." Whilst we undoubtedly have the thoughts and feelings we report, there is no reason why these inner events must give rise to inferences of beliefs, desires and other propositional content. Indeed, as long as we are willing to assume analytically that there is no ontological discontinuity between the within-the-skin world, to use Skinner's terminology and the outer, then we are entitled to treat the inner simply as a series of stimuli and responses, albeit private rather than public. In other words, they can be represented in an extensional way if they are simply understood as constituted by discriminative or other stimuli for particular behavior. We do not, therefore, have to speak of thinking and feeling in intentional terms, and can thus pursue an extensional approach, at least toward the prediction and control of behavior.

We have reached the crux of the argument. On one hand it has emerged that it is legitimate to treat private events as stimuli and responses, that is, extensionally (though this entails the analytic assumption of ontological continuity between these private thoughts and feelings and publicly available elements of the three-term contingency.) What I hope is equally clear is that this formulation is a function of the way in which we use language. Since there is more than one way to use language, it is equally legitimate to someone who accepts the logical distinction between extensional and intentional sentences to argue that the thinking and feeling which Skinner characterizes as private events can be alternatively viewed as intentional because they are necessarily about something: we feel *something*, we think *of* or *that*, and so on. They can be represented as mental, therefore, in the sense that a different kind of linguistic form is needed in speaking of them. As long as we can avoid that linguistic form, we may succeed in formulating an extensional behavioral science; when we employ intentional idioms, we are necessarily invoking intentionalistic explanations. I shall argue that from a pragmatic point of view, each approach leads to similar (if not identical) levels of prediction and influence, if only because the intentional stance relies fundamentally on the contextual in order to achieve these functions. And I also shall argue that at the level of providing as comprehensive and logically consistent an explanation of behavior they also converge, this time because the contextual stance is fundamentally dependent on the intentional in order to accomplish this. Before this, however, it is important to distinguish radical behaviorism's avoidance of intentional terms (and consequently its prerogative as the basis of an extensional science) from the more familiar justification of its uniqueness, its avoidance of mediational or theoretical terms per se. Here, I think, radical behaviorism has been less clear-cut in maintaining its distinctiveness.

Behavior Theory

For, whatever its exponents claim, theory is inevitable in radical behaviorism, at least at the interpretational end of the spectrum. The view that radical behaviorism does not in practice rely on mediational terms has been countered on several grounds. First, inferred events are actually employed in radical behaviorist explanations. In a review of Donahoe and Palmer's (1994) *Learning and Complex Behavior*, Shull (1995) argues that the inclusion of inferred events may make it possible

> to conceptualize some behavior as occurring due to the presentation of a discriminative stimulus or a conditioned aversive stimulus, even though no such stimulus can be found in the environment. Internal events may be inferred to play those roles. Without inferred events, the occurrence of the behavior may be traced to observable antecedents, but the demonstrated molar relationships can often have an ad hoc character instead of being expressions of familiar behavioral processes. For someone who highly values conceptual integration as a scientific goal, then, accounts that rely on inferred events may hold some attractions.

Shull goes on to argue that

> Skinner, of course, made extensive use of these sorts of inferred events in his interpretations of complex phenomena such as "self-awareness", "self-control," "problem-solving," and verbal behavior (for example, Skinner, 1953, 1957, 1969). Autoclitic verbal behavior and editing, for example, were conceptualized as being evoked by stimulation (sometimes conditioned aversive stimulation) arising from the incipient stages of other verbal behavior. Other examples of behavior-analytic accounts based on inferred response and stimulus events include Schoenfeld and Cumming's (1963) analysis of perceptual phenomena, Hefferline's (1962) and Sidman's (1989) analysis of "defense mechanisms" such as repression, Sidman's

(1989) interpretation of "conscience," Keller's (1958) analysis of skill
learning, and Dinsmoor's (1985) interpretation of attentional phenomena.

In this, Skinner appears to differ not as sharply as radical behaviorist
philosophers of psychology have suggested from neo-behaviorists like Hull, Guthrie
and Miller. All of these

> made skillful use of inferred internal responses and stimuli to construct
> parsimonious accounts of complex behavior in terms of acquired S–R
> relationships. Interestingly, Skinner's approach has sometimes been distin-
> guished from those of the S–R theorists on the grounds that Skinner was
> unwilling to infer internal stimulus and response events to mediate
> temporal gaps between environmental cause and behavioral effect. It is
> indeed true that Skinner was often critical of such practices, especially
> when he was in his "prediction and control" mood. But he sometimes
> displayed a "conceptual integration" mood as well, and his interpretations,
> at least in their general style and purpose, would be hard to distinguish form
> those of Hull, Guthrie, Miller and kindred behavior theorists (see the
> exchange between Zuriff and Skinner in Catania and Harnad, 1988, pp.
> 216–217).

Zuriff (1979) notes Skinner's insistence that "postulated inner processes do not
provide adequate explanations of behavior. At best they are merely collateral by-
products of the environmental variables controlling behavior." (Zuriff, 1979, p. 1.)
Nevertheless, he notes Skinner's ingenious interpretations of complex human
behaviors in terms of covert stimuli and responses. Zuriff's argument is that "insofar
as these covert behavioral events exert control over observable behavior, they qualify
as inner causes." He provides ten examples from Skinner's work of internal stimuli
and responses acting as inner controlling variables; often these are intermediate
links in a causal chain that has external variables as its ultimate causes. "Nevertheless, in each example, an inner event is hypothesized to play a causal role, acting
as a link in a causal chain, albeit an intermediate one". (p. 2).

Behavior analysts' interpretations are even more prone to the assumption of
inferred entities. The analysis of verbal behavior, for instance, incorporates as causes
unuttered verbal stimuli. The analysis of the *autoclitic* is a case in point. In Skinner's
analysis of the autoclitic, the speaker is said to tact his or her own behavior before
it is uttered, thereby transforming it into a discriminative stimulus. The discriminative stimulus in question is, however, nothing less than an inferred unobservable.
Smith (1994) concludes that Skinner's theory of verbal behavior falls between a
behaviorist and a cognitive account. Other examples can be found, among which
the "automatic reinforcement" of playing the piano to oneself stands out so strongly
that it is acknowledged as a theoretical term by some radical behaviorists (Parrott,
1986; Reese, 1986) as well as mentalistic critics (Chomsky, 1959). Nor are such

inferences confined to the operant interpretation of verbal behavior. The private events of others, a concept central to the demarcation of radical from methodological behaviorism, cannot but be inferred.[5] They attract all the philosophical problems long associated with the inference of "other minds". Yet Skinner consciously infers the private verbal and emotional responses of others and acknowledges that they may serve as proximal ("non-initiating") causes of behavior (see Skinner's 1988a, 1988b, 1988c, responses to Schnaitter, 1988; Mackenzie, 1988; Stalker & Ziff, 1988). Even if the inferred events are cast by non-behaviorists as cognitive, their lack of propositional content implies that they are not equivalent to the mental entities posited by the intentional stance. Moreover, to the extent that they point to the kind of equivalence proposed by Overskeid (1995), the argument that they are necessarily cognitive is unproven. Smith's assertion that verbal behavior involves cognitive events seems at this stage an *a priori* assumption that is backed up by nothing more than assertion of the conventional folk wisdom of cognitivism in the face of a lack of a more convincing alternative.

The private events of others have in common with intentional attributions that they are inferred entities. In parallel with the operation of the intentional stance, they are ascribed by adherents of the contextual stance on the basis that they are the private events (the thoughts and feelings) that an organism *ought* to have, given its position and behavior, given that is its behavior setting and learning history. They may be self-reported but then so can be propositional attitudes. This raises enormous difficulties for radical behaviorist interpretation. First, we have to recognize that, in providing an account of the behavior of others, *any* appeal to private events is a matter of constructing theoretical constructs to account for observed behavior. Secondly, the status of an individual's privately experienced covert events *as scientific data* must be acknowledged. Kitchener (1996, pp. 116–120) dissects Skinner's categorization of theoretical terms as referring to events (1) taking place somewhere else, (2) occurring at some other level of observation, (3) described in different terms, and (4) measured if at all in different dimensions. Even one's own private events are, *contra* Skinner, (1) taking place *somewhere else* – that is, somewhere beyond the observation of the scientific community and, therefore, even if accepted within that community as relevant to scientific inquiry, of a different epistemological status from other scientific facts; (2) *at some other level of observation* – the evidence for the nature and function of these events is of a different order from that of other scientific facts (those amenable to public scrutiny); they are not open to experimental analysis, for instance; and are (3.–4.) *described and measured in different terms* – clearly the terminology is identical to that used for publicly available stimuli and responses, but the measurement can only be different. In the case of both my own and others' private events, I must make a leap of faith in assuming ontological continuity between the kind of stimuli and responses that can be manipulated in the experimental setting and those that are private. The lack of experimental analysis of private events renders their measurement qualitatively different.

Third, we have to resolve the difference between the private events of radical behaviorist interpretation and the propositional attitudes of intentional explanation. They are epistemologically distinct: private events, because they are *treated as* (that is, spoken of and used as) physical stimuli and responses, belong to an extensional approach to explanation, while propositional attitudes are part of an intensionalistic psychology. These are incommensurable approaches to explanation and there is no question of combining them in some way or of one providing an explanation of events that can simply be substituted for the other. Let us not imagine that behaviorism and cognitivism are converging. However, the general criticisms that behaviorists make of mentalistic explanation – the three main ones are the surplus meaning of the construct, the short-circuiting of explanation, and the tendency toward vacuous explanation – can be applied to attempts at interpreting behavior in terms of private events..

Radical Behaviorism's Claim to Uniqueness

It is the avoidance of propositional content, not that of mediational events, which serves to distinguish radical behaviorism from other neo-behaviorisms. The foregoing analysis does not put radical behaviorism on a par with other neo-behaviorisms such as those of Tolman and Hull, differing from them by degree but presenting the same kind of mediational explanation. Its import is that we must look beyond mediation per se for the essential difference between radical behaviorism and other neo-behaviorisms. The essential distinction is not between systems that employ mediation and those that do not but between those that employ explanatory terms that have propositional content and those that are non-intentional. In view of this claim, it is hardly surprising that those other neo-behaviorisms are the ones that gave rise to cognitivism. The following examination suggests that radical behaviorism is the only neo-behaviorist psychology to provide a basis for an extensional science of behavior.

Tolman's concepts generally appear to have propositional content. Despite his early efforts to operationalize *purpose* in terms that were anchored to observable reality, his later cognitive turn seems to have put him beyond the scope of descriptive behaviorism. Purposes are inferred entities. If a stimulus is present but the organism does not respond, behaviorists such as Guthrie or Skinner would say that no learning had taken place. But Tolman posits cognition as an intervening variable: "The stimulus is perceived but the response does not occur because it is not in accord with the organism's purpose" (Bry, 1975, p.56). *Latent* learning may nevertheless take place, which may serve the organism's purpose as well as stimulus-induced learning. Reinforcement is not necessary to learning, though it may lead to the *expectations* that guide further behavior. Tolman's distinction between learning and performance meant that he needed to make no direct link between stimulus and response. This positing of intervening variables is sometimes said to be more parsimonious than an account that looks for one-to-one connections between stimulus and response.

MacCorquodale and Meehl (1954) find evidence of intentionality in Tolman's conceptualization. They distinguish a data language to which Tolman's dependent and independent variables conform and belong, and a quasi-data language to which some of his intervening variables, those which take the form of hypothetical constructs (that is, have surplus meaning) belong. Tolman (1932) stated that he wished to avoid hypothetical constructs, "in which a construct acquires attributes which exceed the original defining operations", and stressed that his use of intervening variables like "cognition" and "expectancy" were to be understood in terms of the "establishing operations", in which an intervening variable is functionally related to both an empirically specified dependent variable and an empirically specified independent variable. Intervening variables are, therefore, ideally, theoretically neutralized. MacCorquodale and Meehl (1954, p. 183) find, however, that the empirical support Tolman adduces for his intervening variables relies for its power on "the common-sense kind of surplus meaning [that is] informally attached to these theoretically 'neutralized' terms." In order to account for the observed behavior of rats in mazes, Tolman (1932, p. 175) attributes to them the capacity to recognize one part of the maze as the other end of another part. MacCorquodale and Meehl (1954, p. 184) comment that

> recognize is not defined here, nor does it appear in the glossary or index; and surely it is not a word in the data language. The other end of A is a phrase ordinarily in the data language, but used thus only when it describes facts about the maze. In this sentence, however, it occurs in a clause following the word as, where the whole sentence of which it is a part says something, not about the maze, but about the rat's state (or recognition).

We have already noted that Skinner's covert events do not contain propositional content. As Kitchener points out (1977; cf. Kitchener, 1979, 1996; Ringen, 1976), however, Hull's do. Not only does Hull have to treat an r_g as an ordinary response, subject to reinforcement, extinction, etc.; he is also forced to treat it as "expectation ordinarily understood", so that it cannot be an ordinary response at all. As Deutsch (1960) argues, a fractional goal response must be reinforced by the goal response of which it is a part. Thus an r_g is not an ordinary response but an expectancy. "If this is correct, then the Hullian r_g–s_g mechanism for explaining purposive behavior must be judged to be inadequate since it presupposes teleological and cognitive concepts from the start and therefore cannot derive them as 'secondary principles' from neutral a-teleological concepts" (Kitchener, 1977, p. 54).[6]

The intentional nature of anticipatory goal response seems also to be apparent from Zuriff's (1985, pp. 126–7) account in which he uses this concept as a means by which behaviorists deal with the apparent foreknowledge that organisms have of future events. Zuriff, however, seems unaware of the implications of the philosophically intentional nature of r_g when he states that "...behavior under the antecedent control of anticipatory goal reactions not only shows the marks of purposiveness but

also can manifest the foreknowledge, expectations, and intentions of human action."
(p. 127)

Yet, there is good reason for both the dichotomous approach that Shull attributes to Skinner and the unequivocal attitude of other behavior analysts toward the inclusion of mediating events in a science of behavior and in radical behaviorist interpretation. The explicit admission of mediation often leads quickly to the inclusion of intentional idioms, as mediating events cease to be mere building blocks within a theory and take on explanatory functions that necessitate their being about other events or entities. So it is quite easy for an account of behavior in terms of classical conditioning to lead to the understanding that the conditioned stimulus is a *signal for* the unconditioned (), that what a stimulus (S) gives rise to is not a response but to an *expectation of* reinforcement (Bolles, 1972),[7] that mediating stimuli and responses can account for cognitive (i.e., representational) phenomena (Staats, 1996),[8] and so on. The safest means by which such semantic drift can be avoided is to deny the relevance of mediating events altogether, even though on other occasions, notably those of interpreting complex behavior with the tools made available by a relatively simple experimental analysis, their usefulness can be acknowledged. Sometimes the drift is made light of, as in Bolles's (1979, pp. 85–87) account of Tolman's going beyond the definition of learning as the strengthening of S–R connections, involving a single syntactical unit that is both simple and of universal applicability, to posit an organism's map-reading capacity, something that requires description in a syntactically looser form that necessitates the use of terms relating to perception and the formation of expectancies. Whilst admitting the "frankly mentalistic" import of Tolman's words, Bolles seeks to deflect the criticism they attracted to their author by arguing that since he defined terms such as "expectancy" and "demand" behaviorally, that as intervening variables they consti-tuted an explanatory device that was peculiarly psychological in nature and which referred to neither physiological or mental events. Be this as it may, it misses the point that it is the use of intentionalistic language that is at issue here and which marks the deviation from a purely extensional approach to explanation. After all, behaviorism's bounds are not ultimately ontological or methodological.

Chapter 5

Intentional Ascription in Practice[9]

Philosophers and psychologists frequently overestimate the extent to which purported measures of beliefs, attitudes, intentions and other items of intentionality actually predict and explain behavior. Nor do verbal expressions of intentionality, as behaviorists would characterize them, succeed except in the most situationally-bound circumstances. It is a continuing enigma of social cognitive psychology that in the absence of measures of these cognitive and behavioral variables that are *situationally* constrained in the severest fashion the simple correlations that simple theories of behavior would anticipate can rarely be demonstrated (Kuhl & Beckman, 1985; Foxall, 1997a.) This chapter draws attention to this in order to demonstrate that the improving success of social cognitivists in predicting and explaining behavior stems from their adoption of something akin to the intentional behaviorist approach advocated here, that is, the addition of a heuristic overlay based on the intentional stance to the findings of researchers implicitly employing the contextual stance.

The intentional strategy requires the attribution to an assumed rational system of the beliefs and desires it *ought* to have and thereby to predict the behavior of the system; if its behavior proves predictable by this method, we are justified in calling it an intentional system. The question that arises is how this abstract formula is to be translated into a practical means of predicting the behavior of intentional systems. Dennett's (1982, 1991b) means of investigating consciousness, *heterophenomenology*, involves applying the intentional stance to people's verbal behavior, treating it as a text to be interpreted in terms of their beliefs and desires. Much as one examines the text of a character in a novel in terms of what he or she says, what they do and what others say of them, plus background information about the author and his or her other writings, so one can produce an inter-subjective account of the text provided by another person. The heterophenomenology of the person consists in an account of "*what it is like to be* that subject – in the subject's own terms, given the best interpretation we can muster" (Dennett, 1991b, p. 98). The resulting account is, like a scientific hypothesis, subject to testing in the face of the evidence, and hence corrigible.

There is, then, little doubt that Dennett intends the heuristic overlay of intentional ascription to be accomplished on the basis of observation of the system's behavior. This is also a conclusion drawn by some of Dennett's critics such as Webb (1994) who have emphasized the philosophical downside of Dennett's failure to show how behavioral evidence is to be used by the intentional stance. According to Webb, any attempt by Dennett to do so will lead him into either "a radical irrealism or logical behaviorism" (p. 457). These possible consequences do not impinge on the quest to find a practical means of predicting intentional systems. Although I outline Webb's argument here, therefore, the solution for present purposes lies beyond his analysis. Yet his analysis is fruitful for what it reveals of the relevance of the contextual stance to the problem of correct intentional attribution. Failure to consider and take proper account of behavioral evidence will lead to inaccurate attributions of intentionality. The desires and beliefs the system ought to have must in part be derived from "important facts the system has been exposed to" (Webb, 1994, p. 459), or as Dennett (1987a, p. 19) himself puts it, "that the system's experience to date has made available." In the terminology of the contextual stance, this means that the system's learning history and behavioral history need to be taken into account. But how?

A clue is that the correct beliefs and desires arise out of consideration of the logical consequences of the beliefs the system has previously held, which introduces issues that the contextual stance would attribute to learning history plus the current behavior setting and the consequences it portrays as contingent on behaving. The big problem is that Dennett does not give a concise and useable answer to the question of just which of the many available potential consequences of behavior are to be taken into consideration in this process. Dennett raises the problem that the logical consequences of behavior are infinite in number. Webb seeks the answer in the witnessed behavior of the system, a thesis he expands by discussing the three sources of attributable desires identified by Dennett (1987a, p. 20) in what he described as his "flagship" exposition of the intentional stance.

First there are the fundamental desires for basic goods: "survival, the absence of pain, food, comfort and entertainment". Second are those desires that can be rationally deduced from the system's goals and situation. Finally, Dennett introduces a form of witnessed behavior as a source of intentional ascription, one that is confined to consideration of verbal behavior. This raises problems of its own, however, since "The capacity to express desires in language opens the floodgates of desire attribution "(Dennett, 1987a, p. 20). Dennett says little more about this means of belief attribution other than that these are beliefs the agent could not have had without language. As Webb points out, it would be useful here had Dennett made clear "just how we recognize utterances that call for desire attributions and how we know (based on what we hear) which desires to attribute." (p. 460). He notes however that Dennett's proposed method of intentional attribution: it allows for the attribution of desires on the basis of linguistic behavior. Dennett moreover is silent concerning any other attributions on the basis of witnessed behavior, but without some means of making these delimiting ascriptions of content, any attributions made in order to operationalize the intentional stance are likely to be implausible.

If the intentional stance is to be practically applicable as a means of accurate behavioral prediction, it is necessary that the process of intentional ascription be corrigible in the light of accruing information about the behavior of the system and its environment. There is no means to this end other than the incorporation of witnessed behavior. It is interesting that Webb adopts something closely akin to reasoning that is at the heart of radical behaviorism here. Ideally, he argues, only behavior that has actually been witnessed should be considered but this is impracticable. For instance, a person who has never smoked cigarettes before may write on a shopping list "Carton of cigarettes": the attribution of intentionality here cannot depend on whether someone else reads the shopping list. It is thus necessary to consider therefore behavior that is only available in principle (Webb, 1994, p.463). In radical behaviorist terms, the person making the list is a witness to his/her own behavior; it is immaterial that this opportunity is available only to him/her.

An important boundary condition that Webb introduces is that any behavior the intentional stance considers must be displayed at the surface of the system that is being predicted (Webb, 1994, p. 464.) Neuronal activity cannot be brought in to solve problems of the stance: only external behavior is permissible. Using information about brain states would make the intentional stance a subset of the design stance and make impossible the its intended capacity to identify a pattern of behavior more abstract that that given by the design stance. Only behavior that systems display at their surface is thus admissible. This is witnessed behavior. Webb's initial plan is to "incorporate all behavioral evidence available in principle into the intentional stance. An intentional state is thus defined as whatever intentional state would be attributed on the basis of the intentional system's environment and exhibited behavior, where the 'exhibited behavior' is to include all and only the behavior which (actually) occurred prior to its attribution" (p. 464.)

The import of Webb's analysis is that Dennett has shown no means by which the intentional stance can attribute intentionality on the basis of witnessed behavior. Webb suggests that in incorporating some such method, Dennett would reveal himself as a behaviorist, a designation he does not necessarily deny but which he claims to abhor. None of this impinges on the argument being pursued here. My reading of Dennett fully accepts the necessity of attributing intentionality on the basis of witnessed behavior; Webb's analysis is a useful corroboration. Social cognitive psychology has evolved its own method of incorporating both the contextual and intentional stances and provides a means of overcoming the problems Webb raises, at least on a practical level. To this we turn in this chapter which lays the groundwork for two arguments: first, that the program of social cognitive psychology is incapable of implementation without the prior use of the contextual stance, and secondly, that the methods evolved by social cognitivists can be usefully employed to provide the necessary link between the extensional behavioral science and intentional cognitive psychology.

The Attitude Revolution

When Dennett first published *Content and Consciousness* in 1969, attitude psychology, which lies at the heart of social cognitive explanation, had apparently failed. Its subsequent effectiveness is due to cognitive psychologists' adopting the contextual stance as the means of providing the syntactic structure to which they can ascribe semantic content in order to predict behavior. The verbal measures of beliefs, attitudes and intentions which cognitive psychologists had employed and to which they attributed propositional content when using them indexically of mental constructs, simply failed to predict the behaviors to which they referred. Only by introducing elements of the contextual stance into their models have cognitivists been able to predict behavior.

Attitude research is nowadays staunchly cognitive in its theoretical orientation: it is a quest to predict behavior by identifying and understanding the mental structures and processes that allegedly underlie it, giving it shape and direction (Ajzen 1987, 1988; Eagly & Chaiken, 1993; Fishbein & Ajzen, 1975.) As such, it exhibits the intentional idiom, attributing to individuals the attitudes and other belief-based propositional content necessary to predict their actions. Attitude research presents an opportunity *non pareil* to observe the intentional stance in operation in psychology. (Throughout this discussion of recent developments in attitude theory and research, it will be necessary to refer extensively to "attitudes" and "intentions," as the social psychologist does, in the sense of underlying mental structures and relationships. Attitudes and intentions in this sense are always intentional in the philosophical sense: they refer to something else, one always has an attitude *about* something else. A psychological attitude is, therefore, an example of a propositional attitude, as are several other belief-based constructs which will be spoken of in the following account: subjective norms, intentions, perceived behavioral control, and so on. When I refer to the propositional attitudes *per se* I always employ that full term; talk simply of attitudes refers to the particular mental structures I have so designated here.)

I shall argue here that careful examination of these developments in attitude research indicates that the ascription to intentional systems of propositional attitudes such as beliefs and intentions requires the antecedent interpretation of the system's behavior in terms of the contextual stance. That is, human behavior must first be conceptualized as due to the interaction of the current behavior setting and the system's learning history.

There has been a revolution in attitude research over the last three decades. Current emphases in attitude theory and research stem from the dire assessments of the evidence for attitude-behavior consistency published in the late 1960s and early 1970s. Wicker (1969) showed that early attitude research (from the 1930s to the 1960s) generally revealed positive but insipid relationships between attitudes and behaviors. The extent to which attitudinal variance accounted for behavioral variance was small indeed. Rather, as Fishbein (1972) noted, the evidence favored the prediction of attitudes from behavior rather than the expected position. In a judgment that was to foreshadow the role of specificity in future research, Fishbein registered that the relationships probed by earlier research were generally between global measures of attitude toward an object and very particular indices of behavior toward the object.

More recent work has generated much higher correlations for two of the attitude–behavior models which will be described in greater detail below. A meta-analysis of studies using the Theory of Reasoned Action undertaken by Sheppard *et al.* (1988) reported an average correlations between the *behavioral intentions* that are determined by these various cognitive variables and the *behaviors* to which they refer of 0.53; a more recent meta-analysis for this theory reported by Van den Putte (1993) found an average correlation of 0.62. In the case of the Theory of Planned Behavior, Ajzen (1991) reports, for a small selection of studies, an average multiple correlation of 0.71 between the cognitive variables and behavior. (Rather lower correlations have been observed, however, for both theories in a variety of contexts; see for instance Davies *et al.* 2002). The amount of variance in behavior accounted for by variance in the prebehavioral variables posited in these models is thus (for the studies analyzed) within the approximate range 25–50%, a significant improvement on the typical level of "less then 10%" found by Wicker (1969).

The accurate prediction and explanation of behavior require an understanding of why this change has come about. This is not an easy task since, despite the increasing cognitivist rhetoric of those attempting to explain the results of such work, the underlying methodologies are increasingly behavioristic. Those methodologies are of two broad kinds. Some researchers (e.g., Fazio & Zanna, 1978a, 1978b, 1981) have sought a solution to the original problem of understanding the consistency between global attitude toward an object and specific behaviors toward that object. Others (e.g., Ajzen, 1988; Ajzen & Fishbein, 1980; Bagozzi & Warshaw, 1990; Fishbein & Ajzen, 1975) have concentrated on predicting specific behaviors from various combinations of equally specific measures of the reasoning involved in forming attitudes, reacting to social pressure, and assessing one's self-efficacy and one's prior behavior.

Fazio (1990) proposes that these approaches are complementary in that (a) the "global" approach deals with spontaneous attitude elicitation that requires little or no mental processing and that leads directly to action; (hence this approach is known as spontaneous processing theory); and (b) the "reasoned" approach draws attention to the deliberation on the consequences of performing a behavior prior to forming an intention to do so; hence deliberative theory). However, our interest is primarily that research on attitude-intention-behavior relationships conducted in both traditions leads to two conclusions: attitude research has actually pointed up the situational influences on behavior rather than shown that behavior's alleged cognitive precursors are its best predictors; attitude researchers increasingly measure respondents' behavioral histories in order to predict their behavior, though they conceptualize their measures and achievements in cognitive terms.

Spontaneous Processing Theory

Fazio (1986, p. 214) defines an attitude as involving "categorization of an object along an evaluative dimension": specifically, an attitude is an association between a given object and a given evaluation (Fazio, 1989. p. 155.) The definition of attitude in terms of evaluation or affect is evidence of the propositional content ascribed to this construct. Spontaneous processing attitude theory (Fazio & Zanna, 1981) highlights how nonattitudinal factors are increasingly taken into consideration in the prediction of behavior from attitudes to objects. The variations in correlations between attitudes and behaviors depends on the variability in nonattitudinal factors from situation to situation, which is considerable. That is nonattitudinal factors moderate the relationship of attitude toward an object and behavior toward that object (Eagly & Chaiken, 1993). Fazio's model of the attitude-behavior process thus attempts to answer the question "*When* is attitude related to behavior?" rather than the more pervasive why? question. It assumes that social behavior is substantially determined by the way in which the individual perceives the immediate situation in which the attitude object is presented as well as the way the object itself is perceived. Situations are generally ambiguous and the individual's definition of any particular situation depends on how it is interpreted.

Behavior is guided by perceptions of the attitude object but also by perceptions of the situation in which it occurs: that setting is said to determine the event. For instance, behavior toward a particular person (attitude object) naturally depends on the individual's perception of him or her: but the style of that behavior will differ depending on whether the attitude object is encountered in his or her home, or a store, or at a party, or in church. "It is this definition of the event – perceptions that involve both the attitude object and the situation in which the object is encountered – that the model postulates to act as the primary determinant of an individual's behavior" (Fazio, 1986, p. 208.)

"Spontaneous" attitude research draws attention to the conditions under which attitudes have been formed: whether by direct experience with the attitude object, the role of experience in the formation of object-evaluation, and the verbal rehearsal of evaluations prior to behavior. The methodological procedures emanating from the deliberative models are actually measuring learning histories under the guise of addressing cognitive influences. The findings of research conducted within this framework bear this out. Major emphasis is placed on how past behavior is implicated in attitudinal dynamics. The extent to which an attitude guides behavior depends on the manner of its formation. Attitudes formed from direct experience with the attitude object are expected to differ from those stemming from indirect experience (for example word of mouth, advertising) in terms of their capacity to predict behavior. Especially when they have to articulate an attitude, for example to a researcher or to fill out a questionnaire, people draw on past experiences which "are organized and transformed in light of current contingencies" (Rajecki, 1982, p. 78). There is corroborative empirical evidence that the attitudes of people who have had direct experience with an attitude object (target) correlate moderately with subsequent attitude-relevant behaviors; attitudes where such experience is lacking correlate only weakly. Attitude-behavior consistency is higher when the preceding sequence has been behavior-to-attitude-to-behavior, rather than when it has been simply attitude-to-behavior.

A second emphasis is the effect of experience on the efficacy of verbal behavior. Whether an attitude guides behavior depends also on the accessibility of the attitude from memory. Research indicates that: (a) Attitudes formed behaviorally lead to a stronger object-evaluation bond than those formed indirectly and are as a result more easily accessed from memory. (b) The difficulty people encounter in assessing their attitudes (their evaluations of an object) is overcome by engaging in behavior with the object or by observing their own behavior with it. (c) Information gained through behavior or behavioral observation is more trustworthy than that presented by another person or medium.

The influence of repeated verbal expression also receives emphasis. An attitude's strength is also increased through its repeated verbal expression, though repeated expression is also related to attitude polarization. Accessible attitudes are, moreover, activated automatically in the presence of the attitude stimulus – without conscious and volitional cognitive processing. Not surprisingly, therefore, the role of prior knowledge is also stressed. Prior knowledge about the attitude object increases attitudinal-behavioral consistency presumably because such knowledge is attained through direct experience. As will be documented, there is empirical evidence that such verbal repetition increases the chance that the evaluative behavior described as an attitude will become a self-instruction that guides further responding.

It is also most relevant that direct experience with the attitude object is accorded central significance. A feasible deduction from Fazio's demonstration of the significance of direct experience with the attitude object is that the consequences of relevant past behavior are responsible wholly or in part for the probability of current responding in the presence of the attitude object. Current behavior could then be explained as having come under the stimulus control of the attitude object, such control having been established through the reinforcement resulting from previous experience with the stimulus. In other words, the entire episode might be depicted as operant conditioning and investigation might be directed toward identifying the consequences of behavior that accounted for its future probability. However, the explanation that has predominated is cognitive: attitudes formed through direct experience are held to be more accessible from memory than those formed indirectly. And accessibility, measured as verbal response latency (that is the speed with which the attitude is activated or recalled in the presence of the attitude object) is hypothesized to be directly proportional to behavior change. The strength of an attitude, its capacity to influence behavior in the presence of the attitude object, increases with such structural attitude qualities as clarity, confidence, stability and certainty.

Deliberative Theory

We have noted that some researchers have concentrated on predicting specific behaviors from various combinations of equally specific measures of the reasoning involved in forming attitudes, reacting to social pressure, and assessing one's self-efficacy and one's prior behavior. Each of these explanatory variables is assessed through the elicitation of respondents' beliefs, as the following brief account of the principal deliberative models – the theory of reasoned action (theory of reasoned action) and the theory of planned behavior – attests.

In the case of the theory of reasoned action, reasoned behavior that is under the individual's volitional control is assumed to approximate intentions toward its performance (Fishbein & Ajzen, 1975). The theory of reasoned action holds that intentions are determined by two belief-based cognitions: (i) *attitude toward performing the target behavior*, is measured as the respondent's belief that a particular action will have a given outcome or consequence, weighted by his or her evaluation of that outcome. (ii) *subjective norm*, the respondent's perceptions of the evaluations that important social referents ("significant others") would hold toward the respondent's performing the target action, weighted by the respondent's motivation to comply with them. Subjective norm is an attempt to capture the nonattitudinal influences on intention and, by implication, behavior. By permitting this consideration of perceived social pressure to enter the calculation of behavioral intentions, the theory takes account of some at least of the situational interventions that may reduce the consistency of the attitude-behavior sequence.

Consideration of the ways in which the components of the theory of reasoned action are disaggregated and measured by users of this method confirms both the propositional content of the underlying theory and the ways in which these components refer in practice to elements of behavior setting and learning history. *Attitude toward the act* is operationalized as "The person's beliefs that the behavior leads to certain outcomes and his evaluations of those outcomes. [Hence] [a]ccording to our theory, a person's attitude toward a behavior can be predicted by multiplying her evaluation of each of the behavior's consequences by the strength of her belief that performing the behavior will lead to that consequence and then summing the products for the total set of beliefs" (Ajzen & Fishbein, 1980, p. 8, p. 67).

The particular measurement technique involves respondents' engaging in verbal behavior that rates the attitudinal behavior in question according to a small number of its consequences (those representing *salient* behavioral beliefs that have been ascertained in previous qualitative research). In the case of the behavior: *buying organically-grown vegetables*, and its context: *at your usual supermarket next time you shop for groceries*, the required behavior might be elicited thus (the example uses only two belief dimensions for ease of exposition – there would normally be three or four – and shows the reversal of the rating dimension):

Buying organic vegetables when I shop for groceries is

expensive — : — : — : — : — : — : — inexpensive

(-3)   (-2)   (-1)   (0)   (+1)   (+2)   (+3)

environ. harmful — : — : — : — : — : — : — environ. friendly

(+3)   (+2)   (+1)   (0)   (-1)   (-2)   (-3)

In order that the belief statements elicited in this way can be weighted by the individual's strength of expectation that the behavior will actually lead to the stated positive or negative consequence, the respondent will be asked a question such as,

How certain are you that buying organic vegetables will prove environmentally friendly? and will be asked to answer "Not at all certain" (scores 0), "Slightly certain" (+1), "Quite certain" (+2) or "Extremely certain" (+3). Verbal behavior of this kind requires experience, a learning history. That is, in fact what is being measured by means of this technique.

Similarly, *subjective norm* is conceptualized and measured as a set of beliefs about what the respondent believes a significant other thinks about the respondent's performing the behavior in question

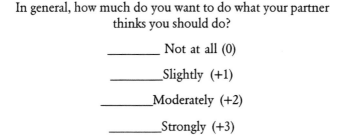

My partner thinks that

I should — : — : — : — : — : — : — I should not

(+3) (+2) (+1) (0) (-1) (-2) (-3)

buy organic vegetables

weighted by the respondent's motivation to comply with the referent:

In general, how much do you want to do what your partner
thinks you should do?

_____ Not at all (0)

_____ Slightly (+1)

_____ Moderately (+2)

_____ Strongly (+3)

Intentions are measured in a way that will by now be familiar:

I will buy organic vegetables on my next shopping trip

probable —— : —— : —— : —— : —— : —— : —— improbable

extremely quite slightly neither slightly quite extremely

The theory of planned behavior incorporates an additional variable, *perceived behavioral control*, in addition to the cognitive variables that form the theory of reasoned action (Ajzen, 1985). Perceived behavioral control is posited – along with attitude toward the act and subjective norm – to determine behavioral intentions. Further, on those occasions when perceived and actual behavioral control coincide or are closely approximate, perceived behavioral control is expected to exert a direct determinative influence on behavior. The theory thus applies to behaviors over which volitional control is limited. This is in contrast to the theory of reasoned action which is adamantly a theory for volitional behavior. Moreover, the extent to which perceived behavioral control adds significantly to the prediction of intentions is apparent from Ajzen's (1991) analysis of the results of several studies employing his theory which shows that the average multiple correlation was .71.

Perceived behavioral control is measured, for example, as

How much control do you have over the kinds
of vegetables you buy?

complete control — : — : — : — : — : — : — very little control

For me, to buy organic vegetables is

very difficult — : — : — : — : — : — : — very easy

If I wanted to, I could buy organic vegetables every time I shop

extremely likely — : — : — : — : — : — : —extremely unlikely

The reasoned approach indicates that in order to obtain high correlational consistency among attitude, intention and behavior these variables must be measured at identical levels of situational specificity. The first source of evidence concerns measurement specificity. The systematic processing group of attitude theories revolves around the belief that the degrees of specificity with which attitudinal and behavioral measures are each defined must be identical if high correlations are to be found between them. Generic attitude measures are therefore consistent with multiple-act measures of behavior toward the attitude object. It follows that the prediction of single acts is only likely to result from equally narrow measures of attitude, those that correspond exactly in level of specificity to the act to be predicted; those, moreover, that are framed as measures of the respondent's attitude toward performing that act in closely designated circumstances (Ajzen & Fishbein, 1980; Fishbein & Ajzen, 1975).

A second source of evidence is the quest for setting correspondence. Ajzen and Fishbein's (1977) analysis of numerous studies of attitudinal-behavioral consistency revealed that high correlations are probable only when the measures of attitude and behavior coincide with reference to the precise *action* to be performed, the *target* toward which the action is to be directed, the *context* in which the action would occur, and its *timing*. Evidence is finally available from the insistence on temporal contiguity. An important recognition was that measures of the cognitive precursors of attitude will be highly predictive only when there is maximal temporal contiguity of the behavioral and antecedent measures (Ajzen & Fishbein, 1980). The greater the temporal gap between attitude or intention and the behavior to which they refer, and hence the extent of situational intervention that potentially separates them, the lower will be their correlative consistency. It is the intention which *immediately* precedes behavior that is predictive.

The implication of the tight situational compatibility required of measures of target behavior and measures of its antecedent cognitive predictors (Ajzen & Fishbein, 1977) is that situational factors are highly significant for the correlational consistency of attitudes/intentions and behavior. Only when the situational influences governing both the prebehavioral and the behavioral variables are functionally equivalent are high correlations found. That the intertemporal period between prebehavioral and behavioral measures must be minimal if high correlations are to be found corroborates this view by pointing to the undesirability of unexpected situational demands which reduce the predictive value of measured intentions. Context and situation deserve a more central place in the explanation of behavior, and this is denied them by the partiality inherent in acceptance of the preeminence of the cognitive paradigm. The explanatory power of past behavior is frequently sufficient to make cognitive variables superfluous; that a behavior analytic theory may be capable of explaining or interpreting the evidence on attitudinal-behavioral consistency in full; and that in any case the reason for including a behaviorist perspective is to identify the consequences that past behavior has produced to account for the consistency of that prior responding and thus to use those consequences to predict future behavior.

This approach has proved successful in as much as the prediction of behavior, albeit under the specialized circumstances to which the theory applies, has been achieved. Hence, the technological achievement of the theory of reasoned action is that as long as its variables are measured under conditions maximally conducive to high correlations, which, as noted, refer to conditions of close situational correspondence, high correlations are usually obtained. However, the deficiencies of the theory of reasoned action identified by researchers all point up the importance of further incorporating behavior setting influences on an individual's behavior.

First among these is the disregard of behavioral outcomes. The theory of reasoned action predicts behavioral intentions and behaviors rather than the outcomes of behaviors: it would for example predict the likelihood of one's studying for a test, not of one's passing it (Sheppard, Hartwick & Warshaw, 1988). The amount of studying actually undertaken is under personal volitional control but whether one's hard studying leads to success in the test depends on factors that lie beyond that control: others in the household or library must cooperate, required books must be available at the right time, the necessary time and effort must have been invested in acquiring relevant study skills, to name but three. Even the individual who is strongly motivated and tries hard may find that circumstances may impede performance and achievement. The second deficiency stems from the recognition of uncompeting behaviors. The theory of reasoned action also concentrates on the prediction of single, specified behaviors which are not in competition with other behaviors. It thus avoids situations of choice within the class of intended behaviors or consequences.

The role of non-attitudinal influences in determining the incidence and consistency of behavior is the third source of deficiency. Most significantly, the theory of reasoned action has been criticized for not taking into consideration the full gamut of nonattitudinal personal and situational factors likely to influence the strength of the attitude-behavior relationship or to enhance the prediction of behavior. The authors of the theory of reasoned action are adamant that behavior is determined by behavioral intention and that all contributing influences are subsumed by the two elements that determine it: attitude toward performing the target act and subjective norm with reference to performing that act. Yet this principle of sufficiency has proved inaccurate in empirical work that has incorporated additional factors to increase the predictability of intentions and/or behavior. Factors not comprehended by the theory which have been found to improve the predictability of behavior include personal norm; self-identity; self-schemas; size and content of consideration set; availability of relevant skills, resources and cooperation; action control; past behavior; amount of reasoning during intention formation; perceived control/confidence; attitude functions.

Finally, deficiencies of the theory of reasoned action become apparent when one considers skills, resources, cooperation. Behavior that requires one or more of these items in order to be enacted is especially problematical. Much behavior requires all three, yet restricting the theory of reasoned action to behavior that is volitional means it requires only motivation on the part of the individual. Studies that have supported the model have dealt with only simple behaviors that require little if anything by way of resources and skills. Fishbein and Ajzen argue that such considerations have an effect on intention and thus were taken care of in their model.

The theory of reasoned action (Fishbein & Ajzen, 1975) probes the respondent's learning history by asking respondents to identify and evaluate (a) the utilitarian consequences of behaving in a particular manner and referring to this as an "attitude"), (b) the individual's socially determined rule-governed behavior ("subjective norm"). The theory of planned behavior (Ajzen, 1985) adds to these a measure of how successful the respondent expects to be; this variable delineates personal rule-formation and -following but is cognitively construed as "perceived behavioral control".

The Turning Point

Social cognitive psychology clearly cannot do without the contextual stance any more than it can avoid the intentional. But equally, as the next three chapters argue, radical behaviorist interpretation is incomplete on the level of explanation (though not necessarily prediction) by dint of its attempt to ignore intentionality. Indeed, an extensional operant interpretation of behavior raises three difficulties for a comprehensive psychology of complex human behavior: the accommodation of what Dennett designates the personal level of analysis, providing an account of the factors responsible for behavioral continuity, and dealing with the problem of equifinality and the need to delimit operant accounts of complex human behaviors. The problem that arises in connection with the personal level of analysis is that neither physiological theories (which operate at a sub-personal level) nor environment-behavior theories (which operate at a super-personal level) capture what the person as a whole knows (what pain is, for instance.) In the case of behavioral continuity, the problem is that radical behaviorism lacks a mechanism to account for the continuity of behavior between situations and over time. Continuity is sought in the discriminative and other setting stimuli that are constant form setting to setting. This is problematic in accounting for such phenomena as generalization and discrimination. Finally, the problem stemming from considerations of equifinality and delimitation is that of ambiguity surrounding the behavioral response enacted, the precise discriminative stimuli that should be held responsible for it, and the particular consequences that should be implicated in its shaping and maintenance.

These problems are examined in relation to three approaches to radical behaviorist interpretation each of which illustrates a particular difficulty. First, Skinner's solution to the problem of providing an extra-laboratorial account of behavior is to assume that such behavior is determined by the consequences of previous behavior of a similar kind. Skinner seeks to avoid teleology by concentrating on history. Hence the person gazing at his desk, moving papers to look underneath them, is according to Skinner "looking for his glasses". He can say this only because the last time he behaved in this way he came across them. His knowledge of what he is doing is gained from the same source as our knowledge of what he is doing: external observation. Second, Hayes' solution is to define in greater depth the stimulus basis of the behavior setting by showing how stimuli transfer their functions one to another by participating in relational frames. Third, Rachlin's solution is to claim that the causes of behavior are its final consequences, the effects it has on the environment, and these are nested within each other or to change the metaphor spreading out as do the ripples on a pond when a pebble is thrown into it. Each element of the contextual stance – history, behavior setting, and consequences – is thus explored. In examining them, there is no intention to criticize the approaches to radical behaviorist interpretation which are used to exemplify each of the problems of interpretation and the solutions offered by an intentional framework. Indeed, the analysis strengthens the position of each as an approach to extensional behavioral science. The aim is only to draw attention to the role of intentionalism in order to enhance their explanatory contribution.

Chapter 6

The Personal Level

Radical behaviorist interpretation fails to consider the personal level of analysis as surely as does the subpersonal analysis provided by physiology. It is simply not a part of the function of either physiology or extensional behavioral science to address this level. Nor is it feasible at the super-personal level which a purely extensional operant interpretation admits. It should be possible nevertheless to include a personal level of analysis in a framework of interpretation which embraces the findings of behavioral science but also admits a further heuristic overlay of intentional interpretation. If neuroscience provides the sub-personal level of analysis on to which ascriptive content can be overlain to arrive at the personal level of analysis required by Dennett's "physiological psychology," then a similar procedure can be followed to arrive at the personal level by ascribing content to the findings of extensional behavioral science. Moreover, a comprehensive social psychology requires it. In this way, we can talk more completely about cognition and affect, thinking and feeling. The personal level we posit here in contradistinction to the super-personal level of environment–behavior relations is that which Dennett defines in contrast to the sub-personal level of brains and neurons.

We should understand it, as he does, as the "level of people and their sensations and activities" rather than that of "brains and events in the nervous system" (Dennett, 1969, p. 93), *and also* rather than the environment and its events. The experience of emotion is to be understood at this level rather than that of the stimulus–response or the response–stimulus configuration which has been the focus of its study in operant psychology. Just as there are no neural events or processes that capture the experience of pain as we speak of it in everyday discourse, so there are no environmental events or processes that capture emotionality. Even to speak of mediating stimuli and responses in order to capture this personal level is arbitrary and fails to do justice to the non-mechanical, personal level at which emotion is known. There will of course be environmental correlates of emotionality but their study, as part of an extensional science of behavior does not embrace the unanalyzable sensation to which emotional language refers. The ascription of emotion requires that extensional level of scientific analysis – indeed it cannot do without it – but it is an overlay necessary to its full psychological understanding. There is an equivalent to knowing what pain is (that is not caught in physiological terms) in the environment-behavior sphere: knowing what reinforcement is in the context of what the behavior setting stimuli signal. This knowing comes from or at least is associated with the person's history of reinforcement and punishment. As the person who has felt pain knows what pain is, so the person whose behavior has been reinforced and punished knows what these effects are. But this knowing is unanalyzable: it is a feature of the personal level rather than either the physiological or environmental level. This personal level is not captured by any extensional analysis be it biological or behavioral. But that is not the verdict of radical behaviorists, who seem to have complicated the point out of all recognition.

We have distinguished three sources of knowledge into which the results of operant research may enter. The first is that of *behavioral science*, aka behavior analysis, the experimental analysis of behavior. It is extensional and super-personal in its scope, methodology and domain. The second is that of *radical behaviorist interpretation* as it has been practiced among others by Skinner, Hayes, and Rachlin. It attempts to provide an extensional account of complex behavior based on the extension of principles of behavior gained in the laboratory to naturalistic settings without incorporating intentional idioms. This strategy fulfills well the predictive purposes of those who embrace it but it fails on three counts to provide an adequate explanation of complex behavior. Third is *intentional behaviorism*, an interpretive mode based on the findings and theories of behavioral science plus the heuristic overlay provided by intentionalism. This strategy is not intended to predict behavior but to fill in the gaps left by radical behaviorist interpretation through the addition of an additional layer of intentional interpretation.

This chapter and those following are concerned primarily with radical behaviorist interpretation and why it needs this "heuristic overlay." We begin with Skinner's attempt to make sense of first-person accounts of behavior in terms of operant conditioning.

Skinner's "Third-Person" Account

Skinner's approach to interpretation is to seek the explanation of an individual's current behavior in his or her history of reinforcement and punishment, i.e., *learning history*. Despite the way in which the three-term contingency is usually symbolized as showing the factors that cause a response as the consequences that necessarily follow it, Skinner does not try to explain behavior by reference to future events. He avoids teleology by explaining current behavior in terms of the consequences that have followed similar responding in the past. Hence,

> When we see a man moving about in a room opening drawers, looking under magazines, and so on, we may describe his behavior in fully objective terms: 'Now he is in a certain part of the room; he has grasped a book between the thumb and forefinger of his right hand; he is lifting the book and bending his head so that any object under the book can be seen.' We may 'interpret' his behavior or 'read a meaning into it' by saying that 'he is looking for something' or, more specifically, that 'he is looking for his glasses.' What we have added is not a further description of his behavior but an inference about some of the variables responsible for it. There is no *current* goal, incentive, purpose or meaning to be taken into account. This is so even if we ask him what he is doing and he says, 'I am looking for my glasses.' This is not a further description of his behavior but of the variables

of which his behavior is a function; it is equivalent to 'I have lost my glasses,' 'I shall stop what I am doing when I find my glasses,' or 'When I have done this in the past, I have found my glasses.' These translations may seem unnecessarily roundabout, but only because expressions involving goals and purposes are abbreviations. (Skinner, 1953, pp. 89–90).

It is first necessary to contrast this with Skinner's view of cognitive explanation. Such explanation of behavior by reference to some conception of the inner world of the individual, his or her private experience, becomes under the influence of the behaviorist philosophy of psychology one which refers by contrast to his or her contact with prior contingencies. The strategy of cognitive psychology, according to Skinner (1977), is to move the contingencies of reinforcement inside the person, inside the head. The behavior analyst seeks always, by contrast, to locate the causes of behavior in the environment. So the individual who is "looking for his glasses" is engaging not in an internal problem solving activity but in behavior that in the past has led to the location of the spectacles (Skinner, 1953, p. 89–90). The person who thinks such and such or feels this or that is simply in touch with discriminative stimuli that happen to be "within the skin" rather than in the external environment (Skinner, 1974). These stimuli are not autonomous: they have been learned through the operation of the external environment and are therefore no more than "collateral" responses, that have been produced by the same external contingencies that are responsible for the overt behaviors that correlate with them. A sportsman's feelings of confidence when he plays tennis well are not the causes of his continued good performance but inner responses that result from the same external events that determine his achievements on court. Although he may find it tempting to report his performance as resulting from his changed beliefs, goals or emotions, or from his "inner game of tennis," his words would be easily translated by the radical behaviorist interpreter into an account based on his supposed learning history.

But Skinner's insistence on an objective, third-person account in a science of behavior that readily accepts private events raises a more fundamental difficulty.

"First-Person" Accounts

The behaviorist strategy of "discovering" a learning history in order to interpret complex behavior evidently accords with the philosophy of behaviorist explanation. Although it eschews the mentalistic fictions Skinner so strongly repudiated, it nevertheless extends the analysis of human behavior beyond the confines of a scientific enquiry. "Looking for" one's glasses thus becomes a re-enactment of behavior that preceded their being located in the past. Malcolm (1977) argues that mental terms do not refer to something that can be observed, whether within or outside the individual: terms such as "intend" are not referential in the sense that they point to something to be observed. Although he does not say so in as many words, his view is consonant with Dennett's position that intentions must be ascriptional, though this tells us nothing about their ontology. It is also reminiscent of the irreducibility thesis (Dennett, 1969, p. 30): no sentence fashioned according to extensional logic can capture the meaning of an intentional sentence. He makes some important deviations from Skinner's – and indeed Dennett's – insistence that science requires that an objective third-person account be given of behavior. By following Malcolm's reasoning here, it is possible to critique both of the central philosophies with which we are concerned, to see their conceptual similarities and contrasts, and to advance toward an *intentional behaviorism* which is capable of combining their merits.

Clearly, Dennett and Malcolm come from somewhat different philosophical positions. It is in fact Dennett's third-personal view that is here closer to Skinner's: the view that what we know about ourselves is based on essentially the same information as is what others know of us, something which he develops considerably in his treatment of heterophenomenology and consciousness (Dennett, 1991b; see also Dennett, 2003). But that need not detain us here, for here they are arguing something very similar in relation to behaviorism. If Malcolm were taking an unequivocally subjectivist stance with respect to intentionality I would not pursue the similarities in what they are saying. But although he uses the term 'first-person' account which Dennett avoids, there is something in Malcolm's insistence that mental terms must have external referents in the contingencies of reinforcement that ensures his inclusion in this part of my critique of behaviorism's being unable to supply the personal level of analysis. Dennett escapes the problem of how to deal with a personal level of explanation whilst assuming the third-personal stance of science by being willing to ascribe intentionality to the system whose behavior is to be predicted and explained. But there is no such let out for the radical behaviorist. Malcolm, despite speaking in terms of the first-personal perspective, essentially deals with the way in which that intentionality must be assumed and ascribed.

Malcolm's reasoning in coming to his conclusions is both sympathetic with Skinner's (in particular the insistence that socalled mentalistic terms can and must be traced to their environmental contingencies) and critical of Skinner's argument that the individual's description of his thoughts and feelings and that provided by another person are identical third-person accounts. Hence, he points out first that Skinner does not necessarily deny that people have purposes, intentions, and so on (to which mentalistic terminology refers) but that the terms are to be understood in a particular way. Skinner portrays mentalistic terms as explanatory fictions. It is not that he wants to claim that people are never thirsty or discouraged but that such words usually conceal an appeal to the independent variables that actually determine and explain behavior (see Skinner, 1953, p. 36). This means that statements that appear to explain behavior in mentalistic terms, for example, that it is the result of incentive or purpose are reducible to statements that embody the functional relationships that are fundamental to operant conditioning and thus to radical behaviorist explanation (Skinner, 1953, p. 87).

Malcolm also points out that Skinner is against explanations of (operant) behavior that proceed in physical or physiological terms. Rather than appeal to internal physiology in order to test its propositions about behavior, it should seek confirmation in the external physical consequences and outward behavior. Looking within diverts attention from the actual causes of behavior. "The practice of looking inside the organism for an explanation of behavior has tended to obscure the variables which are immediately available for a scientific analysis. These variables lie outside the organism, in its immediate environment and in its environmental history" (Skinner, 1953, p. 35). Skinner's attempts to reformulate psychology by explaining what mentalistic terms actually *mean* in the sense of the environmental causation to which they refer, is a philosophical contribution which identifies the misleading expressions found in ordinary language. "These expressions have a disguised meaning. They are 'abbreviations'. Skinner's task is to unpack these abbreviations by making explicit the behavioristic variables to which they refer in a 'concealed' way and which give them whatever intelligibility and usefulness they have." (Malcolm, 1977, p. 94).

Skinner is, of course, entirely right to point this out: as we have seen, even the operation of the intentional stance inescapably requires prior contextual analysis. When he writes that feelings of confidence, or believing, or perceiving, for instance, can be related to the environmental contingencies that are related to behavior (see Skinner, 1974), he is making the valid point usually not considered by cognitive psychologists that a contextual analysis of these events is often possible. Dennett's empirical excursion into cognitive ethology (Dennett, 1988), bear this out as does the work of the social cognitivists of attitude–behavior relations. Indeed, these latter examples suggest that the prior contextual analysis is essential to the use of the intentional stance. However, this does not make the intentional stance invalid: the contextual stance cannot handle all so-called psychological terms simply by means of translating them into the language of behavior analysis. The intensional cannot be so treated.

Skinner is arguing here against introspectionism, "the basic assumption of which is that each of us learns from his own case what pain, anger, fear, purpose, and so on *are*." After Wittgenstein, Malcolm argues that there is no possibility of our understanding each other's psychological language and thus such introspectionism leads to a kind of solipsism: worse, "it leads to the result that one's identification of one's own inner experience might be wrong without one's ever being the wiser" (Malcolm, 1997, p. 95). The behaviorist refutation of introspectionism shows that "our concepts of mental states and events cannot be divorced from human behavior." Skinner himself admits that we must take on the responsibility to show how a private event is connected to the person's description of it. "The intelligibility of psychological words must be based on something other than the occurrence of those words" (p. 96).

However, he argues, the fallacy of behaviorism, which is common also to physicalism, is the view that when a person uses a psychological sentence such as "I am excited", he is basing this at least partially on personal observations of states or events in his own body. Malcolm (1977, pp. 96–7) comments: "The truth is that it would be a rare case in which a person said that he was excited on the basis of noticing that his hands were trembling or his voice quavering. I do not say that it is impossible for such a case to occur... In the normal case, however, a man does not *conclude* that he is excited. He says that he is, and he is; but his utterance is not the result of self-observation." He also employs the following argument (which is germane also to Rachlin's teleological behaviorism which will be discussed in Chapter 8): "The point comes out very strikingly when we consider first-person reports of bodily sensations, for example, 'I have a headache.' It would be completely mad if I were to say this on the basis of noticing that my face was flushed, my eyes dull, that I was holding my head, and had just taken some aspirin. If someone were to say, *on that basis*, that he has a headache, either he would be joking or else he would not understand how the words are used. The same is true of a first-person perception sentence, such as 'I see a black dog'."

He argues further that behaviorists have erred by assuming that a psychological sentence expressed in first-personal terms is identical in content and method of verification to the corresponding third-personal sentence. We verify that another person is angry by the way the veins stand out on his neck, by the redness of his face and by his shouting. But we do not verify our own anger in this way. We do not as a rule attempt to verify it at all. Despite the ontological differences between Malcolm and Dennett, this echoes to some extent what Dennett is saying about one's knowing what pain is, being able to discriminate pain, but not to be able to give reasons for it or define what is meant by being in pain. Malcolm contends that verification is simply not a concept or operation that applies to many first-person psychological reports, those which are not founded on observation. While introspectionism supposes that they depend on observations of internal mental events, behaviorism supposes them to be founded on observations of either external events or of physical events taking place within the speaker's skin. In this respect both methodologies are in error as a result of imagining that a first-person psychological statement reports on something the speaker has observed or thinks he has observed. (Malcolm, 1977, pp. 97–98).

An individual's statement of purpose or intention belongs in a different class from one made by someone else on the basis of observing that individual. If we see someone turning out his pockets and recall that on previous occasions he has done this before producing his car keys from one of them we can reasonably conclude that he is looking for his car keys this time too. But it would be odd indeed if he himself were to work out what he was doing by observing that he was emptying his pockets as he had done in the past when looking for his car keys. If he announced that he must be looking for his car keys at present because he was doing what he had done in the past when finding them had eventuated, we should think him most odd, crazy, to be treated in future with circumspection.

Malcolm (1977, p. 99) also draws attention to speech acts such as "I was about to go home" which for Skinner present the problem that it "describes a state of affairs which appear to be accessible only to the speaker. How can the verbal community establish responses of this sort?" (Skinner, 1953, p. 262) Skinner's explanation is that as the speaker has previously behaved publicly, private stimuli have become associated with the public manifestations. "Later when these private stimuli occur alone the individual may respond to them. 'I was on the point of going home' may be regarded as the equivalent of 'I observed events in myself which characteristically precede or accompany my going home.' What these events are such explanation does not say." (Skinner, 1953, p. 262) Malcolm comments, "For Skinner 'private stimuli' would mean of course physical events within the individual's skin. The fact that Skinner regards this hypothesis as a possible explanation of the utterances, even though he does not know what the private stimuli would be, shows how unquestioningly he assumes that such a remark as 'I am on the point of going home' must be based on the observation of something." (Malcolm, 1977, p. 99). But the statement "I am on the point of going home" is not a prediction based on the observation of anything. "The announcement 'I am about to go home' is normally an announcement of intention. Announcements of intention are not based on the observation of either internal or external variables…" (Malcolm, 1977, p. 99).

Statements of intention are undoubtedly related to external events and someone who said he was about to go home would normally have a reason for doing so, for example, that it was time for dinner. But this does not mean that going home or making the utterance is under the "control" (in Skinner's sense) of dinner time. In Skinner's technical sense of control, y is under the control of x " if and only if x and y are connected by some *functional relationship*," and if control is given this sense then neither intentions nor statements of intention are "controlled" by anything (Malcolm, 1977, p.100). On the one hand, behaviorists' resolution in proposing that psychological language (that which deals with so-called mental phenomena such as believing, intending and wanting) has to be conceptually linked with public phenomena is entirely correct. (This is what was argued above, on the basis of psychological practice rather than philosophical argument, in terms of the demonstration that social cognitivists have to use the contextual stance as a starting point.) Otherwise, to put the matter in the terminology of behavior analysis, the verbal community could not teach children to use such terms appropriately. The psychological terms must have some external referent in preverbal behavior. But, on the other hand, "the employment of psychological terms outstrips their foundation in preverbal behavior. Someone who has satisfied us that he understands certain psychological terms begins to use them in first-person statements *in the absence* of the primitive, preverbal behavior that had previously served as the basis for judging that he understood those terms. He tells us that he feels ill, or angry at someone, or worried about something when we should not have supposed so merely from his demeanor. The interesting point is that in a great many cases we will *accept* his testimony. We conclude that he is angry when, if we had been judging solely on the basis of nonverbal behavior and visible circumstances, we should not have thought it. We begin to use his testimony as a new criterion of what he is feeling and thinking, over and above and even in conflict with the earlier nonverbal criteria." (Malcolm, 1977, p. 101)

There would of course be a radical behaviorist riposte to the effect that through contact with the person who "has satisfied us that he understands certain psychological terms," we had developed a learning history with respect to his verbal behavior that we had tried and tested according to the contingencies. Having done so we would again accept his verbal testimony since we had a learning history of doing so. However, the point is that this is an explanatory fiction, an untestable extrapolation of learning principles to a sphere where by its very nature we can have no empirical evidence for or against our assertions. This is not science. In fact we abandon the contextual stance at this point and rely on the intentional stance. We are using it whenever we 'trust' someone or interpret behavior in terms of trust when we have no access to a learning history. We cannot do without the intentional stance any more than social cognitivists can do without the contextual stance. They employ this stance by virtue of their observations of the contingencies to which they add propositional content; behavior analysts employ it (at least in their interpretation of complex behavior) in the absence of observations of the contingencies because the contingencies simply are not empirically available. Hence, "The first-person psychological sentences must be correlated with behavior up to a point. But they quickly go beyond that point. People tell us things about themselves that take us by surprise, things which we should not have guessed from our knowledge of their circumstance and behavior. A behaviorist philosopher will say that if we had known more about their history, environment, and behavior, we should have been able to infer this same information. I do not believe that there are any grounds for thinking so. The testimony that people give us about their intentions, plans, hopes, worries, thoughts, and feelings is by far the most important source of information we have about them. To a great extent we cannot check it against anything else and yet to a great extent we credit it. I think we have no reason to think that it is even a theoretical possibility that this self-testimony could be adequately supplanted by inferences from external and/internal physical variables." (Malcolm, 1977, 101–2.)

"Within the whole body of language the category of first-person psychological sentences has peculiar importance. The puzzling status of human beings as subjects and persons is bound up with these first-person utterances, which possess the two striking characteristics I have pointed out: first, they are not, for the most part, made on the basis of any observation; second, in many cases they cannot be 'tested' by checking them against physical events and circumstances *other than* the subject's own testimony. If we want to know what a man wants, or what he is thinking about, whether he is annoyed or pleased, or what he has decided, the man himself is our best source of information. We ask *him*, and *he* tells us. His own testimony has a privileged status in respect of this sort of information about himself, and *not* 'because he has had an extended contact with his own behavior for many years.'" (Malcolm, 1977, p. 102) "I have argued that behaviorism fails to perceive self-testimony in a true light. It mistakenly assumes that when a man tells you what he wants, intends or hopes, what he says is based on observation and therefore he is speaking about himself as if he were an *object of his own observation*. ... In short, behaviorism fails to perceive that self-testimony is not replaceable, even in principle, by observations of functional relations between physical variables." (Malcolm, 1977, pp. 102–3)

Hayes, Wilson and Gifford (1999) attempt to show that the concept of private events can address an individual's own account but they do not address the specific problems raised in this chapter. The truth is that psychological first-person reports or utterances lie beyond the bounds of behaviorism. They cannot be subjected to a behavioral analysis. We can indeed parse such sentences in functional terms as Schnaitter (1999) has suggested but how does this aid in explaining them or how they are related to the private events that give rise to them? The examples based on the kinds of locutions employed in applications of the theories of reasoned action and planned behavior which were discussed earlier indicate that it is entirely feasible to make the necessary translation of terms. But what can we do with these behavioral translations by way of interpretation without adding inferences that cannot be verified, for example, about the origin of the mands and tacts they include? While the technique makes it possible to specify the rules that people reveal in their responses to standard methods of attitude measurement in extensional language, the question arises: how are we to use this behavioristically-consistent locution in interpretation? It may appear to have some advantage in that it may be said to reveal the otherwise-elusive learning histories of those whose behavior we seek to delineate in terms of its environmental correlates. But the burden we place on the extensionalized statements of intentions to reveal a history of reinforcement and punishment is quite unrealistic, leading as it does to untestable propositions about the past.

We could always ask: why not confine our interpretations of people's psychological statements to a functional analysis of their verbal behavior involved in uttering such sentences? This would presumably be on the model of what Schnaitter (1999) suggests, so that a statement like "I believe eating green vegetables is healthy" could be functionally parsed into its autoclitic and tact-ful components. (Schnaitter's proposal is further examined in Chapter 7). But these functional categories, though interesting for armchair analysis, have no empirical foundation other than the observational (anecdotal) examples attached to them in *Verbal Behavior*. In other words they function exactly as do explanatory fictions from other sources, they allay enquiry, and so on. Analyzing a statement as a tact or mand, for instance, is to invent a learning history and behavior setting for the person who uttered it by proposing the contingences that led to the utterance and that will guide behavior based on it. This is sufficient for speculative analysis but it is not science. Our aim must be to bring science and interpretation closer to one another. Merely translating from one system to another does not bring this goal nearer. Radical behaviorists need to be aware of the two approaches to the use of psychological terms and to determine which they will take. The choice is between believing that I know I have a headache because I look in the mirror and note the way I am screwing up my face or that I base this knowledge on some means that does not involve observing either internal or external phenomena; that I conclude I must be looking for a book because I have observed myself systematically eyeing my bookshelves in the past, or that I simply know that I am searching for the dictionary.

Each of these intentional activities must of course be linked in some way to external events and another person to whom I cannot communicate verbally will judge from my behavior that I am in pain or looking for a book. But this is not the information I use to come to such conclusions. Behavior analysts, in other words, either incorporate the personal level of analysis in their interpretations of complex behavior or confine their analyses to what is externally observable. There is no objection then to radical behaviorists pursuing the extensional route to interpretation, but none either to the incorporation of an intentional overlay of interpretation being used to supplement this. The entirely extensional approach is surely absurd in this context. The addition of an intentional overlay makes for a more convincing interpretation, a fuller and richer account of what is going on. In a pragmatic spirit, we may pursue both. But let is be aware of the consequences. If we adopt the intentional overlay, we are employing two approaches that in themselves are incommensurable but we have found a necessary way to incorporate the essential level of analysis for psychology: the personal level. We must not, as Wundt was reputed to do, seek a science more than we seek a psychology.

And these Three are One

The foregoing argument stands, however, in need of some refinement before it can be accepted. First, note that the accounts of Dennett and Skinner are largely identical in that they presume a third-person perspective. Second, Malcolm's account differs from both in proposing a first personal perspective. The Skinnerian view that first person and third-person viewpoints coincide, that private events are observable in just the same way as are public events, albeit by only one person, suggests a reconciliation that suffices for present purposes between Dennett's views and those of Malcolm. I want to retain elements of the arguments of all three authors, but I emphasize here that Malcolm's view of a (what he calls a first-personal) viewpoint is inescapable insofar as it points to sources of knowledge available to the individual that are beyond those gained by a deliberative examination of the contingencies.

Both Skinner and Dennett argue that we can only know our pains and other private events by directly and yet still objectively: as a third person would, even though we are the only one present. I should argue, however, that this applies equally to knowing the kinds of intention that Malcolm posits, even though they are of a different source. There is good reason for retaining and using this third-personal view, but as Malcolm is at pains to point out, this kind of third-personal knowing does not exhaust our knowing of our private events. There are sources of information available to the individual that go beyond those gained by an examination of past behavior and its consequences, and of the current contingencies. Naturally, the radical behaviorist riposte to this is that this source is still the individual's learning history, an unconscious accumulation based on previous behavior and its consequences, which by appearing to have a spontaneous and immediate effect on behavior gives rise to the notion of an extra-environmental source of motivation. But the point is not to defend such a mystical source; rather it is to agree with Malcolm that the individual does not contact his or her motivation solely or even usually by a process of third-personal examination of previous behavior and the current contingencies.

Hence, the contradiction that is apparent on one level between the first-person perspective of Malcolm and the third-person perspective of Dennett need not, I think, prove problematical for the present argument. First, note that the argument is aimed at behavior analysts for whom the first-person/third-person distinction is redundant: both are objective, the first based on the availability of data to a single individual rather than a group. Since it is only logical positivism that insists on truth-by-agreement, and behavior analysis does not fall into this camp, the two sources of knowledge coincide methodologically. Both have certain similarities with the radical behaviorist approach they critique. Hence, Dennett argues that the information available to the individual to determine his own beliefs and desires is the same evidence available to others to ascertain them. We can ascertain them through the technique of heterophenomenology which is a detective process of analyzing the behavior of the target person including his verbal behavior, what others say of him and how they act toward him. Heterophenomenology is the ultimate strategy that derives from the intentional stance. We have seen that this is the way in which users of the intentional stance use the contextual stance. Malcolm accepts that mental events such as beliefs and intentions must have some external referents which – in our terms – would enter into the learning history and behavior setting. Nevertheless, he denies that the individual examines his own situation in order to conclude what his intentions are: he just knows that it is time to go home; he does not need to work this out from external information: I have always gone home when the light has got dim in my office, etc.

I want to retain elements of all three arguments but I emphasize here that Malcolm's view of a (possibly first personal) viewpoint is inescapable because there sources of knowledge available to the individual that are beyond those gained by an examination of the contingencies. Radical behaviorists could always argue that this is our learning history, an unconscious accumulation based on our previous behavior and its consequences, which by appearing to have a spontaneous and immediate effect on our behavior gives rise to the notion of an extra-environmental source of motivation. But I am not arguing that there is such a source of motivation. I am just arguing along with Malcolm that the individual does not contact that motivation by a process of third-personal examination of his previous behavior and the current contingencies.

Several implications derive from this analysis.

First, note that the argument pursued here ties in well with the attitude theory and research considered earlier (see also Foxall 1997a, b) in which the individual develops spontaneous attitudes through experience with the attitude object (culminating in self-rules acquired in the course of a learning history). Malcolm's intentions are the result of a process akin to what Fazio and Zanna call the spontaneous development of attitudes; the self-examination that Skinner attributes to the man looking for his glasses has much in common with the deliberative approach to attitude and intention formation to which Fishbein and Ajzen have drawn attention. We can combine these into an account of learning that begins with other-rule following and consequent deliberation on events as a surrogate for a learning history for the acquisition of which there has as yet been no opportunity, and which culminates in the development of self-rules which give the impression of spontaneity (Foxall, 1997a, b). At this broad and somewhat abstract level in which we are not directly concerned with an actual person whose behavior we are attempting to explain or predict, such an interpretation is consistent with both extensional behavior analysis (in which deliberation for instance is cast as a behavior) and with an extensional cognitive approach (in which it refers to the intrapersonal processing of information with intentionalistic overtones).

Second, if we are to pursue a radical behaviorist interpretation of a particular individual's behavior, however, it becomes incumbent upon us at some stage to assign particular self-rules to him or her in order to render intelligible his or her past actions and possibly to predict future conduct. Such assigned motivations, even if they reflect the interpreted person's own verbalizations of the rules he or she has constructed and followed, can have no meaning except to the interpreter: he/she has no objective evidence on the basis of which to assign them other than a theory of how the person's assumed experience will have led him/her to accumulate such self-rules. This is no different in essence from the intentionalist's ascription of intentionality. Pragmatically we are doing the same thing. There are, of course, empirical techniques that may appear to overcome this problem by purporting to provide a purely extensional behavior analytic access to the self-rules that the individual has constructed. One of these is the "Silent Dog technique" (Hayes, 1986), which involves the elicitation of verbal protocols during the performance of a task. Another is through the application of relational frame theory in which we ascertain the emergent relations between words and from which we may claim to reconstruct the self-rules in question. While relational frame theory can claim that it has access to learning history by virtue of the emergent relations it uncovers this is an act of faith: the only sure route to knowledge of a learning history is observation/experimentation: all other routes are somewhat conjectural, to be derived from a sure scientific footing by all means, using as far as we can rigorous canons of scientific judgment, but ultimately unconnected to the facts by other than by means of a theoretical language (Zuriff, 1985) that has elements of arbitrariness rather than scientific certainty. The same is true of the method of the silent dog. We do not know that we are tapping verbal behavior indicative of the person's learning history: any presumption that we are is based on the prior assumption of a particular explanatory viewpoint. In this case we have two valid viewpoints and methodologies to which to turn: the contextual stance and the intentional stance.

In both cases, we are making a leap from the words given to us by the individual in a laboratory setting and construing them as indicative of something else. This is precisely the technique of the social cognitivist who attributes attitudes, intentions and other cognitions to an individual on the basis of his or her verbal responses. In both cases we ascribe/assign on the basis of what the subject does, says, what is said of him/her, our idea of the behavior (and thus the dispositions or intentions) that would be consistent with his/her having had a particular learning history. We are ascribing to the person whose behavior we wish to pre- or post-dict verbalizations such as "I think that or I believe that catching an earlier bus to the office in the morning will enable me to complete my assignments before lunch". Yet doing this is inconsistent with the behavior analytical scientific approach of avoiding explanatory fictions. It is in fact adopting the intentional stance. For self-rules are the domain of intentionality *par excellence*.

In the case of other-rules, the tracks, plys and augmentals we encounter daily in the social and physical environment can be localized to that external environment: a spouse's admonition to "Take care out there" as one sets out for the academy is a preparation for the slings and arrows of intellectual civilization that can be said to exist in those environments; the road sign that prohibits a particular driving behavior itself contains the rule "No right turn". However, self-rules are not like this. Where are they? In the process of radical behaviorist interpretation which we are discussing they exist in the verbalizations of the investigator albeit generated from the verbal behavior of the interpreted person and other clues. The formulation of these clues into a rule that is attributed to the individual as a motivator of his behavior is either the ascription of intentionality itself or something so close that its recognition should give behavior analysts serious pause for thought. Naturally, it is also the case that there is no way of getting to the intentions that ought to be ascribed to a system without going through exactly the same procedure: i.e., constructing a learning history for the person and predicting its reactions to the current behavior setting. As we have seen this is what social cognitive psychology does. However, it is not always possible to construct such a history for the adult human on the basis of either observation or personal verbal report. The use of the intentional stance is inevitable in these circumstances. There are two spheres of inquiry in which this inevitability is especially pertinent for radical behaviorist interpretation: the problem of behavioral continuity, and the problem of equifinality and delimitation which are the subject of a later chapter.

It is possible from this consideration of the epistemological similarities and dissimilarities of these stances to propose some general conclusions about the interpretation of complexity. The contextual stance and the intentional stance each make pre-empirical assumptions about the relationship of private events to overt behavior. The contextual stance assumes that private events are always independent variables whilst behavior always a dependent variable: private events can never therefore be said to cause behavior. Now a scientist setting out to discover pragmatically how aspects of the world can be advantageously predicted and influenced could not make such an assumption: his pragmatic approach to the world will turn out to be what it will be, regardless of any a priori assumptions about causality that might be enjoined upon him by this or that pre-empirical philosophical position. The intentional stance assumes, for purposes of prediction and explanation, a causal relationship between (ascribed) personal events and behavior. Each runs into difficulties. Users of the contextual stance are sometimes forced to adopt private events as causes of behavior, for example when private discriminative stimuli and private reinforcers are assumed to control private or public behavior, or when the verbal behavior that inheres in rules, especially self-rules, is assumed to act as a discriminative stimulus or establishing operation that enters into the control of other verbal or non-verbal behavior. And adherents of the intentional stance must admit that sub-personal cognitive psychology has proved to be less than reliable as a predictor of behavior. Each comes in practice to resemble the other a little. Perhaps more than a little.

Dennett's characterization of the intentional has two dimensions. The first is linguistic, based on the nature of intentional sentences (we have seen that he amalgamates the perspectives of Brentano, Chisholm and Russell into a single account based on the properties of language.) Second, he isolates the personal level of analysis which is open only to the individual who, in describing mental events, knows what pain, for instance, is without being able to define or analyze it further. It is, of course, open to behavior analysts to reject both of these on the basis of their philosophy of science. The first can be disposed of as Quine disposes of it by rejecting intentional language because it does not by definition match up to the requirements of science, which is by its very nature extensional. The second can be "retained" by behavior analysts as some kind of private event, acceptance of which is used to differentiate radical from methodological behaviorism but which is *de facto* considered no further because behavioral science lacks the technical means to incorporate it into an experimental analysis. Neither of these is satisfactory even at this methodological level. The intentional use of language exists as part of the *parole* which behavior analysts ought by the very dictates of their science to be interested in elucidating; it also produces explanations that cut across those of behavior analysis and which should therefore be of primary interest to the conscious explication of behavior from a radical behaviorist point of view. They have at the very least to show that they can produce satisfactory explanations of both public and private behavior without resorting to the use of intentional idioms. However, the implications of the argument of this chapter is that intentionality poses a problem – and an opportunity – for operant interpretation that is far closer to home.

The point of the three-stage model introduced early in this chapter is not simply that we *could* if we chose develop a link between the contingencies and the personal level of analysis: it is that radical behaviorist interpretation already does so (and thus mirrors the social cognitive strategy). Intentional behaviorism is not something I am advocating so much as something I am pointing to as the present reality of both social cognitivism and radical behaviorist interpretation.

Chapter 7

Behavioral Continuity

The plausibility of an extensional radical behaviorist interpretation depends vitally upon its capacity to account for the continuity of behavior. Why should behavior that has been followed by a particular ("reinforcing") stimulus in the presence of a setting stimulus be reenacted when a similar setting is encountered? Why should a rule that describes certain physical or social contingencies be followed at some future date when those contingencies are encountered? Why can I tell you now what I ate for lunch yesterday? The whole explanatory significance of learning history is concerned with the continuity of behavior between settings and this implies some change in the organism, some means of recording the experience of previous behavior in such a way that it will be available next time similar settings are encountered. There is no other way in which the individual can recognize the potential offered by the current behavior setting in terms of the reinforcement and punishment signaled by the discriminative stimuli that compose it. Broadbent's *Behaviour* (1961/1978) remains a most readable and authoritative account of what amount to problems of behavioral continuity and the theoretical and empirical ingenuities to which they led in the history of behaviorism. It is the fascinating story of behaviorists' attempts to explain the emission of behavior in the rat that has not been previously reinforced but which is nevertheless consistent with an intentional account. Similar difficulties arise in the purely operant explanation of human choice, all of which raise the specter of accounting for behavioral continuity.

Although he does not use the term "behavioral continuity," Bandura (1986) provides a clear description of the problem. The arguments against radical behaviorism he puts forth center on the impossibility of providing an account of behavioral continuity that does not refer to cognitive processing. So long as people are assumed to act automatically in response to the environmental consequences of their past behavior or their thoughts are conceptualized as no more than intervening events themselves under environmental control, so long will any "internal link in the causal chain" be eschewed and agency assumed to reside in the environment (p. 12.) Yet there are instances in which environmental causation is assumed to act without any mechanism by which it produces behavior over time being shown to operate.

First, consider his treatment of the fundamental behaviorist principle that behavior is controlled by its immediate consequences. Bandura points to Baum's (1973) demonstration that the rate of emission of behavior is related to the aggregate of its consequences. Such "molar" behavior is actually a feature of Skinner's own approach since it is learning history rather than present stimuli alone that determine behavior. In fact, it was Herrnstein (1997) who most obviously defined and built upon this phenomenon. Defining choice not as an internal deliberative process but as a *rate* of intersubjectively observable events that are temporally distributed, Herrnstein's dependent variable was not the single response that needed contextual explication in terms of a single contingent reinforcer: it was the relative frequency of responding, which he explained by reference to the relative rate of reinforcement obtained from the behavior. Animals presented with two opportunities to respond (pecking key A or key B), each of which delivers reinforcers (food pellets) on its own variable interval (VI) schedule, allocate their responses on A and B in proportion to the rates of reward they obtain from A and B. This phenomenon, known as "matching," has been replicated in numerous species including humans and has found applications in behavior modification and organizational behavior management, to name but two relevant fields. In particular, it provides a framework for the behavioral analysis of consumption (Rachlin, 1989, 2000). However, Baum's (1973) molar approach to which Bandura makes reference is sufficient to suggest that organisms use data on how often a response is reinforced over a long period of time and that their behavior is then regulated according to the aggregate level of reinforcement. Such integration, Bandura asserts, requires cognitive skills. It actually suggests the need for a subsumptive level of analysis, cognitive, environmental. physiological, behavioral or otherwise such as that for which Smith (1994) called. The absence of any convincing evidence for these (when cognitive is given a specific ontological status) leaves the ascription of intentional content as the only safe possibility given the current state of knowledge.

A second consideration to which Bandura draws attention is that when behavior is learned on intermittent schedules, only a small proportion of responses receive reinforcement and reinforcements are occasional: perhaps only every 50th or 500th response is reinforced. Yet the behavior strengthens for very long periods and eventually diminishes or is entirely extinguished. The question is whether such integration or behavioral continuity can be explained without positing some non-environmental determinant, presumably cognitive. Something other than external causation is necessary to account for what happens in between. Bandura invokes the distinction between the acquisition of a skill and its performance which in turn evokes the question of what is learned. Cognitive processes are again implicated. Despite the fact that reinforced performance is uncommon on such schedules, skill is acquired which nevertheless permits the behavior in question to continue.

Bandura points out too that most complex behavior is learned by modeling rather than by experienced reinforcement (1986, pp. 74–80). He is highly critical of operant attempts at interpreting observational learning within the framework of the three-term contingency, which portray the process as one in which the modeled stimulus (S^D) is followed by an overt matching response (R) which produces a reinforcing stimulus (S^R). The elements of the three-term contingency are often missing from actual instances of observational learning. When the observer performs the matching response in a setting other than that in which it has been modeled, when neither the model's behavior nor that of the observer is reinforced, and when the modeled behavior is performed by the observer after the passage of time (which may be several months), the operant paradigm is unable to explain the behavior. As Bandura (1986, p. 74) points out, "Under this set of conditions, which represents the pervasive form of observational learning, two of the factors (R–S^R) in the three-element paradigm are absent during acquisition, and the third factor (S^D, the modeling cue) is absent from the situation in which the observationally-learned behavior was first performed." Observational learning of this kind also requires some mechanism to aid integration of vast amounts of information. Acquisition of novel behavior particularly requires such integration of modeled information. Bandura maintains that learning through modeling requires four processes: attentional, retentional, reproductive, and motivational. Certainly, observational learning is a process that must be comprehended at the personal level of analysis. Neither subpersonal nor super-personal can cope with it.

Learning that involves rule acquisition and following must also require these four procedures in some way or other. The individual acquiring rules from others must pay attention to the behavior of others, verbal or nonverbal. Somehow this has to be retained, compared for instance with earlier-gained knowledge and experience. Then it must somehow be translated into overt behavior when the situational immediacy that makes the behavior in question possible or even likely. For Bandura, all of this argues for cognitive representation and processing and it becomes all the more urgent to develop this line of reasoning if understanding rather than prediction and control is the primary goal of scientific endeavor. Though it is an empirical question whether the inclusion of cognitive processing will increase the predictability of behavior, in fact, we must keep an open mind on whether they add to predictive accuracy. Their primary aim is to aid understanding, to allow a complete account of human behavior acquisition and maintenance. The environmental variables alone *might* contribute more to simple prediction and control. However, the evidence is that, alone, cognitive factors add little to prediction (Foxall, 1997a).

Can the required account of behavioral continuity be achieved by introducing the moderating effect of thought into the explanatory scheme? Bandura argues that a fundamental principle of radical behaviorism is that thought cannot affect action. He argues that, contrary to this, most external influences on behavior act via cognitive processing. People develop beliefs about what is happening to them (i.e., the likely consequences of their behavior) and the beliefs come to influence their behavior. Moreover, "One can dispense with the so-called internal link in causal chains only if thought cannot affect action," (p.13). It is a moot point, however, whether thought's influencing behavior is or is not part of radical behaviorist explanation. Strictly, thought is a collateral response, the effect of the same environmental events that determine the overt responses with which the thoughts are associated. However, even Skinner came to recognize thoughts and other private events as "non-initiating" causes in the sense that they might act as discriminative stimuli for covert and overt behaviors but remained ultimately dependent on external environmental stimuli for their power as did the events of which they were local or proximal causes. Other radical behaviorists, as we have seen, have held that a private event can function as any of the elements in the three-term contingency – hence, a thought can reinforce other covert or overt behaviors – though this remains a subject of deep controversy. More particularly, however, the role of thought in rule-governed behavior is of interest here. Rules may inhere in thought and thought, like other verbal behavior that embodies or expresses rules, may thus control responses. This is an interesting departure from the behaviorist view that behavior can predict other behavior but not be the cause of it.

As it stands, Bandura's claim that cognitions determine behavior is not substantiable since, especially if the last mentioned causal statement of radical behaviorism is allowed, the overt behaviors to which he refers might be caused by covert behaviors rather than mental events. However, given that the ontological status of thought and its empirical availability are not obvious, the situation is open to rational cognitive ascription since there may be no other means by which to establish behavioral continuity and to predict future actions. It seems of little importance to the argument whether we simply ascribe intentionality as does Dennett on the basis of rational behavior or make the ontological claims for it that Bandura does on the basis of empirical psychological research: the imperative of behavioral continuity that is raised here requires one or other of these solutions. In the absence of ontological certainty, the first seems preferable, but either way the argument is one that radical behaviorists must face up to.

In his final criticism of radical behaviorism, Bandura draws attention to the principle that behavior is influenced by its enactive consequences. He argues that, on the contrary, the *anticipated* consequences are more effective in predicting and controlling behavior. Hence, "When belief differs from actuality, which is not uncommon, behavior is weakly influenced by its actual consequences, until more realistic expectations are developed through repeated experiences" (p. 13). There is ample corroborative evidence for this from studies of rule-governed behavior in behavior analysis as well as from more cognitively-based investigations. The question is how the findings will be interpreted.

Symbolic Behavior

The import of the phenomenon of stimulus equivalence which was discussed above is that the emergent relations have not been reinforced in the course of subjects' training. Sidman's attribution of equivalence to the basic process of reinforcement begs the question posed by Rumbaugh (1995, p. 369): "reinforcement of what?" As Rumbaugh further points out, "There is no 'equivalence' response in the traditional sense to be reinforced during training. Although equivalence relations do emerge, they are neither obviously nor directly reinforced as such during training, during which time other very specific responses are, indeed, selectively reinforced" (*ibid.*) His solution is to propose a third type of behavioral response: in addition to respondents and operants, there are *emergents* (Rumbaugh, 1997).

Sidman's understanding of equivalence as the result of evolutionary contingencies implies that the brain is responsible for the production of emergent behavior. Rumbaugh (1995, p. 372) finds that his cognitive view closely resembles Sidman at this level: "Frankly, I believe that my view that the brains of many animals, and primates in particular, have been selected via evolutionary pressures to organize (e.g., relate) sensory and perceptual input and to coordinate those, in turn, with response systems for successful adaptation appears to be far more compatible with Sidman's view than I had earlier thought." Both seem close, at this fairly general level, to Dennett's view of the brain producing evolutionarily appropriate efferent responses to afferent stimuli by the exercise of intelligence.

Dennett's reasoning with respect to the personal and subpersonal levels of analysis is also pertinent. The discrimination of emergent relationships is a phenomenon that can occur only at the personal level: it is something that the personal as a whole does. It is, moreover, unanalyzable. There is no way in which the subject to the training summarized above can tell why C is the "correct" answer when the stimulus is A. The similarity to the experience of pain as a personal-level phenomenon is strong: *knowing* that A must be matched with C, C with A, is something that the person just does. There is no way to explain it, whatever neuroscience comes to reveal, that can deal with this personal level except the appropriate mental language.

Now the present analysis is not intended to offer a critique of relational frame theory or competing explanations of symbolic behavior such as the naming account of Horne and Lowe (1996) per se: as extensional science and interpretation they will stand or fall in terms of their capacity to predict and control/influence behavior. These are appropriate goals for an extensional account and where these accounts are in conflict with one another a choice can be made between them based on their comparative predictive validities. The point is that when we are called upon to make an interpretation of complex behavior that is more than merely plausible, it is necessary to attend to the problem of how continuity between learned relational frames and current situations comes about. There will naturally be correlates of these temporal and spatial relationships that can be expressed in terms of physiology, rule-governance, verbal behavior, and so on, but since each of these is itself a component of the extensional enterprise, none can fill the gap. That gap requires an additional level of interpretation which must necessarily be intentionalistic. The difficulty faced by a purely extensional account is conveyed by Biglan's (1995, p. 67) summary of the positive functions performed by the phenomenon of functional transformation:

> Much of the power of the concept of relational framing is in the concept of the transfer of function. The concept specifies how language comes to establish the functions of stimuli that have never directly been experienced. A person's sensitivity to the world increases enormously as framing introduces a huge number of connections that were never directly trained.

Events become reinforcing through relational framing even though the person has had no direct experience with them. An event becomes aversive after the listener is told it is like another event that already has that effect. An event becomes a discriminative stimulus simply because of its verbally mediated relationship to another event.

Descriptively this works; pragmatically it fulfills the goal of extensional science that phenomena be predictable and subject to influence or control. There is no argument with that. But it is essential that the behavior analyst acknowledge here that it brings us back to the problem of explaining how behavior is acquired in the absence of reinforcement, back to the realm of Skinner's "automatic reinforcement," "seeing in the absence of the thing seen," and whatever else cannot be accounted for within the strict confines of laboratory science. Filling in the gaps requires that we resort to intentional idioms that propose what the individual whose target behavior is to be explained rather than just predicted and influenced believes and desires.

Not does the claim that relational framing itself accounts for the temporal and other gaps that must be filled if behavioral continuity is to be explained (Biglan, 1995; Hayes, 1992) identified carry weight. For, of itself, it invokes intentional interpretation:

Hayes (1992) suggests that relational framing may account for human abilities to bridge such temporal gaps. When an organism does something to achieve a long-delayed consequence, the organism must *somehow be able to discern that* the delayed event was relevant to a given behavior. He points out that all instances where nonhuman species are able to make this connection involve processes that narrow the possible relations between the consequent event and behavior. For example, nonhuman organisms have been shown to avoid foods that make them ill hours later. Presumably, organisms responsive to such contingencies could be selected because such responsiveness did not interfere with responding to other features of the environment. In other words, ingestive behavior could be sensitive to long-delayed responses of the alimentary canal because such sensitivity contributed to the avoidance of poisoning and did not prevent responses to other contingencies. (Biglan, 1995, p. 69; emphasis added)

It is entirely consistent with the behaviorist thesis that knowing can be understood as behavior. But, even if "knowing that" is redescribed in terms of relational framing which identifies it with different sources of environmental control from those that govern "knowing how" (Hayes, 1992; see also Hayes, 1997), there remains room for an understanding of knowing which alludes to the personal level of experience on which the individual can describe his or her knowing that but cannot further analyze it, which accounts for the individual being able to make the relational connections between verbal expressions in ways that leads to their being treated as equivalent (or whatever) in that they have similar behavioral consequences, and which delimit the range of applicability (content) of the relational frame. This is the function of the heuristic overlay to which Dennett refers.

It might be objected to this analysis that even if intentional idioms are required *pro tem* as we await the ability of physiology or more elaborate principles of verbal behavior to provide more complete explanations, they need not become a permanent feature of behavioral analysis. This would be to misunderstand the role of the intentional overlay which is to provide access to a level of explanation beyond that of extensional science. Whatever advances physiology and the analysis of verbal behavior make to extensional behavioral science, they will not address this level which refers primarily to explanation, plausible interpretation, and the inevitability of gaps that can be filled only by an a-ontological ascription of intentionality. Let us examine these elements of extensional science in greater detail.

The Appeal to Physiology

The radical behaviorist does not deny that change occurs within the organism as a result of behavior, but maintains that it is physiological change. The nature of Skinner's reasoning on this point is interesting and germane to the argument pursued here. He notes that Pavlov was "interested in how the stimulus was converted into neural processes and in how other processes carried the effect through to the muscles and glands... The 'physiological activity' was inferential. We may suppose, however, that comparable processes will eventually be described in terms appropriate to neural events. Such a description will fill in the temporal and spatial gaps between an earlier history of conditioning and its current result." (Skinner, 1953, p. 54). This hope that physiology will fill in the gaps "eventually" was expressed some fifty years ago. Has it done so? Can it perform this role?

Still, in 1974, Skinner was prophesying that "some day the physiologist will give us all the details" (Skinner, 1974, p. 249). Midgley and Morris (1998) argue that Skinner can deal with the problem of behavioral continuity by reference to "a changed organism," "temporal gaps," and "causal chains." They trace his explanation to phylogenic and ontogenic contingencies of selection of which innate and acquired behavior are functions. Organisms were biologically changed by their exposure to such contingencies: phylogenic contingencies promote genetic differences among organisms, while ontogenic contingencies promote neurological changes that ensure organisms are "different from their earlier selves" (Midgley & Morris, 1998, p. 121). "In both cases, biologically changed organisms (and replicated genes, with phylogenic contingencies) fill the temporal gap in the causal chain between past contingencies and current or future behavior" (*ibid.*) They quote Skinner: "The physiologist of the future will tell us all that can be known about what is happening inside the behaving organism. His account will be an important advance over a behavioral analysis, because the latter is necessarily 'historical' – that is to say, it is confined to functional relations showing temporal gaps. Something is done today which affects the behavior of an organism tomorrow. No matter how clearly that fact can be established, a step is missing, and we must wait for the physiologist to supply it. He will be able to show how an organism is changed when exposed to contingencies of reinforcement and why the changed organism then behaves in a different way, possibly at a much later date. What he discovers cannot invalidate the laws of a science of behavior, but it will make the picture of human action much more nearly complete" (Skinner, 1974, pp. 236–7.)

The same reasoning is derived from Skinner by Lee (1988) who speaks in terms of "action at a distance" to describe the problem of accounting for behavioral continuity: "Skinner insisted that the temporal gap between past contingencies and current performance at the psychological level is mediated by the physiology of the organism. Presumably, past contingencies change the organism so that it behaves differently now. Describing this physiological mediation of the effects of past contingencies is properly the task of the physiologist" (Lee, 1988, p. 162).

Burgos and Donahoe (2000) make the same point backed by the same quotation. But their attempt to delineate the behavior analytic from physiology and cognitivism is more elaborate, and their use of experimental physiology more sophisticated. Setting themselves the task of explaining why retention occurs as part of selection by consequences, they argue that three possibilities arise for explicating complex behavior: first, principles of behavioral variation and selection may themselves be sufficient to offer a complete explanation in which case there is no problem of explaining retention; second, inferences about what is happening within the organism may be drawn in the absence of an experimental analysis; third, retention principles can be drawn from an experimental analysis of the internal processes. The first they characterize as just saying nothing, which appears to be the familiar Skinnerian strategy of just leaving things to the physiologists and trusting that the answers will one day appear in the neuroscience laboratory. The second they designate bizarrely as "cognitivism" which "violates the thesis according to which retention principles must be derived through a direct experimental analysis." (pp. 40–41.) The third, their chosen strategy, seeks the required retention principles in the experimental analysis of neuroscientific phenomena. But before examining this, what are we to make of their understanding of cognitivism expressed in the second option? Of all the branches of psychology to make advances in the last half century, the study of neurocognition stands out precisely because of its exponents' willingness to embrace experimental method in the attempt to understand the internal physiological processes that account for overt behavior. Whilst it is difficult to see how cognitive neuroscience could conceivably be characterized in this way, more important is the third strategy these authors identify, one which has formed the basis of a broad approach to interpretation in the behavior analytic tradition (Donahoe & Palmer, 1994).

The difficulties with this are twofold. First, although a materialist philosophy of science must put its faith in a physiological basis of continuity, even though it is not presently demonstrable, that physiology will produce the kind of linkages

Skinner seeks from it can right now be no more than faith; the device seems like one designed to bring inquiry to an end while stipulating what cannot be admissible as a gap-filling element. It would be more in keeping with what we know of the tentative nature of science to acknowledge this than to argue and act *de facto* as though the necessary scientific findings were a current fact. Second, whilst it may be reasonable to believe in general terms that neuroscience will identify the physiological correlates of behavior at the level of extensional science, there is no reason to believe that such science can produce the kind of interpretive device required to produce explanations of behavior at the personal level. In fact, Dennett has argued persuasively that it cannot, and his arguments have not been convincingly met by behaviorists. It may be useful here to remind ourselves of Dennett's reasons for making the distinction between the subpersonal level revealed by physiology and the personal level which is the realm of psychology. Action at a distance is repudiated as a genuinely scientific explanation by other behavior analysts. Malott and Malott (1992, p. 244) are of the opinion that "the notion of distant, physically-separated causes just does not seem plausible, though one can argue in support of their possibility, just as one could argue in support of the possibility of ghosts". Of course, there may well be physiological change when behavior occurs that his implications for the way in which the organism will behave when next it encounters similar stimulus conditions. The question is whether knowledge of this is sufficient to explain the behavior on subsequent occasions including its prediction and control. We have already noted Dennett's objection to the use of physiology as an exclusive basis of psychology, that the heuristic overlay of intentional concepts adds an interpretive level that makes what is going on more intelligible. I do not wish to advocate that at this stage save to point out that it seems self-evident: it adds an interpretive overlay that not only makes the activities of the nervous system more intelligible in terms of ordinary language but may well make them and the behavior of the organism at the personal level more predictable. This remains an empirical matter for now but it is one to which we shall return.

The most intriguing fact about Skinner's embracing physiological mediating events is that he uses this as a device to bring inquiry to a premature end by denying the need of an intentionalistic analysis and thereby precluding the search for explanations of behavior as opposed to descriptions. Physiology is the concern of the physiologist, not that of the psychologist or behavior analyst. The behavior analyst's job is done when the physiologist has been presented with an "assignment" that reflects the environmental determination of behavior. Thus Skinner avoids speculation about the kind of theoretical structures, events or states that he abhors, be they mental, neural or hypothetical. But if physiology is an uncertain means of establishing a basis for behavioral continuity, what other constructs might fill the gap? The leading remaining contenders are private events and rules.

The Appeal to Private Events

Can radical behaviorism rely on private events to provide or support an extensional interpretation of complex behavior by accounting for the continuity of behavior? Malott and Malott (1992) pose the question whether private events should be included in the causal chain. They note that some behaviorists such as Hayes and Brownstein (1986), and Rachlin (1974) hold the view that private events cannot be considered causes of public events. Hayes and Brownstein argue, for instance, that only those events that can enter into the prediction and control of behavior can be considered causes of behavior and, as we have seen, this exempts private events from this category. Others, however, have argued the reverse. Malott and Malott (1992, p. 250) conclude for instance that private events can sometimes function as causes, for example, in mental arithmetic where each response serves as a covert cue (discriminative stimulus) for the next. Malott's view is that Hayes and Brownstein are right to insist that the analysis of covert events make contact between the private elements in the chain of causation and the environmental events that control/cause both the private event and the overt/public responses associated with it. This is fine, but I agree with Malcolm that whereas there must usually be some public events associated with (what he calls) psychological sentences, other, intentional usages are automatic, not associated with anything internal or external that can be observed, monitored or have conclusions drawn from it. Nevertheless, if there is to be a radical behaviorist interpretation of complex behavior that is itself extensional in nature and scope then private events must carry much of the burden of the behavioral construal of events that are not amenable to an experimental analysis. If *radical* behaviorism is to give an interpretive account of complex behavior, it must resort to inferred entities. There are two options: either extensionally-defined but nevertheless inferred and hence explicitly theoretical *private events*, or intentional idioms, which are also theoretical but which make no extensional claims.

We have already seen that private events are theoretical terms of the kind Skinner repudiated. Since the defining essence of radical behaviorism lies in its eschewal of propositional content rather than of theoretical entities as Skinner defined them, this is not problematic for the present analysis. Their non-intentional nature rests entirely on the kinds of sentence in which we incorporate them, the kinds of explanatory work we make them do. If it is possible to construct interpretations is purely extensional terms, which are more than merely plausible, but in some way testable in terms of the accuracy of the predictions or postdictions to which they lead, then so be it. Are private events up to this task, especially in view of the lack of a substantiable learning history for most of the persons for whom such an interpretation would be sought? Even though Skinner claims that radical behaviorist interpretation is different in several essential respects from the experimental analysis of behavior – he implies, for instance, that interpretation will not be subject to the same canons of scientific rigor as apply to experimental analyses – radical behaviorist interpretation belongs in a radical behaviorist framework only if it adheres to the basic explanatory mode of radical behaviorism, if it shares with the experimental analysis of behavior this philosophy of psychology. Radical behaviorist interpretation cannot do without, at present, some allusion to private events. But, notwithstanding Smith's (1994) inclusion of private events within the extensional framework of radical behaviorism, they remain problematical in this regard. There are several reasons for believing that they do not belong within the framework of extensional behavioral science to which the experimental analysis of behavior aspires and within which it can largely be fitted.

First, private events are cast as responses in behavior analysis, collateral responses to those visible to all that are produced by publicly-available stimuli, differing from them only in being private or covert (e.g., Skinner, 1974). Thoughts and feelings come into this category. But to claim that these are behaviors is to make an ontological assumption that can be neither substantiated nor falsified by scientific analysis (see also Harzem, 2000). Second, private events are not subject to an experimental analysis. Their being apparent to only the person to whom they are occurring has not been seen by radical behaviorists as a barrier to their entering into a scientific analysis since radical behaviorism rejects the requirement of logical positivism that scientific observation be amenable to public scrutiny. This is a fine point because having differentiated his *radical* behaviorism from *methodological* behaviorism on this point (Skinner, 1945), Skinner makes little further use of the private events he has uniquely conceptualized. They rarely enter into behavior analysis because they cannot be experimentally manipulated. In the interpretation of complex (especially verbal) behavior they sometimes perform the role of saving the theory by allowing an extensional account to be given of, for instance, the ways an individual might formulate for him/herself rules of conduct not provided by others. This may be permissible but it is important that if it is sanctioned by the scientific community, the ontological and methodological status of such events be made explicit. While my own private events may be sufficiently in evidence to me to enable me to incorporate them into some sort of limited analysis of my own behavior, those of other people are at best inferences (Skinner, 1988d). Like the perennial philosophical problem of other minds, which can be resolved only by the most severe application of Occam's razor, the problem of other people's private events can be swept away only if the very notion of private events is abandoned.

Third, private events therefore resemble the "explanatory fictions" identified by Skinner as the very conceptual mechanisms that bring inquiry to a premature end. They resemble both the mediating events that are invented to provide explanations for observed stimuli and response patterns, and those which we have seen enter readily into radical behaviorist interpretations of private behavior, verbal behavior, decision making, and so forth. Since they are usually characterized extensionally in the accounts behavior analysts give, they are clearly within the scientific purview of radical behaviorism's distinct approach to the science of behavior. The question for a pragmatic science is, how useful are they in this role? Do they permit prediction? control? plausible interpretation? Fourth, there is no legitimate logic or means by which private events can be ascribed to other people – even if we are capable of accurately discriminating them within ourselves. At best, they can only be inferred from other people's behavior (including verbal) which Skinner among others has resolutely set his face against as an explanatory device. They have no ontological status in this interpersonal context (perhaps none at all if they are not intersubjectively available) that would allow us to justify their attribution as part of an extensionally-based behavioral science. Private events simply have no place in extensional science. Fifth, private events are in any case incapable of providing an extensional account: they are by their very nature *about* something else: thinking and feeling are always intentional in this sense. We cannot maintain their integrity as constructs, concepts or variables within a science of behavior.

It appears that, at best, private events are an attempt to come to terms with the need for a personal level of analysis. They cannot succeed because the personal level cannot be accessed through extensional science.

The Appeal to Rules

Perhaps the burden ascribed to private events can be assumed by rules. Malott (1989) argues that rules are capable of providing the continuity easily ascribed otherwise to "action at a distance". Since the rules that guide individual action can for the most part in contexts requiring interpretation only be arrived at by speculation, we are hardly on scientific ground when we infer them, often from the very behavior we are attempting to explain by them. The radical behaviorist account of the origin of rule-governed behavior is also dubious since it assumes that rules are simply learned in the course of acquiring a learning history. A history of being reinforced by following the rules laid down by others makes one more likely to follow the rules provided by similar people in similar situations. As Zuriff (1985, p. 129) expresses it, "Both the construction and the following of rules are behavior, and presumably they arise because they proved reinforcing in the history of the community and the individual." This is a plausible surmise but its use in the reconstruction of the environmental factors responsible for any particular sequence of complex behavior is likely to be unamenable to canons of judgment that call for the judicious use of evidence. The belief that rules provide for the continuity of behavior is not usually subject to scientific test and therefore cannot be the basis of a scientific account. Seeking to avoid the rigor that would normally be expected of a scientific statement by calling it interpretation rather than science, to be adjudged according to its sounding plausible rather than there being evidence for it will not do. It is a contravention of the very principle by which Skinner has sought to condemn cognitive and other structuralist accounts of behavior.

The Appeal to Verbal Analysis

A preliminary case for the necessity of considering radical behaviorist interpretation to be deficient in these respects is made by an examination of behaviorists' treatment of the kinds of sentence by which responses to the questions asked in the course of attitude research were exemplified above. How would radical behaviorists explain this verbal behavior? Can they present, in the language of extensional science, an account of this aspect of human behavior which makes no causal reference to intentionality? The elements of the three-term contingency are specifiable extensionally and are capable of producing a science of behavior that is logically independent. The question raised here is whether this approach can deal adequately with human behavior that seems to express intentionality and especially with the language of intentional sentences that are rife in the folk psychology that all agree we use daily to make sense of our social interactions or at least to steer us through them. Can it deal also with the kinds of analysis proposed by cognitive scientists whose formulations consist in the verbal ascription of intentionality?

The claim has certainly been made that radical behaviorism can deal in an extensionalistic manner with verbal behavior which cognitivists interpret in terms of the intentional idiom. Schnaitter suggests what he calls "a tentative behavioral interpretation of the intentional idioms" (1999, p. 243), exemplifying this approach by a functional analysis of the sentence "I believe it is going to rain". This expression consists of a tact – "it is going to rain" – and an autoclitic – "I believe". An autoclitic, a category derived by Skinner (1957) in his functional analysis of language, is "a unit of verbal behavior that depends on other verbal behavior for its occurrence and that modifies the effects of that other verbal behavior on the listener" (Catania, 1992, pp. 363–4). It includes the use of grammatical terms such as prepositions which qualify the sense of the verbal stream in which they are embedded.

In the behavioral interpretation proposed, the autoclitic modifies the tact which lies at the heart of the sentence. "'I believe' is a response *following from* the tact 'It is going to rain'" (Schnaitter, 1999, p. 243). It need not, therefore, be the case that "I believe" is a "response directed *toward* the tact" which would be the intentionalistic interpretation. All of the statements used in the measurement of the variables contained in the theories of reasoned action and planned behavior can be translated in this manner.

Attitudinal beliefs were measured in the example given earlier in terms of responses to the statement

"Buying organic vegetables is expensive/inexpensive."

Behavior analysis can provide a non-intentionalistic understanding of what is going on here which makes clearer the role of the contextual stance in the elicitation and use of these responses. Following Schnaitter's (1999) methodology for providing a behavior analytical interpretation of intentionalistic sentences, the verbal behavior of a respondent to this kind of inquiry is a kind of tacting or naming and the stated rule is a track (Zettle and Hayes, 1982). From this, it is possible to derive an interpretation of the individual's relevant learning history since, according to the logic of radical behaviorism, it would be difficult to understand how a person could be capable of engaging in tacting/naming and tracking of this sort without a behavioral repertoire based on a learning history that is the basis of his or her answers.

Subjective norm, measured in the example in terms of responses to the statement

"My partner thinks that I should/should not buy organic vegetables"

can be similarly expressed in the non-intentional terms of manding and pliance, and these verbal responses can once again be attributed to an appropriate learning history.

A statement used to elicit behavioral intention such as

"I will buy organic vegetables on my next shopping trip"

can be construed as eliciting a tact which is modified by the autoclitic "I intend to" or "I will" (the present tense of "to will" (which is a propositional attitude in the intentionalistic interpretation) rather than the future tense of "to be".) Such a locution expresses an augmental (there is no corresponding functional element in the verbal behavior of a speaker). The augmental is "I *will* buy organic vegetables!" There is nothing intentionalistic about this expression: the response "I will" follows from the tact; it is not directed toward it.

Finally, the verbal responses to which social cognitive psychologists attribute the mental process or state they call perceived behavioral control is explicable in behavior analytical terms without resort to propositional content: as response such as "I believe that I can achieve this" is simply a tact "I can achieve this" modified by the autoclitic "I believe". The motivating force with which this is held and expressed may transform the expression into an augmental.

In itself, this approach is entirely consistent with principles of behaviorist interpretation, especially as they are evinced in Skinner's (1957) *Verbal Behavior,* which concentrates on the verbal behavior of the speaker, and in recent work on the verbal (rule-following) behavior of the listener (e.g., Hayes, 1989.) It is valuable in so far as it demonstrates that a consistent interpretation of verbal behavior is feasible that is devoid of propositional content; it demonstrates the capacity of a functional analysis of verbal behavior to cope with this aspect of language on its own level. As such it is on a par with the reasoning that underlies the application of the intentional stance. But it has a drawback due to its provenance: whatever its persuasive impact on intentionalists, it may seem less than plausible to behavior analysts on account of the impossibility of subjecting it to an experimental analysis or other empirical means of generating data consistency with its premises and conclusions. Like much behaviorist interpretation in the mold of *Verbal Behavior,* it is plausible to those who accept the basic principles of behavior analysis. But can behaviorism satisfactorily handle intentionality in this way?

The answer has to be that while Schnaitter's procedure maintains the extensional consistency of a behaviorist account of this aspect of language (or verbal behavior), it does not deal with the entire range of human experience available to psychology. Specifically, it does not handle the personal level of analysis. In this regard, it is similar to the broader approach to explanation of which it is part. Nor does it account for *how* rules delivered verbally at one time influence behavior much later and in different circumstances. Nor yet for how the same rule can produce vastly different responses, different rules the same behavior. Parsing sentences functionally will not do.

Prediction and Plausibility

Even if we had all the facts about an individual's past behavior and the reinforcing/punishing consequences it had produced, it would not be possible to explain fully why a particular individual now has a known probability of again behaving in a given way. Simply to say, as Skinner would, that it does not matter, that it is not a question for the behavioral scientist but can be left to the physiologist has limited merit: whatever the physiologist turns out to be able to contribute here, it will always fall short of accounting for the personal level of analysis. Since behavior is always simultaneously reinforced and punished (Alhadeff, 1982), the individual always has the options of behaving or not behaving. Unless we can ascribe rationality to him, we do not even know which direction he will move in – toward which reinforcer. We cannot possibly predict or explain which one will win out unless we know his goal (desire) and the information he has (beliefs) about the consequences of behaving in a particular way in the current behavior setting. There are three sources of the required intentional ascription: observe past behavior and extrapolate (i.e., project the person's behavioral history), ask him, or attribute intentions on the basis of some logical scheme that relates the behavior of the individual to his position (learning history and behavior setting). We need the contextual stance to describe these positional factors and the intentional stance to ascribe appropriate content.

We have examined three modes of radical behaviorist interpretation, each of which has been used to exemplify a particular shortcoming of the genre when it is judged not in terms of its predictive capacity but rather its explanatory completeness. Explanatory completeness is central to the plausibility of an interpretation. Any purely extensional operant interpretation of behavior raises three difficulties for a comprehensive psychology of complex human behavior: the accommodation of what Dennett designates the *personal level of analysis*), providing an account of the factors responsible for *behavioral continuity*, and dealing with the problem of *equifinality* and the need to delimit operant accounts of complex human behaviors. The problem that arises in connection with the personal level of analysis is that neither physiological theories (which operate at a sub-personal level) nor environment-behavior theories (which operate at a super-personal level) capture what the person as a whole knows (what pain is, for instance.) In the case of behavioral continuity, the problem is that radical behaviorism lacks a mechanism to account for the continuity of behavior between situations and over time. Continuity is sought in the discriminative and other setting stimuli that are constant form setting to setting. Finally, the problem stemming from considerations of equifinality and delimitation is that of ambiguity surrounding the behavioral response enacted, the precise discriminative stimuli that should be held responsible for it, and the particular consequences that should be implicated in its shaping and maintenance. Any radical behaviorist interpretation must address not one of these problems but all three, but it is now time to examine the third in greater detail.

Chapter 8

Equifinality and Delimitation

An experimental analysis of behavior necessitates the close delineation of the variables in terms which it proceeds. "Stimulus," and "response," "learning history," and "rate," must be specified sufficiently closely that they can be unambiguously, consistently and inter-subjectively applied to this or that aspect of the events occurring within the experimental space. Strictly-speaking, the results and conclusions of such experimentation apply with total precision and assurance only to that space, and predictions of the generalizability of behavior observed within the experiment will be most accurate when they take the form of projections of acts taking place within similar environments. Interpretation is required when such projection becomes discontinuous, when the terms used with precision in one sphere must be applied elsewhere with less than full assurance that they can be entirely disambiguated, consistently employed, or capable of evoking the high degree of mutual agreement which the operant chamber presents. And, on occasion, terms may be required in the process of interpretation that fail to evoke analogues which can be experimentally tested. The problem of interpretation arises because it is a process that cannot yield the precision of delineation normally available to the experimenter. However, although it is inevitable that interpretation will entail concepts, methods and criteria that go beyond those appropriate to the experimental analysis of behavior, it is incumbent on the interpreter of complex behavior to delimit the scope of his or her account of complexity, to show how the difficulties inherent in behavior whose various consequences exhibit equifinality have been overcome. If there are no safeguards of this kind, if we cannot circumscribe the range of outcomes of a particular act to which its enactment can be attributed without straining credulity, then we remain unsure what constitutes a cause of the complex behavior we observe outside the laboratory and what does not. And this problem remains, whether our aim is to take our interpretations back to the laboratory or to test them by means of non-experimental methodologies.

The ease with which we are able to construct interpretations of the everyday actions we behold in the terminology of the three-term contingency compounds the difficulty of reliable delineation. Hence, the behavior of the professor we see entering the faculty club is readily explicable by reference to an easily constructed learning history. Since we have lunch with him there twice a week, the notice "Faculty Club" and the time shown by the clock on the building's façade can safely be said to be discriminative stimuli for his current behavior, elements of the environment that set the occasion for his entering, ordering and eating a meal leading to an increase in the likelihood that he will enact similar behaviors on other occasions. So far, so good: based on our expert knowledge of these contingencies of reinforcement, we shall make accurate predictions of this professor's behavior in these and similar circumstances. And, although we cannot subject his activities to an experimental analysis, we can interpret what we see of them in terms we have validated in our work. However, he may well be entering the faculty club in order to pursue his extramarital *amour passionel* with the catering manager, something he has done without our knowledge on the remaining days of the working week for the last seven years. In this case our prediction will fail and our interpretation of his behavior, though entirely plausible, may cause us embarrassment when the catering manager exposes the professor's indiscretion in the tabloids. Our difficulty lies in not having been able to subject the professor to the same rigorous observation in the course of his acquisition of a history of reinforcement and punishment which is available to the animal experimenter.

In experimental studies of the behavior of organisms whose whole world of learning is coterminous with the operant chamber, learning history is often unproblematical. First, it is known: the rats and pigeons typically used in such experiments can be trained from a very early age; all that needs to be known about their history of reinforcement is accessible by the experimenter in whose charge they find themselves. Second, it is simple: the effects of differing schedules of reinforcement and punishment are easily described and taken into consideration in further research. Third, it can often be ignored: the current contingencies represented by the behavior setting are sufficient to determine behavior or at least to render it predictable and controllable by the experimenter. There remains the problem of incorporating the animal's learning history into this account, of course; since learning history is so central an explanatory factor in radical behaviorism it cannot be right to ignore it altogether. But this does not seem to exercise experimentalists whose scientific goals (prediction and control) are sufficiently fulfilled without recourse to the abstract. But these difficulties cannot go so easily unnoticed by the interpreter of human behavior in radical behaviorist terms, who is left to enquire: how can learning history be taken into consideration in the case of human beings whose previous responding is simply not accessible, and how can we better understand the interaction of that learning history and the stimulus elements of the current behavior setting to produce the situation, the intersection of time and space that explains the response made?

There is simply no means by which the learning history of an adult human can be established even approximately unless he has lived all his life in the most closed of settings. Hence, there is no unequivocal means of deciding what pattern of reinforcement is responsible for the maintenance of an observed pattern of behavior which is amenable only to an interpretive account, i.e., the complex behavior that cannot be reduced to a laboratorial analogue. The import of this problem of equifinality (Lee, 1988) is that if radical behaviorist interpretation is to mean anything other than vaguely-guided speculation, on a par with any other amateur psychology, its practitioners must find a means of bringing to it some greater measure of the scientific rigor characteristic of the experimental analysis of behavior. But if the ascription of terms of contingency to the contextually-enrapt behaviors we observe seems easy, it must also be admitted that some behaviors may be neither predictable nor amenable to plausible construal within the bounds of this philosophy of psychology or, for that matter, any other single framework of conceptualization and analysis. If learning histories for the purpose of accurate – as opposed to merely plausible – operant interpretations of complex behavior are not empirically available, we ought surely to be circumspect when proffering constructions of observed activity in terminology we know only from another sphere of inquiry.

An operant class is an equifinal class: it may include responses that are topographically quite different but which belong together because they are functionally equivalent, that is, produce identical consequences (Lee, 1988, pp. 135–7). Obtaining a record by mail order has a form that is entirely distinct from asking for the same product in a record shop, but both responses belong to the same equifinal class because they have the same outcome. A response that closely or exactly resembles another belongs to a different equifinal class if it produces functionally different results. Two consumers may enter the same store at the same time in exactly similar manners but their responses belong to different operant classes if the first is reinforced by the purchase of a product while the second is reinforced by information about the availability and price of that product. Lee (1988, p. 136) gives the example of seeing a person walking down the stairs at a particular time of the morning. He or she might be going to the library, to morning coffee, or any of a dozen other places of reinforcement. But such equifinality is a problem for the would-be interpreter for it makes ascription of the behavior to a particular operant class difficult if not impossible. Innumerable interpretations might be made: we do not have to go as far as the example of the professor entering the faculty club to recognize that even simple everyday construals of observed behavior in operant terms eludes us because we have no access to the person's learning history or even the full complement of stimuli comprising the setting in which the observed individual's behavior is taking place. It is difficult to see how such interpretations as we might venture in these circumstances could carry much by way of plausibility let alone validity and reliability. As I argue in this chapter in regard to the kind of interpretation proposed by teleological behaviorism, it is impossible to define the bounds of behaviorism other than by the incorporation of intentional idioms.

Teleological Behaviorism

Rachlin's (1994) extensional interpretation of observed behavior, *teleological behaviorism*, follows Aristotle in distinguishing efficient from final causes. Efficient causes precede their effects and consist in the set of internal nervous discharges giving rise to particular movements; they would include internal physiological and cognitive precedents of activity. The analysis of efficient causes yields a mechanism that answers the question "*How* does this or that movement occur?" (Rachlin, 1994, p. 22). Final causes are consequences of behavior. Final causes may inclusively fit into one another as the causal web extends outward from the individual who behaves: "eating an appetizer fits into eating a meal, which fits into a good diet, which fits into a healthy life, which in turn fits into a generally good life. The wider the category, the more embracing, the 'more final' the cause." (Rachlin, 1994, p. 21). The analysis of final causes is an attempt to answer the question "*Why* does this or that movement occur – for what reason?" (p. 22). The process of finding the causes of behavior is one of fitting the behavior into an ever-increasing molar pattern of response and consequences. The dependent variable in Rachlin's scheme is not a single response, however, but a temporally extended pattern of behavior. Similarly, the causes of behavior are extended, a series of consequences nested within one another from the closest to the most remote. We have seen that, from these extended patterns of behavior and consequence, can be discerned emotional and "cognitive" behaviors: indeed, the emotion or thinking or believing or knowing *is* the pattern of extended behavior. Rachlin's work in behavioral economics is highly relevant here because an important cause of behavior is the utility function that describes the entire sequence of extended behavior of the individual (Rachlin, Battalio, Kagel & Green, 1981.)

In some respects this is pure radical behaviorism and for the purposes of this investigation it states very clearly the essential position of radical behaviorism as a philosophy of psychology. It has, therefore, some similarities to the interpretive stance adopted by Skinner, though it also differs from his thought, principally in its treatment of private events. Rachlin is a radical behaviorist to the extent that he avoids dualism and his truth criterion is pragmatic (Baum, 1994, p. 39). Unlike conventional radical behaviorism, however, Rachlin's system has no time for private events or intrapersonal phenomena; yet, unlike both radical and methodological behaviorism it freely employs mentalistic terminology. The reason is, as we have just noted, that in Rachlin's theory, behavior is always external to the individual even when it is thinking and feeling; its ultimate cause is represented by the individual's utility function, an entirely observable measure of the ultimate range of external consequences it generates (Rachlin, 1989). Rachlin asserts that mind is behavior, sequences or patterns of behavior rather than single acts. This molar view (common in behavioral economics: see inter alia Baum, 1973; Herrnstein, 1997) means that mental phenomena such as attitudes, intentions and even pain are all defined by extended patterns of behavior. We know that our friend is in pain because of the behaviors he emits: grimacing, groaning, holding his arm, and so on. According to Rachlin, this is exactly the information our friend also has to go on in order to know that he is in pain. Bem (1972) speaks of attitudes in similar vein: I must like brown bread because I see myself eating a lot of it – this is exactly the same information on which my wife bases her view that I like (have a positive attitude toward) brown bread. It is a third person account that is unconcerned with the first-person access I have to my pain or to my experience of liking brown bread.

Rachlin is not saying that this is the sole permissible ontology: he is simply concentrating on what is of interest to him to the general exclusion of the notion of intrapersonal causation (see also Baum, 2000). That is, he is concentrating on the Aristotelian idea of final (external, succeeding the behavior for which it is responsible) causation as opposed to the more familiar efficient (inner, preceding) causation that underlies cognitivism (Stout, 1996). But he neither rules out the latter, nor suggests that it is inadmissible. Teleological behaviorism thus eschews the problems of private events, mediating variables and propositional attitudes at a single stroke. In insisting on public corroboration of the facts of science, however, it adopts a tenet of logical positivism that is absent from radical behaviorism. Skinner's notion of private events, said by him to be admissible to science because they are observable, albeit by one person, is a very different proposition, though as we have seen it leaves the private events it posits in order to differentiate itself from other (predominantly methodological) behaviorisms almost entirely unanalyzed.

The Scope of Radical Behaviorist Interpretation

There are two reasons why Rachlin's teleological behaviorism cannot provide a comprehensive approach to the explanation of behavior, one that can incorporate both an experimental analysis and a plausible interpretive system. (I am not here offering a comprehensive critique of Rachlin's teleological behaviorism: I merely suggest that interpretations based on his system are unbounded and require an intentionalistic overlay of interpretation in order to be useful. As far as I know, there is little by way of critical comment on Rachlin's system from behaviorists or others, which is a commentary on the level of philosophical debate among behaviorists or about behaviorism. For informed philosophical criticism of Rachlin's book, *Behavior and Mind*, however, see Lacey (1995/1996).) The first is that the search for final causes introduces a degree of imprecision and arbitrariness (since the final causes we advance may frequently be unamenable to empirical examination) that is unacceptable. This is the problem of context, specifically that of finding the appropriate context by which to judge the consequences of the behavior under interpretation. The second is the inability of teleological behaviorism to provide a personal-level analysis of behaviors such as pain. This is the problem of the privacy of personal experience, specifically that of incorporating first-person accounts in a science of behavior.

We have noted that teleological behaviorism is a system of explanation in terms of final causes, the external consequences that determine the rate of behavior and to which the terminology of mental events may be attached. A whole series of final causes may each be nested within one another, diffused over time, the whole sequence being necessary to a full explanation of the behavior that produced them. But, since the events that explain a behavior are temporally extended, the compilation of its explanation may require the elapse of a significant period before the full complexity of the behavior's consequences can be noted and understood (Rachlin, 1994, pp. 31–2). The search for final causes as ultimate explanations may, nevertheless, be convoluted and unscientific in the sense that the propositions employed in explication of a behavior may never be brought into contact with the empirical events that could substantiate them or lead to their refutation. Take, for example, the commonplace idea that Nylon was so-called because of the locations of the laboratories that developed it in *New* York and *Lon*don. If, as seems likely, this tale is an urban myth, it still provides a final cause for the naming of the material.

However, again assuming the story is no more than mythical, there is an important sense in which it is untrue: no one actually had this reason for naming Nylon in mind (or in their verbal behavior) at the time it was named. Its intension must be sought elsewhere. In other words, the extension we might in ignorance attribute to "Nylon" supports the myth (the final cause argument) while the intension of the term does not. The idea that the material was named for the cities of New York and London provides a plausible extension, but one that is untestable. The kinds of final cause that Rachlin enjoins upon us may be like this.

Similarly pursuing teleological explanation, Stout (1996) quotes Aristotle to the effect that causation lies in identifying what a thing or action is "for the sake of". He comments: "If walking is good for health, and my walking can be explained by that reason, walking about is done for the sake of health. If a flower is for the sake of attracting insects and that is why a plant has one, then the presence of the flower is teleologically explained. If my going to the bank is for the sake of getting out some money, and that explains why I go to the bank, then the action is teleologically explained." (p. 81) So, of course, is the bank. Yet a teleological explanation for the bank in terms of its being for the sake of the individual who wishes to get money out of his account is partial to say the least. The intensional meaning of building a bank, and of building it at that particular place, is also required for a full explanation. The frequently-misquoted observation that the final cause of the human nose is snuff makes the argument well. (What Coleridge actually wrote was "You abuse snuff! Perhaps it is the final cause of the human nose." *Table Talk*, 4 January 1823.)

Rachlin's search for plausible extensions fails because, first, the extension identified is untestable (at least during the period of the interpretation) and, second, it leaves out of the picture the personal level of analysis which seeks to identify the intensional basis for the interpretation. To say that a or the (final) cause of the physics research undertaken by Rutherford and his colleagues that included the splitting of the atom was the death of millions of Japanese civilians is a travesty. The two events are undoubtedly linked but the invocation of a causal relationship between them is hardly adequate to account for either. More complete explanations must be sought at the intensional level. Of course, this may lead equally to speculative interpretations that are untestable. But, it deduces them (its interpreted "causal" mental mechanisms) from a logical framework of goal-directed activity based on evolutionary reasoning, and it does not ignore the personal level of analysis.

Rachlin gives the example of our seeing a snippet of film showing a man swinging a hammer in order to explain Aristotle's conception of final causation (Rachlin, 2000, pp. 58–9; see also Rachlin, 1994, pp. 82–3, which is the subject of the review by Lacey quoted below.) What, he asks, is the man actually doing? He might be swinging a hammer, hammering a nail, joining pieces of wood, laying a floor, building a house, providing shelter, supporting his family, being a good husband or father, or being a good person. All of these may be descriptions of his behavior, all may be true. But in order to arrive at the final judgment of what the man is doing we must look through the movie of the man's entire life. "The validity of any of the above descriptions may be settled by moving the camera back or showing more film – earlier and later" (p. 59.) The whole point of my criticism, the whole problem of the behavioral interpreter, is that there is no such thing as this comprehensive movie, no means of obtaining the complete behavioral history of this individual. We only get snippets of film and we need to find a means of interpreting it that is readier-to-hand than the supposed universal observation. Lacey (1995/1996, p. 69) hints at the kind of extra interpretation that is required: "Insofar as building a house is constituted by an extended behavioral pattern, a particular act is part of the pattern only if it is performed because the builder believes that it will contribute towards her goal of a house being built through her own agency. In this analysis, which is Aristotelian, intentional categories are essential for defining the behavior pattern. The applicability of intentional categories to states of an organism cannot be grounded in the operant processes of discrimination alone."

The mode of expression which Lacey adopts here can possibly be clarified as follows. The behavior of the builder is predictable only insofar as we ascribe to her the desire to build a house and the belief that placing this brick will lead to building a wall, that building the wall will contribute to the fabrication of a room... and so on. We need some mechanism for attributing these desires and beliefs: we do so partly on the basis of an idea of rational behavior in the circumstances and partly by inference from the builder's behavior pattern including her verbal behavior. This displays an initial analysis based on the contextual stance (the operant behavior she displays is likely to result in this consequence which will increase the probability of her doing such and such next...), which is overlain by an intentional heuristic based on optimality, the assumption of desires and beliefs appropriate to the situation, and the ruling out of consequences that are improbable or non-maximizing, in other words are impossible ends to attach to her behavior. We can immediately rule out the possibility that she is building a staircase to heaven, therefore, or a marble palace, or a headquarters building for the Society for the Protection of Small Disingenuous Wooden Italians with Extensible Noses. But can teleological behaviorism? It may be significant that the predictive capacity of this approach is greatest in the context of the narrowly-defined and measurable utility functions of everyday economic life rather than in broader circumstances.

Perhaps it is a little unfair to criticize the quest for final causes as explanations of behavior: it is the very complexity of the interpretive task that renders precision and warranted assertibility not simply arduous but impossible. It is the apparent unwillingness of the system's exponents to acknowledge this that is the cause for concern. Rachlin (1994, p. 32) observes that "If a behavioral analysis ultimately fails, the failure will be due to the complexity of the task. It will be like the failure to predict and control the weather precisely rather than any intrinsic inaccessibility or opacity of its subject." But it is not the complexity of the task that daunts it; it is the inability of any system on its own to reconstruct all of the relevant elements by which a behavioral interpretation must proceed. In the case of an ultimately intentional approach, the reconstruction of a learning history and the construal of the behavior setting is a vital prerequisite. In the case of an extensional approach such as Rachlin attempts, the bounds of "plausible" causation can be set only by a construal of the intentional meaning of the acts in question. In order to identify the consequences that are relevant to a specific behavior it is necessary to specify the *context* of the act under interpretation. (One does not have to be a card-carrying contextualist to find the idea of the "act in context" a useful summary of the paradigm). Radical behaviorism has no mechanism by which to identify the context of any relevant behavior that takes place beyond the closed setting of the laboratory. It has no concept of the open setting and how its influences on behavior can be expected to differ from those obtaining in closed settings. If behavior analysis and the extensional science of behavior which is its basis cannot supply some means of delineating the contextual boundaries of the behavior it seeks to explain, where is such demarcation to come from? At least an approximation to it can be obtained by considering the intensional meaning of the behavior.

The objection is not to the pursuit of final causes as an end in itself – especially one that promises much insofar as it proposes to reduce causality to the economist's device of the individual's utility function – but that it leaves out a level of analysis that is essential to a complete interpretation of human experience. Rachlin (2000, p. 19) is clear on this point: "If other people with all their senses functioning were present, if the lights were on, and if they still could not see or hear you do something, then (according to teleological behaviorism) you have not done it." This is allowing what we claim to be able to see or hear to be determined by a priori assumption and argument rather than by the empirical means available to us. It is reminiscent of scholastic philosophy rather than modern science. Yet what Rachlin is arguing is that our experience is limited by a certain view of what constitutes scientific observation.

Chapter 9

Intentional Behaviorism

The strategy that Dennett advocates for the addition of content to physiological research may be followed in the case of operant behavioral science in order to generate a psychology of the person that takes environment–behavior relationships into consideration. The question arises: on what basis is content to be ascribed to theories and findings at the super-personal level in order to arrive at a psychology of the person that takes environment–behavior relationships into consideration? In order to find an answer to this question it is necessary to go back to Dennett's strategy of ascribing content to the sub-personal theories and findings of neuroscience, and it may be worthwhile reviewing its central themes now. At the same time, if the analogy between a subpersonal : personal level linkage and a superpersonal : personal level linkage is to be confirmed, it should be possible to show how the reasoning that develops for adding content to the extensional findings on environment–behavior relationships applies to the resolution of the problems of personal level psychology, behavioral continuity, and delimitation.

The strategy of ascribing content to the theories and findings of extensional behavioral science cannot be pursued in the absence of a convincing rationale. Recall that Dennett's strategy is to assume that the sequence of events that are to be intentionally explained are appropriate from an evolutionary perspective; the next step is to propose structures that will account for these appropriate sequences. The environmental significance necessary for the brain to discriminate useful from unuseful neural events is extrinsic to those neural events, the brain's necessary distinctions cannot stem solely from extensional descriptions of extrinsic stimulation and past behavior. The brain has to be able to discriminate and store fortuitously appropriate structures. Some close analogy of natural selection must be sought to provide for the capacity of the brain to do this. The necessary capacity could itself be an outcome of the evolution of species. An intentional system has to be able to discriminate and respond to the environmental factors that impinge upon it and to do this it must be able to "interpret peripheral stimulation." This entails producing within itself not representations but states or events that "co-occur" with the conditions or objects in its perceptual field. Information abstracted from the environment will nevertheless remain non-intelligent unless something else it added to it; what must be added consists in the detection of afferent and efferent links.

The links between the subpersonal–personal and superpersonal–personal levels of analysis can in each case be characterized in Skinner's (1981) term "selection by consequences." The first is dependent on an evolutionary history that produced phylogenic consequences which determine the structure of the brain and its functioning, the neural afferent–efferent relationships to which content is added in the process of intentional ascription in order to delineate the personal level of analysis. The second depends also, indirectly, on this process since it is through natural selection that the organism's capacity to change as a result of contact with environmental consequences presumably came about. However, in a more direct way, this link is the result of ontogenic consequences through which behavior is shaped in the course of a lifetime. Again there is a need for intentional ascription, even if (or possibly, especially if) operant behavior instantiates physiological change within the organism. Donahoe, Palmer and Burgos (1997, p. 196) state that "In a stable context, control by consequences (as opposed to antecedents) stands as a behavioral law, but we propose (at another level of analysis) that the effects of those consequences are implemented by changes in synaptic efficacies," an idea they trace back to Watson. But this argument merely addresses the subpersonal–personal levels of linkage that Dennett proposes, and has no direct bearing on the relationship between the super-personal–personal levels which are proposed here as a function of ontogenic development.

Intentional Ascription Revisited

We have seen that an extensionally-based system of radical behaviorist interpretation attempts to account for these necessary linkages by resorting to (a) physiological mechanisms, (b) private events, and (c) rules, and that there is no reason for taking any of these seriously at the explanatory level since they do not provide the necessary continuity even in the terms required by an extensional science of behavior. The required interpretative device is that of content-ascription in terms of the desires and beliefs it would be rational for the individual to have in view of his or her situation defined by the intersection of his or her learning history and the behavior setting he or she faces. Both evolutionary reasoning and the behavioral analysis of matching phenomena suggest that the contingencies with which an individual will have come most obviously into contact in the course of phylogenic and ontogenic histories will be those producing behavior that tends toward optimization of outcome. In any situation, therefore, we can assume beliefs, attitudes and intentions that are consistent with this objective. As long as the conceptualization and – at the level of empirical research – measurement of these cognitive constructs is in line with those pursued by attitude theorists, there is a convincing rationale for the attribution of content to the findings of extensional behavioral science based on the contextual stance (that is, the location of behavior at the intersection of learning history and behavior setting.) These constructs directly link the elements of the contextual stance with the process of content ascription.

Dennett criticizes "S-R theorists" for being unable to show how a novel stimulus can arrive at or select the appropriate response. (Although behavior analysts are immediately likely to interpret reference to "S–R theorists" as not applying to them, the following argument is just as applicable to operant psychology as to S–R psychology and it is clear that Dennett is including operant and respondent behaviorisms in the same category here.) He continues by pointing out that an animal might detect a stimulus but not "know" what the appropriate response is (the stimulus in question could as well be discriminative stimulus as unconditioned or conditioned.) No afferent can be taken by the brain to have significance A unless it is recognized by the efferent side of the brain has having it, i.e., until the brain has produced the appropriate response. The content of a neural event or state depends not only upon its "normal state of stimulation" but also whatever additional efferent effects it produces. The determination of these factors necessarily takes us beyond the extensional description of stimuli and responses.

Content can be ascribed to a neural event only when it is a link between an afferent and an efferent – and not just that but a link in an *appropriate chain* between afferent and efferent. The content is not something one discovers within this neural event but an extra interpretation. The ultimate justification for such ascription is provided by evolutionary thinking – the intelligent brain must be able to select the appropriate response to a specific stimulus. Why should this be less the case for the link between extensional operant analysis and the personal level of analysis than for that between physiology and that level? A totally biological theory of behavior would still not be able, Dennett claims, to account for *what the person is doing*. Intentional ascription simply describes what a purely extensional theory would describe, nothing more, but in a different way. This different way may be useful to the physiologist, however. Neuroscience that does not view neural events as signals, reports or messages can scarcely function at all. No purely biological logic can tell us why the rat knows which way to go for his food. Nor can any purely contextualistic logic reveal this in the absence of some sort of "Dennettian overlay." In neither case does the proposed intentional ascription detract from the extensional version of events but adds an interpretation that provides greater intuitive understanding of the system.

The import of intentional ascription must, however, in the course of the present argument, go thus far and no further. It retains the a-ontological assumption about cognitive events, states, processes and structures with which, along with Dennett, we began. There is no justification for uncritically accepting the entire apparatus of the information processing account of behavior be this based on cognitive conjecture or neurophysiology. The justification of intentional behaviorism lies in the necessity of connecting efferent–afferent processes in some way that (a) physiology cannot, (b) behavioral science cannot, and (c) that aids the coherent explanation and prediction of behavior. What Dennett calls a centralist theory, therefore, has two explanatory components. The first is an extensional account of the interaction of functional structures; the second, an intentional characterization of these structures, the events occurring within them, and states of the structures resulting from these. The links between the extensional account and the intentional interpretation consists of a hypothesis or hypotheses describing the evolutionary source of the fortuitously propitious arrangement in virtue of which the system's operation in this instance makes sense. These hypotheses are required in principle to account for the appropriateness which is presupposed by the Intentional interpretation, but which requires a genealogy from the standpoint of the extensional, physical theory. Despite the inevitable imprecision of this approach, the challenge is to make the case that the ascription of content to the theories and findings of behavioral science can be of use to the behavior analyst, and in particular, to the process of radical behaviorist interpretation.

As Gunderson (1972) summarizes Dennett's argument, humans are not simply neurophysiological organisms but also persons who exhibit complex behaviors. Dennett's case for the ascription of content rests on the understanding that because some neural events, states and structures are about other things, that is, intentional, it is possible to ascribe content to them. The basis of the contextual stance is similarly that humans are persons as well as organisms whose behavior is determined by the contingencies of reinforcement. Moreover, some of the environmental elements on which our behavior is contingent are *about* things, i.e., are such that it makes sense to attribute content to them, to add an extra layer of interpretation that is relevant to the personal level. Whereas Dennett speaks of only two levels of analysis, however, we have distinguished three. We have noted his argument for a *personal* level, at which the individual as a whole discriminates such "mental" entities as pain, and a *subpersonal* level of brains and neurons, at which level the physiological correlates of pain behavior can be detected. "..[T]he terms in our mentalistic vocabulary are nonreferring. Rather like 'sakes' or 'miles', [or centers of gravity] mentalistic terms in appropriate contexts tell us something, but succeed in doing so without thereby referring to any entities any more than the words 'sakes' or 'miles' refer to sakes or miles." (Gunderson, 1972, p. 593). At the superpersonal level we turn to the environmental contingencies that shape and maintain responding in order to find an extensional basis for the ascription of such content. Several factors distinguish this level from both the personal and the subpersonal level based on neuroscience that Dennett identifies.

First, the superpersonal level cannot capture anything of the personal level including some essential components of what it is to be human, such as being able to discriminate pain. No matter how we grimace and howl and hold our painful heads, no matter what consequences these overt actions have by way of producing sympathy or medicine or exemptions from work from others, these superlevel events are entirely separate from the discrimination of pain. Second, the superpersonal level constitutes an extensional approach to the science of behavior, one which can explain much behavior at that level but which is incapable of dealing with the things that can only be discriminated at the personal level: pain, that it is time to go home, and other intentional matters. Only by the addition of a heuristic overlay of interpretation can these personal level matters be accommodated. Third, even though neither level reduces to the other, it is incumbent upon us to show how they are linked if we are to make legitimate and convincing interpretive ascriptions. The link, moreover, must be consistent with evolutionary reasoning. There are several strands to be considered here. (a) The capacity for operant reinforcement is bestowed by natural selection. What Skinner (1981) calls "selection by consequences" is the analogy/homology that links the two processes at least at the level of phylogenic and ontogenic consistency. (b) In the case of linking the personal and subpersonal levels, the links must supervene (i.e., add appropriate interpretation) between the afferent and efferent processes of the brain. The corresponding processes in operant conditioning are stimuli and responses: the heuristic overlay of intentionality must link these in ways that an extensional account cannot. There are three such ways: (i) to elucidate the personal level, (ii) to demonstrate continuity of behavior from setting to setting, (iii) to solve problems of equifinality by delimiting operant interpretations that (attempt to) proceed solely at the extensional level. These considerations bring the interpretation within the scope of an evolutionarily consistent framework of conceptualization and analysis. How? The animal that is to be successful in negotiating its environment must be able to discriminate discriminative and other setting stimuli in order to act appropriately (with behavior that will be reinforced).

There is no more reason to believe that a physiological account will eventually be available to show how this occurs any more than there is a possibility that a physiological account will be able to demonstrate an individual's discrimination of pain. The discrimination of appropriate behavior occurs at the personal level. The recognition of appropriate inaugurating stimuli is a similar process. At the very least, the intentional mode of explanation cannot be abandoned until the physiological link is demonstrated: to trust in eventual physiology is superstitious in a way in which the ascription of intentionality is not if the latter strategy results in more effective predictions of behavior. Physicists who shun the concept of center of gravity in favor of a belief in some distant more physical explanation would be showing a similar level of superstition. That physicists are not embarrassed to include centers of gravity in their predictive work should be an example to the psychologist.

Intentional Behaviorist Interpretation

The alternative to an extensional system of radical behaviorist interpretation, then, is the amalgamation of extensional operant behavioral science and Dennett's intensional stance by which content would be ascribed to its theories and findings in order to provide a basis for radical behaviorist interpretation. The reality of this may be closer to us than we have imagined. The point is sometimes made that radical behaviorists often incorporate the language of intentionality in their popular accounts of behavior, the implication being that the extensional operant account is thereby diminished, perhaps incapable of adequately describing the events that are the subject of the accounts in question. Skinner (e.g., 1974) argues that in order to communicate to a non-specialist audience, it is useful to adopt everyday language, as does the professional astronomer speaks of the sun "rising" and "setting" when addressing children. Many behaviorists have taken this at face value and not concerned themselves further with the charge that the use of such language necessarily invokes a theoretical stance which is inevitable in the explanation of behavior. In view of the import of the current argument, this is a serious matter that behavior analysts ought not to ignore so easily.

The accounts in question are generally interpretations rather than reports of experimental work and this suggests that at least at the level of interpretation intentional language is inevitable not only to communicate to pedestrians but to express the ideas involved in accounting for complex activity in operant terms. "Thinking" and "feeling," the very stuff of private events, are almost always spoken of in intentional language: we do not just think, we think *about* or think *that*; we do not just feel, we feel *that*; and so on. We can treat such events as stimuli and responses that do not differ in kind from those that are publicly available – though this is to make an enormous ontological leap that can never be the subject of a scientific analysis – but to insist that thoughts and feelings are simply discriminative stimuli (or establishing operations, or other source of antecedent stimulation), associating them in the process with a physiological level of extensional analysis, is to leave out entirely the personal level to which Dennett draws attention, the level without which no psychological explanation can be complete.

The suggested program is not a call for the use of mediating events or the kinds of theory that Skinner repudiated. Even less is it a regurgitation of the sometimes argued notion that the intentional and contextual stances might be conjoined or a synthesis generated that would combine "the best of each." This is not possible in practice because their respective intentional and extensional bases are incommensurable (Foxall, 1999). But the adding of content to an extensional account is not a synthesis or amalgamation. It is not adding anything to the findings and theories derived from the experimental analysis of behavior. Rather, it is the derivation of another level of interpretation in order to facilitate understanding and prediction by taking the personal level of experience into account.

In order to advance the debate between cognitivists and behaviorists, this account takes Dennett's thesis about the relationship between extensional science and intensional psychology at face value. To do this is to share, again for the sake of argument, (a) his assessment of the (literal) shortcomings of purely extensional science as a means to understand behavior: such science simply does not go far enough in the quest to explain all behavior, and (b) his judgment that the link between the two is found in the imperatives of evolution. Extensional behavioral science is, like physiology, an autonomous approach to knowledge in its own right but it is incapable of explaining all human behavior within its own theoretical and methodological purview, nor even that it can engender plausible interpretations (that is expressed in non-convoluted language) of all behavior. It is here that an important parallel with Dennett's analysis leads to a major conclusion: the extensional science of physiology is to Dennett's intensional physical psychology what an extensional behavioral science is to the intensional psychology of social cognition. In other words, the extensional science provides the evolutionary basis

for understanding behavior biologically to which intensional cognitive interpretation verbally ascribes an a-ontological, initially non-empirical dimension which
yields predictions of certain behaviors that the extensional approach of itself can
neither explain nor predict. What is true for the center-piece of social cognitive
psychology – attitude research – is likely to be generally the case.

The strategy of ascribing optimality (rationality) to systems in order to predict
their behavior is a methodological simplification that involves further ascription –
of posited entities such as beliefs, attitudes and intentions which, as we have seen,
have the function of fine-tuning the prediction by linking it to the system's
environmental history and behavior setting. The three stages of the intentional
strategy make its dependency on the prior application of the contextual strategy
clear. Dennett takes pains to avoid this conclusion. He denigrates (radical)
behaviorism by, first, casting it as a simplistic S-R paradigm, and, secondly, by
asserting, in the absence of any adduced evidence, that it has proved unsuccessful
in predicting behavior. The first of these caricatures fails to engage with the operant
behavior analysis of the last thirty years, especially the analysis of behavior at the
molar level, the post-Skinnerian analysis of the verbal behavior of the listener, etc.
The second ignores a mass of empirical evidence. Both overlook the possibility of
radical behaviorist interpretation, that is, the use of the contextual stance to account
for the behavior that is not amenable to an experimental analysis. Indeed, the use
of the intentional stance is advocated here only in the context of radical behaviorist
interpretation. It is important that the extensional science of operant behavior
analysis continue its program for two reasons: first, to provide an evolving and
expanding base for the content ascription to which content can be ascribed in the
process of interpretation; secondly, to provide alternative, competing and challeng-
ing explanations. Insofar as the growth of knowledge depends on "the active
interplay of competing theories" (Feyerabend, 1975), it is essential to have (i) a
thriving experimental analysis of behavior, (ii) operant interpretations which
themselves attempt to function on an extensional level only, and (iii) operant
interpretations that contain the intentional overlays necessary to provide accounts
of behavior at the personal level. Their interaction is, indeed, a *sine qua non* of
intellectual progress. Hence, what characterizes the intentional behaviorist approach is the incorporation of both the contextual and the intentional stances into
a single framework of analysis. Social cognitivists must reconstruct desires and
beliefs in the context of the individual's rationality by considering its situation. The
contextual stance facilitates this reconstruction by *de*constructing the notion of
situation in terms of (a) a learning history, (b) the current behavior setting, and (c)
their interaction. This is both consistent with and a means of operationalizing
Dennett's view that the organism will have those desires and beliefs that are
appropriate to it given its situation.

Intentional behaviorism differs from the other systems of explanation in its
comprehensive inclusion of the various elements of the contextual and intentional
stances, as well as in the understanding that the ascription of intentionality

reinforces rather than detracts from the prior existence of an extensional behavioral science. It follows Dennett's subtle recognition that the addition of an intentional layer of interpretation does not discover anything new but tells another story about the theories and findings produced by operant psychology. The result is not just an extra story that maps on to the original in a one on one fashion: rather it extends the scope and relevance of the interpretation. Moreover, intentional behaviorism recognizes that social cognitive psychology proceeds in a similar manner, and raises the possibility that psychology will find a platform on which it might unite.

Some Consequences

In a spirit of methodological pluralism, I have not argued *against* any particular approach to the generation of knowledge but rather for the expansion of the behaviorist's canon of interpretive methods and for the cognitivist's recognition of the role of contextual factors in interpretations of human behavior involving intentional idioms. Progress will result more readily from the active interplay of competing methodologies (or "paradigms") than by the attempt to enforce orthodoxy (Feyerabend, 1970). It would be entirely in keeping with this were the extensional approach to operant interpretation to continue to attract attention and effort, building upon the kinds of verbal behavior analysis which translates the statements of social cognition into the functional categories of Skinner's *Verbal Behavior* and those of the analysis of rule-governed behavior (e.g., Zettle & Hayes, 1982). The inclusion of private events into such accounts is not ruled out, either: although there are difficulties with their present state of conceptualization and deployment, scientific progress is always open to conceptual extension and refinement and there is nothing that says they must be finally abandoned at this stage. Equally, however, the attempt to provide behavioral explication in terms that rule out private events is an endeavor which can be expected to contribute to the growth of knowledge through such active interplay. The point is to encourage critical, informed debate that forges new conceptualizations and searches for empirical knowledge that would not have been generated within the confines of a single methodology. The major innovation to be commended to behavior analysts is the alternative methodology in which the personal level of analysis is opened up by the ascription of intentional content to the findings and theories of the extensional science of behavior that is based on experimental and quasi-experimental analysis. This completes the project begun by Dennett by linking that personal level with the super-personal level of analysis in which behavior is understood in terms of its environmental contingencies.

If the argument is accepted, however, behavior analysts have at the very least to cede a kind of analysis to those who embrace the intentional idiom, that is, to recognize intentionalistic psychology as legitimate, feasible and perhaps even useful (to us). Of course we might argue with Quine that the very opacity of the intentional sentences only shows that they should be ignored but this argument has not convinced the majority of philosophers of mind or cognitive scientists.

Moreover, the existence of propositional sentences opens up the possibility of a far richer psychology of behavior that can cope with intentionality without relying on mediating variables. If the argument is accepted (that is, the account of what intentionalistic cognitivism is doing) then we should embrace the use of attitude measurement as a basis for establishing learning histories and the effects of behavior settings in interpretive accounts. We cannot have it both ways: If "cognitive" measures of verbal behavior (a) refer to learning history and behavior setting variables, (b) do not use exclusively cognitive variables to predict behavior, and (c) rely rather on situational variables to do so, then similar techniques can represent learning histories in radical behaviorist interpretations. While the extensional apparatus of the experimental analysis of behavior is appropriate to the closed setting of the laboratory, the explication of behavior in the relatively open settings encountered in everyday life requires tools that are appropriate to it: the ascription of intentionalistic content to the behavioral science of experiment and quasi-experiment presents a way forward in such explication that can be commended to behavior analysts at least for active consideration.

Finally, if the argument is accepted, the relationship between intensionalistic and extensionalistic accounts becomes clear. It is that proposed by Dennett to link physiology with psychology. Physiology provides an extensional science which can proceed in its own terms without recourse to intentionalistic attribution. But it is thereby limited: it cannot provide explanations of such phenomena as pain which are properties of the entire person. Similarly, behavior analysis provides an independent but limited science of behavior to which propositional content can be applied. Cognitive psychology in adopting the intentional stance is always dependent on the prior existence and coherence of the contextual stance. The prediction of behavior may, and the comprehensive interpretation of behavior in operant termsdoes, require the ascription of propositional content to the outcomes of extensional behavioral science. This solution to the problem of the relationship of behavioral science to intensional psychology means adopting the strategy apparently employed by social cognitivists, namely the ascription of content to the findings of science. This approach retains the contextual stance – we have argued that social cognitivists have been unable to leave it out; we can hardly now claim that it is not there. Such a strategy would, however, involve the abandonment of an intellectual project which involved the combined pursuit of an extensional behavioral science and that of a fully extensional mode of radical behaviorist interpretation. The reason is that it would overlay on the findings of such a science the propositional content which belongs to a different – probably incommensurable – paradigm. More positively, it would contribute to the solution of age-old problems of intentionality, incommensurability and interpretation. This approach makes no ontological claims about cognition but stresses the incommensurability of explanations of behavior based respectively on the intentional stance and the contextual stance. It nonetheless draws attention to the inescapability of each of these for the other. Such a strategy avoids the ontological problems that inhere in a simplistic amalgamation of environmental and intrapersonal causes of behavior as they are apparently incorporated into a single scheme of interpretation.

What is suggested here differs from the frequent tendency in for instance cognitive behavior theory and therapy to speak of thoughts and imaginings as "cognitions" but to take little notice as a result of the methodological implications of doing this. *Radical behaviorism* and the *psychological behaviorism* of Staats (1996) do not include intentionality at all. In deriving the mental processes and states of the individual on the basis of its extended (publicly available) behavior, Rachlin's (1994) *teleological behaviorism* ignores setting elements, (e.g., we do not surmise that you are angry because you are in what is usually a frustrating situation, but because you shout and jump about). It considers behavioral history (in the sense of the sequence of behavior that is observed) but not learning history (it is not concerned with the stimuli that have produced behavior in the past). It is the final, not the efficient causes of behavior that are at the heart of teleological behaviorism, whilst intentional behaviorism seeks efficient causation in the propositional attitudes it ascribes. Staddon's (2001a) *theoretical behaviorism* proposes state changes in the organism when behavior occurs. In this it follows Skinner but, whereas Skinner leaves the question of what and how to physiologists and does not trouble about them again, Staddon suggests that these theoretical questions cannot be ignored in science: indeed they are an inevitable component of the scientific procedure. Even physics proceeds by positing unobservables. He does not trouble whether the changed internal states are physiological or cognitive (or not) but argues that they constitute efficient causes of further behavior. However, theoretical behaviorism relies neither on the intentional stance nor the contextual; nor is it concerned with the sphere of radical behaviorist interpretation with which we have been specifically involved here. Other attempts to amalgamate behavioral and cognitive psychologies tend to overwhelm one causal perspective with the other – so, for example, Bandura's (1986) *social cognitive theory*, closest to Tolman's purposive behaviorism, tends in practice to subsume psychology within a cognitive framework, but without suggesting a mechanism of amalgamation, whilst Staats' (1996) *psychological behaviorism*, closest to Hullian behaviorism, tends to subsume cognitive phenomena within behavioral. The intentional behaviorism perspective alone retains the essential contributions of both systems, each of which may proceed in its own terms, whilst emphasizing the advantages of the sort of combination that Dennett proposes. It also completes Dennett's program by explicating the super-personal level of analysis and its contribution to understanding the personal level.

The main contrast to be drawn, however, is with radical behaviorism. How are behavior and its consequences related? As we have seen, Skinner and Rachlin propose the alternative approaches of fabricating a plausible learning history and proposing the final causes of an extended pattern of behavior. The difficulty with the first is that without some intentional ascription to identify the rational motives or intentions of the behaving person, it becomes absurd. The difficulty with the second is that, without some intentional ascription to delimit the range of consequences that can count as causes, it becomes absurd.

A traditional way of attributing proximal motivation to the behavior and/or circumscribing the range of effects of behavior that might explain it is the attribution to the organism of internal processes or events or states which are represented in some way in the theoretical causal chain. In intentional behaviorism, however, the theoretical link is made explicit as ascribed intentional content. "Cognitive" is for many behavioral psychologists a loaded term: there is no reason why they should not speak of intentional behavior and intentional behavior analysis. But the term is carefully chosen. Intentional ascription is simply the most straightforward method of making attributions of proximal motivation that circumscribe the consequences of behavior that may usefully be used in its explanation. Nor should this come as a surprise. Radical behaviorists who have considered the problem of behavioral consistency and resolved it by speaking of physiological change within the organism have thereby already accepted the idea of ascribing something to the individual in order to explain his/her behavior: the fact that their physiological ascriptions are not related to any known physiological correlates of behavior just makes their proposition bizarre. The ascription of unknown physiology does nothing to reveal additional levels of analysis whereas that of cognitive content at least makes the personal level available to the behavioral scientist, and provides a means of circumscribing the chain of behavioral consequences in terms of which behavior might be interpreted.

Radical behaviorism defines its scientific goals exclusively as prediction and control: its pragmatic program eschews the search for "understanding." If it went no further than this it would succeed or fail on its own terms. But it goes further, claiming that the demonstration of behavior-environment correlations is tantamount to showing that other modes of explanation, those for instance that seek understanding based on the cognitive mediation of behavior, are redundant. This is to suggest that behavior analysis provides sufficient understanding and it is on this ground that radical behaviorism is vulnerable. As a technology, it may, on the basis of what it includes, achieve the merit that effective applications confer. As a science, however, it is open to criticism for what it excludes. But if uncritical acceptance of environmental determinism leads to one problem of epistemology, it is certain that the kind of unfettered, asituational cognitivism which is common in some quarters is equally partial and problematical. This is the problem with what Dennett calls "pure intentionalism," the lack of external referents for explanatory variables that derive entirely from intentional reasoning.

Beyond the Bounds

The foregoing analysis has enabled us to spell out the bounds of behaviorism. While the experimental analysis of behavior can form the basis of an extensional behavioral science, radical behaviorist interpretation requires special treatment. An extensional radical behaviorist interpretation would require that private events be extensionally delineable. Only dogma can cast them as such: consisting in feelings and thoughts, they are inescapably intensional. Given the content-ful way in which we talk about thoughts and feelings, the behaviorist can treat private events only with the most discursive locutions in order to avoid the idea that they rely on their propositional content in order to contribute to the interpretation of complex human behavior. The importance of behavior analysts' coming to terms with the claims of intentionalism lies in the absurdity of their explanatory position should they continue to seek an interpretive system that they suppose to be based uncomplicatedly on the extensional behavioral science they have forged in the laboratory. It is an absurdity recognized by all but themselves. As a result, psychologists in general are failing to recognize the role of environmental influences on their subject matter by not realizing that the cognitive ascription of meaning to their empirical findings rests upon the exercise of the contextual stance. Behaviorism's greatest lesson for psychology – that the language of private events, however we characterize them ontologically and methodologically, must be systematically related to events external to the individual. So long as behaviorists ignore the corresponding truth that their system provides a basis for interpretation only if it embraces the ascription of content to their findings so long is the promotion of a more unified psychology impeded.

It is important to emphasize the a-ontological position here accorded intentional or cognitive events. One sphere in which behaviorists and cognitivists seem determined to talk past each other is that of verbal behavior which can be construed either extensionally or intensionally. Many behaviorists are determined to see only one interpretation in such cases; many cognitivists, only the other. A case in point is Skinner's writings which advocate say a new way of looking at language (his *Verbal Behavior*, 1957) or of organizing society (his *Beyond Freedom and Dignity*, 1971). Skinner's interpretation of what these books comprise is samples of his own verbal behavior which are entirely under contingency control. The interpretation placed on Skinner's words by cognitivists such as Lacey (1995/1996, p. 64.) is intentionalistic: Skinner is advocating *that*, proposing *that*, and so on. Of course, since this is not an argument based on empirical evidence and its interpretation but merely one based on the interpretation of the structure and function of sentences, each can be correct. The questions that arise are merely pragmatic: when is one or other useful (i.e., when can our aims be achieved using behaviorist or cognitive psychology alone, and when are both required (i.e., when does our required interpretation demand intentional behaviorism?) It may well be that the sphere of discourse in which the extensional construal of language can be usefully employed is very small, whilst that in which an intentional construal is very large; but at least the present formulation preserves the possibility that each can be useful, and indeed suggests that there is some place for both: what use is actually made of them is a matter to be decided by practical concerns.

The disagreement is worth pursuing if the behaviorist and cognitivist in question take a conventionally realist position in which case the argument is over whether cognitions have any physical existence. Since the brand of intentionality advocated here is a-ontological, this dispute does not arise. It is based solely on the view that different kinds of sentence can be and are used to describe each interpretation of the kind Lacey mentions with respect to Skinner's books or for that matter any kind of advocacy. This is in line with the approach taken by Dennett in *Content and Consciousness* (1969). This has implications for the strategy one adopts for changing behavior, however. Should behavior be changed by attempting to change beliefs, attitudes or intentions, or by changing situations? Since the beliefs that an individual has are simply those ascribed to it on the basis of what beliefs it ought to have given its position, what is the point of changing those beliefs in order to change its behavior? If, however, one changes the situation by altering the pattern of available contingencies and the stimuli that signal their availability contingent upon the performance of certain specified behaviors, then the individual's behavior is likely to change as a consequences, and one can alter the beliefs that can be appropriately ascribed to him or her. Part of changing the situation might involve changing the individual's verbal behavior but that is not the same thing as changing his or her beliefs or other cognitions.

Assuming that the ascription of cognitive (intentional) events permits the prediction of behavior is not to say that behavior is caused by mental events. This is the root of both Dennett's and Skinner's behaviorisms. Therefore, changing behavior by seeking to change mental events may be inappropriate. It may be possible to alter motor behavior by changing *verbal* behavior, be it private or public but this is not to say that the verbal behavior in question is determined by underlying mental events such as attitudes. It may be learned on its own schedules as the radical behaviorist says. But it may have a greater causal effect than the radical behaviorist assumes. It is also likely that unless the external environment changes in line with the changes in verbal behavior the changes in motor behavior will not be sustained. This is in line with operant research on instructed behavior and with attitude theory and research (Foxall, 1997a).

Radical behaviorist interpretation cannot fail to be more complete and accurate if it takes into consideration the nature of its innate bounds and the role that intentionality can play in defining and overcoming them. The first challenge for behavior analysts is that of building on the considerations drawn out in this monograph in order to produce more intellectually and practically satisfactory interpretations of complex behavior. All explication of empirical observation requires some interpretation, of course: even the application of the elements of the three-term contingency to the observed sequence of events in the most rigorously defined experiment in the operant laboratory cannot avoid theoretical consider-ations and even theoretical terminology altogether. The second challenge for behavior analysts is to decide how far that scientific process, the fundamental experimental analysis of behavior which lies at the heart of their discipline, can continue to ignore and avoid intentionality.

In a nutshell, I have not argued that radical behaviorism needs to change its approach to the analysis of behavior, even complex behavior. The kind of explanation that I have noted which depends on utilizing the intentional stance is not one that inheres in the radical behaviorist tradition and I am not attempting the proselytizing task of trying to transform this tradition. I am simply pointing out (a) the prevalence of intentional explanation as a rival and opposing force to radical behaviorism, the consequent need to understand it, to be prepared for its arguments and to comprehend their ramifications for radical behaviorist interpretation, (b) the gaps that exist in radical behaviorist explanation and the questions that can be raised about the capacity of the usual radical behaviorist approaches (contingency shaped behavior, rule-governed behavior, physiology) to fill them, (c) that the intentional stance and the contextual stance predict most complex human behavior about as accurately as one another, (d) that the gaps will never be filled by their very nature at the level of extensional science, (e) that the intentional stance is highly dependent on the prior use of the contextual stance, (f) that the way is open if we wish to take it to harmonize psychology by employing both the intentional and the contextual stance at the level of interpretation of complex behavior, and (g) that this has methodological but not ontological implications for behavioral science.

Both Rachlin and Dennett take pains to emphasize that the interpretations to which their various systems give rise are necessarily non-specific and tentative. This is in the nature of the interpretation of complexity itself rather than in the systems. Hence, none of what I have written may allow us to explain the behavior of the professor entering the faculty club with the certainty of avoiding his suing us along with the tabloids, but it is may give us greater confidence to interpret his behavior according to a comprehensive system of explanation.

The End-Point

The inextricable relationship between the contextual and intentional stances is apparent from the following accounts, by an intentionalist and a behaviorist, respectively. In the first, the contextual stance surely precedes the intentional, whilst in the second the order is reversed. Each author nonetheless emphasizes just one of these. First, Dennett (1987a, p. 251) illustrates what he calls the *Sherlock Holmes method* with a quote from Cherniak (1981, p. 161):

> In "A Scandal in Bohemia," Sherlock Holmes' opponent has hidden a very valuable photograph in a room, and Holmes wants to find out where it is. Holmes has Watson throw a smoke bomb unto the room and yell "fire" when Holmes' opponent is in the next room, while Holmes watches. Then, as one would expect, the opponent runs into the room and takes the photograph from where it was hidden. Not everyone would have devised such an ingenious plan for manipulating an opponent's behavior; but once the conditions are described, it seems very easy to predict the opponent's actions.

Holmes' opponent, Irene Adler, is thus revealed to *want* the photograph; to *believe* it to be located where she goes to get it; to *believe* that the person who yelled "fire" *believed* there was a fire...; to *want* to retrieve the photograph without letting anyone *know* she was doing this, and so on (Dennett, 1987a, p. 251). By contrast, legal scholar Richard Posner (1990, 1995), who describes himself as a behaviorist "in the sense of being a determinist," argues that juries act behavioristically in attributing *premeditation* to an accused:

> Not only do we punish the premeditating criminal more severely for reasons having nothing to do with free will, but in deciding whether a crime is premeditated we employ – oxymoron though it may seem – a behaviorist account of deliberation. We examine the circumstances of the crime: Was it concealed? Had the criminal made arrangements for a getaway? Had he obtained the means of committing the crime in advance? Were those means suitable to the end (suitably lethal, in the case of murder?) Did the criminal have much to gain from the crime? (Posner, 1990, p. 175)

Such a step is at best heuristic, since:

> "Conscious" choice can be redescribed in nondeliberative terms as cost-benefit analysis, utility maximization, or means-end rationality; even some philosophical accounts of deliberation do this. It is thus possible, if paradoxical, to understand premeditation in behavioral terms, as a roundabout way of describing the criminals who are most likely to succeed (Posner, 1990, pp. 175–6.)

QED? Over to you, *Koko*.

Notes

1. I have elsewhere sought principles of interpretation that would render complex economic behavior intelligible in operant terms whilst remaining within the framework of extensional science (Foxall, 1990, 1996, 1997a, b, 1998, 2002a, b; Foxall & James, 2002, 2003; Foxall & Schrezenmaier, 2003; Foxall, Oliveira-Castro & Schrezenmaier, 2004; Foxall & Yani-de-Soriano, 2004; Soriano & Foxall, 2003). This work is analogous to the extension of the conceptualization of verbal behavior from a mere extrapolation of the findings of animal research to the human situation to Skinner's reconceptualization of verbal behavior in terms of rule-governance and the later emphasis on the verbal behavior of the listener (Hayes, 1989). The aim and achievement in both cases has been the better prediction of behavior as well as the extension of the behavior analytical interpretation of complex environment-behavior contingencies. But in this essay I draw attention to broader considerations in the interpretation of complexity, the inescapability of adopting a theoretical position prior to as well as during the process of re-reading a complex situation through eyeglasses that have been forged and perfected in respect of a more accessible context.

2. See also Dennett (1996). Cf. Stich (1981), Churchland (1981), and the peer commentary on "Intentional systems in cognitive ethology" (Dennett, 1983). More general peer commentary can be found in Dahlbom (1993); *Philosophical Topics* (1994); Ross, Brook and Thompson (2000), and Brook and Ross (2002). Reviews of *Content and Consciousness* include Anon. (1970), Audi (1972), Blake (1969), Dent (1970), Franklin (1970), Gunderson (1972), Kane (1970), Kelley (1990), McKim (1970), Nagel (1995), Rice (1971), Smart (1970). Alternative accounts are presented by Anscombe (1957), Chisholm (1957), and Searle (1983).

3. See Dennett, 1969, p. 29; 1994; 1996, p. 38–39; Dennett & Haugeland, 1987; cf. Bratman, 1994; Guttenplan, 1994; Harman, 1998; Perry, 1994; Searle, 1994.

4. In *Content and Consciousness*, Dennett employs the device of capitalizing the initial letter of intentional when it refers to the philosophical concept, thereby distinguishing it from everyday intentionality. Although he did not retain this usage in later writings, he maintained it in the second edition of *Content and Consciousness* and it is thus retained in the quotations from that source.

5. If it is feasible in radical behaviorism to infer the private events of other people in order to render their behavior more intelligible, one could of course ask why the strategy cannot be extended to the private events of nonhumans or machines. However, sufficient unto the day...

6. Kitchener's (1977, p. 54) full comment here is instructive: "The most damaging criticism of the r_g–s_g mechanism for purposive behavior is an objection raised by J. A. Deutsch (1960). Deutsch argues (convincingly in my opinion) that Hull is forced to treat r_g as an ordinary response, subject to the well-established experimental laws of conditioning, extinction, etc. At the same time, however, Deutsch claims, Hull is also forced to treat an r_g as an expectation ordinarily understood and, consequently such a response cannot be an ordinary response at all. [*Footnote*: Cf. Hull's remarks: 'When r_g às leads to S àR$_g$, i.e., when the anticipation of food leads to the actual eating of food, we have what we shall call the *realization of an anticipation*' (1952, p. 133).] For example, Hull believes an r_g (e.g., salivation) was an 'anticipatory response' to the goal stimulus (food). However, Deutsch suggests, responses can be reinforced in various ways and one way of reinforcing the r_g in question would be by means of the goal stimulus water. Water should therefore reinforce an r_g (even though this r_g is a fractional part of the original goal response of eating). But such an account is inadequate to explain certain kinds of maze behavior. The results can only be explained, according to Deutsch, if it is assumed that a fractional goal response must be reinforced by the goal response it is part of (and not by different goal responses). But to assume this is to assume an r_g is not like an ordinary response at all but rather is equivalent to the ordinary notion of expectancy (along with the associated notions of the confirmation or frustration of such an expectancy.) If this is correct, then the Hullian r_g–s_g mechanism for explaining purposive behavior must be judged to be inadequate since it presupposes teleological and cognitive concepts from the start and therefore cannot derive them as 'secondary principles' from neutral a-teleological concepts."

7. Berridge (2000) makes the progression from mediationism to intentionalism clear in his description of the history of behavioral psychology. Bolles's (1972) account of behavior in terms of the expectation of hedonic consequences of Bolles follows the S–S theory of Tolman rather than the S–R theory of Hull but suggests that what is learned are S–S associations of a particular kind and function: an association is leaned between a conditioned stimulus (CS) and a subsequent hedonic stimulus (S*) that elicits pleasure. The first S does not elicit a response but an expectation of the second S (S*). This explains why animals sometimes act as though they have received a reward when they have not: e.g., the raccoon that washes a coin as though it were food, "misbehavior," or autoshaping, or schedule-induced polydipsia. Berridge (2000) argues that useful as this is it fails to explain why the animal still approaches the reinforcer (say food) rather than waiting for it to appear and enjoying the S* in the interim. He discusses the approach of Bindra (1978) who proposes the hedonic transfer of incentive properties to the CS. Bindra accepts the S–S* theory but argues that the S does not simply cause the animal to expect the S*: it also elicits a central motivational state that causes the animal to perceive the S as an S*. The S

assumes the motivational properties that normally belong to the S*. These motivational properties are incentive properties which attract the animal and elicit goal-directed behavior and possibly consumption. Through association with the S*, the S acquires the same functions as the S*. An animal approaches the CS for a reward, finds the signal (S) attractive; if the CS is food, the animal wants to eat it. If it is an S for a tasty food S*, the animal may take pleasure in its attempt to eat the CS (Berridge, 2000, p. 236; see also Bouton & Franselow, 1997). But if CSs were incentives one would always respond to them whether or not one were hungry. The question is to explain how CSs interact with drive states. Toates (1986), therefore, builds on the Bolles–Bindra theory by positing that both cognitive expectancy and more basic reward processes might occur simultaneously in the individual. All of these theories are necessarily intentionalistic since they deal in expectancies.

8. Staats (1996) goes beyond the Skinnerian and Hullian systems to propose an approach to human environment that incorporates both classical and operant conditioning. The contribution of Staats's behaviorism is that it combines the roles of classical and operant conditioning into a single system in which a stimulus performs three functions. The first function of a stimulus is to elicit an emotional response (S —> r). In classical conditioning, the emotion-eliciting function of an unconditioned stimulus is transferred to a neutral (subsequently conditioned) stimulus and, in higher conditioning, this function may be further passed to any number of originally neutral stimuli that become in turn conditioned elicitors. Emotion-eliciting stimuli are those that reinforce motor responses enacted prior to their presentation (R —> S). This is the second function of the stimulus; it is thus the capacity of a stimulus to elicit an emotional response that determines what can be a reinforcer. These two functions of a stimulus show how classical and operant conditioning are related in the environmental production of emotional and motor responses. The third function of a stimulus inheres in its ability to elicit approach-avoidance. Associated with each emotional response is an emotional stimulus or stimulus function which elicits the motor response (S —> r —> s —> R). Approaching an object that elicits a positive emotional response is often reinforced. As a result, any positive emotion-eliciting stimulus will come to elicit approach. This mechanism, once learned, generalizes to any stimulus that elicits a positive emotional response. While a stimulus that elicits positive emotion elicits approach, avoidance is elicited by a stimulus that elicits negative emotion. In this incentive or directive function, the stimulus brings on approach-avoidance which thus follows it; contrast this with reinforcement in which the stimulus follows the environment it strengthens. Although he goes further than most behaviorists who embrace cognitive phenomena in anchoring cognition in behavior, Staats nonetheless proposes a theory in which representative images (which are *of* or *about*) other phenomena cause behavior.

9. I have presented the argument summarized in this chapter in greater detail in the context of consumer psychology: see Foxall (1983, 1997a, b, 2002b). The attitude–intention–behavior models discussed in this chapter are in fact examples of intentional systems theories, unlike sub-personal cognitive psychology which transcend the predictive goal of folk psychology by proposing causal structures to account for behavior at the cognitive level. See Dennett (1987a, Chapter 3.) Cf. Yu and Fuller (1986). This distinction will have implications for the development of intentional behaviorism that are beyond the scope of the present essay.

References

Ajzen, I. (1985). From intentions to actions: a theory of planned behavior. In J. Kuhl and J. Beckman. (Eds.) *Action control: From cognition to behavior* (pp. 11–39). Berlin: Springer-Verlag.

Ajzen, I. (1987). Attitudes, traits, and actions: dispositional prediction of behavior in personality and social psychology. In L. Berkovitz (Ed.) *Advances in experimental social psychology, 20* (pp. 1–63). San Diego: Academic Press.

Ajzen, I. (1988). *Attitudes, personality and behavior.* Milton Keynes: Open University Press.

Ajzen, I. (1991). The theory of planned behavior. *Organizational Behavior and Human Decision Processes, 50,* 179–211.

Ajzen, I. & Fishbein, M. (1977). Attitude-behavior relations: a theoretical analysis and review of empirical research. *Psychological Bulletin, 84,* 888–918.

Ajzen, I. & Fishbein, M. (1980). *Understanding attitudes and predicting social behavior.* Englewood Cliffs, NJ: Prentice-Hall.

Alhadeff, D. A. (1982). *Microeconomics and human behavior.* Los Angeles, CA: University of California Press.

Allen, C. & Bekoff, M. (1997). *Species of mind: The philosophy and biology of cognitive ethology.* Cambridge, MA: MIT Press.

Amsel, A. (1989). *Behaviorism, neobehaviorism, and cognition in learning theory: Historical and contemporary perspectives.* Hillsdale, NJ: Erlbaum.

Angulo, M. C., Staiger, J. F., Rossier, J., & Audinat, E. (1999). Developmental synaptic changes increase the range of integrative capabilities of an identified neocortical connection. *Journal of Neuroscience, 19,* 1566–1576.

Anon. (1970). Status of the mental. *Times Literary Supplement,* 12 February, *3546,* p.152.

Anscombe, G. E. M. (1957). *Intention.* Oxford: Blackwell.

Audi, R. (1972). Review of Dennett: *Content and consciousness. Philosophy Forum, 12,* 206–208.

Baars, B. J. (2003). The double life of B. F. Skinner. *Journal of Consciousness Studies, 10,* 5–25.

Bagozzi, R. P. & Warshaw, P. R. (1990). Trying to consume. *Journal of Consumer Research, 17,* 127–140.

Bandura, A. (1986). *Social foundations of thought and action: A social cognitive theory.* Englewood Cliffs, NJ: Prentice-Hall.

Bandura, A. (1997). *Self-efficacy: The exercise of control.* New York: W. H. Freeman and Company.

Baum, W. (1973). The correlation based law of effect. *Journal of the Experimental Analysis of Behavior, 20,* 237–153.

Baum, W. (1994). *Understanding behaviorism: Science, behavior, and culture.* New York: HarperCollins.

Baum, W. (2000). Alive and kicking: A review of *Handbook of behaviorism. Journal of the Experimental Analysis of Behavior, 33,* 263–270.

Bechtel, W. (1978). Indeterminacy and intentionality: Quine's purported elimination of propositions. *Journal of Philosophy, 75,* 649–662.

Bechtel, W. (1988). *Philosophy of mind: An overview for cognitive science.* Hillsdale, NJ: Lawrence Erlbaum Associates.

Bem, D. (1972). Self-perception theory. In L. Berkovitz (Ed.) *Advances in experimental social psychology,* 6 (pp. 1–61). San Diego, CA: Academic Press.

Berridge, K. C. (2000). Reward learning: Reinforcement, incentives, and expectations. In D. L. Medin (Ed.) *The psychology of learning and motivation, 49* (pp. 223–278). San Diego: Academic Press.

Biglan, A. (1995). *Changing cultural practices: A contextualist framework for intervention research.* Reno, NV: Context Press.

Bindra, D. (1978). How adaptive behavior is produced: A perceptual–motivation alternative to response reinforcement. *Psychological Review, 81,* 199–213.

Blake, A. G. E. (1969). Review of *Content and consciousness* by D. C. Dennett. *Systematics, 7,* 261–3.

Bolles, R. C. (1972). Reinforcement, expectancy, and learning. *Psychological Review, 79,* 394–409.

Bolles, R. C. (1979). *Learning theory.* Second edition. New York: Holt, Rinehart and Winston.

Bouton, M. E. & Franselow, M. S. (Eds.) (1997). *Learning, motivation, and cognition: The functional behaviorism of Robert C. Bolles.* Washington, DC: American Psychological Association.

Bratman, M. E. (1994). Intention. In S. Guttenplan (Ed.) *A companion to the philosophy of mind* (pp. 375–379). Oxford: Blackwell.

Brentano, F. (1995). *Psychology from an empirical standpoint.* London and New York: Routledge. (First published, Leipzig, 1874).

Brewer, W. F. (1974). There is no convincing evidence for operant or classical conditioning in adult humans. In W. B. Weimer, & D. S. Palermo (Eds.) *Cognition and the symbolic processes* (pp. 1–42). Hillsdale, NJ: Erlbaum.

Broadbent, D. E. (1961). *Behavior.* London: Methuen. (Reprinted in 1986 by Greenwood Press, Westport, CT.)

Brook, A. & Ross, D. (Eds.) (2002). *Daniel Dennett.* Cambridge: Cambridge University Press.

Brown, J. R. (2001). *Who rules in science? An opinionated guide to the wars.* Cambridge, MA: Harvard University Press.

Bry, A. (1975). *A primer of behavioral psychology.* New York: NEL.

Burgos, J. E. & Donahoe, J. W. (2000). Structure and function in selectionism: Implications for complex behavior. In J. C. Leslie & D. Blackman (Eds.)

Experimental and applied analysis of human behavior (pp. 39–57). Reno, NV: Context Press.

Catania, A. C. (1992). *Learning*. Third edition. Englewood Cliffs, NJ: Prentice-Hall.

Catania, A. C. (1998). *Learning*. Fourth edition. Upper Saddle River, NJ: Prentice-Hall.

Catania, A. C. & Harnad, S. (Eds.) (1988). *The selection of behavior. The operant behaviorism of B. F. Skinner: Comments and consequences*. New York: Cambridge University Press.

Catania, A. C., Matthews, B. A., & Shimoff, E. (1982). Instructed versus shaped human verbal behavior: interactions with nonverbal responding. *Journal of the Experimental Analysis of Behavior, 38*, 233–248.

Chance, M. R. A. (1960). Köhler's chimpanzees—How did they perform? *Man, 60*, 130–135.

Chance, P. (1999). Where does behavior come from? A review of Epstein's *Cognition, creativity, and behavior. The Behavior Analyst, 22*. 161–163.

Cherniak, C. (1981). Minimal rationality. *Mind, 90*, 161–183.

Chisholm, R. (1957). *Perceiving: A philosophical study*. Ithaca, NY.

Chisholm, R. (1960). *Realism and the background of phenomenology*. Glencoe: The Free Press.

Chomsky, N. (1959). Review of Skinner's *Verbal behavior. Language 35*, 26–52.

Churchland, P. M. (1981). Eliminative materialism and the propositional attitudes. *Journal of Philosophy, 78*, 67–90.

Churchland, P. S. (1986). *Neurophilosophy: Toward a unified science of the mind/brain*. Cambridge, MA: MIT Press.

Dahlbom, B. (1993). *Dennett and his critics: Demystifying mind*. Oxford, UK and Cambridge, MA: Blackwell.

Dahlbom, B. (1993). Mind is artificial. In B. Dahlbom (Ed.), *Dennett and his critics* (pp. 161–83). Oxford: Blackwell.

Davey, G., C. L. & Cullen, C. (1988). (Eds.) *Human operant conditioning and behavior modification*. Chichester: Wiley.

Delprato, D. J. & Midgley, B. D. (1992). Some fundamentals of B. F. Skinner's behaviorism. *American Psychologist, 47*, 1507–1520.

Dennett, D. C. (1969). *Content and consciousness*. London: Routledge.

Dennett, D. C. (1978). *Brainstorms*. Montgomery, VT: Bradford.

Dennett, D. C. (1981). Three kinds of intentional psychology. In R. Healy (Ed.), *Reduction, time and reality*. Cambridge: Cambridge University Press. (Reproduced in Dennett, 1987a).

Dennett, D. C. (1982). How to study human consciousness empirically, or nothing comes to mind. *Synthese, 59*, 159–180.

Dennett, D. C. (1983). Intentional systems in cognitive ethology: The "Panglossian paradigm" defended. *The Behavioral and Brain Sciences, 6*, 343–390.

Dennett, D. C. (1987a). *The intentional stance*. Cambridge, MA: MIT Press.

Dennett, D. C. (1987b). Reflections: Interpreting monkeys, theorists, and genes. In D. C. Dennett, *The intentional stance* (pp. 269–286). Cambridge, MA: MIT Press.

Dennett, D. C. (1988). Out of the armchair and into the field. *Poetics Today, 9*, 205–221. (Reprinted in Dennett, D. C. (1998). *Brainchildren: Essays on designing minds.* Cambridge, MA: MIT Press.)

Dennett, D. C. (1991a). Real patterns. *Journal of Psychology, 88*, 27–51. (Reproduced in Dennett, 1998).

Dennett, D. C. (1991b). *Consciousness explained.* New York: Little, Brown and Co.

Dennett, D. C. (1994). Dennett, Daniel C. In S. Guttenplan (Ed.), *A companion to the philosophy of mind* (pp. 236–244). Oxford: Blackwell.

Dennett, D. C. (1995). *Darwin's dangerous idea: Evolution and the meanings of life.* New York: Simon and Shuster.

Dennett, D. C. (1996). *Kinds of minds: Toward an understanding of consciousness.* London: Weidenfeld and Nicolson.

Dennett, D. C. (1998). *Brainchildren: Essays on designing minds.* Cambridge, MA: MIT Press.

Dennett, D. C. (2003). *Freedom evolves.* London: Allen Lane.

Dennett, D. C. & Haugeland, J. C. (1987). Intentionality. In R. L. Gregory (Ed.), *The Oxford Companion to the Mind* (pp. 383–386). Oxford: Oxford University Press.

Dent, N. J. H. (1970). Review of Dennett: *Content and consciousness. Philosophical Quarterly, 20*, 403–404.

Deutsch, D. (1997). *The fabric of reality.* Harmondsworth: Penguin.

Deutsch, J. A. (1960). *The structural basis of behavior.* Chicago: Chicago University Press.

Dinsmoor, J. A. (1985). The role of observing and attention in establishing stimulus control. *Journal of the Experimental Analysis of Behavior, 43*, 365–381.

Donahoe, J. W. & Palmer, D. C. (1994). *Learning and complex behavior.* Boston, MA: Allyn and Bacon.

Donahoe, J. W., Palmer, D. C., & Burgos, J. E. (1997). The S-R issue: Its status in behavior analysis and in Donahoe and Palmer's *Learning and complex behavior. Journal of the Experimental Analysis of Behavior, 67*, 193–211.

Dretske, F. (1988). *Explaining behavior: Reasons in a world of causes.* Cambridge, MA: MIT Press.

Eagly, A. H. & Chaiken, S. (1993). *The psychology of attitudes.* Fort Worth, TX: Harcourt Brace Jovanovich.

Epstein, R., Kirshnit, C., Lanza, R., & Rubin, L. (1984). Insight in the pigeon: Antecedents and determinants of an intelligent performance. *Nature, 308*, 61–62.

Fazio, R. H. (1986). How do attitudes guide behavior? In R. M. Sorrentino & E. T. Higgins (Eds.), *Handbook of motivation and cognition: Foundations of social behavior* (pp. 204–243). Chichester: Wiley.

Fazio, R. H. (1989). On the power and functionality of attitudes: the role of attitude accessibility. In A. R. Pratkanis, A. J. Breckler, & A. G. Greenwald (Eds.), *Attitude structure and function* (pp. 153–180). Hillsdale, NJ: Erlbaum.

Fazio, R. H. (1990). Multiple processes by which attitudes guide behavior: the MODE model as an integrative framework. In M. P. Zanna (Ed.), *Advances in experimental social psychology, 23* (pp. 75–109). San Diego, CA: Academic Press.

Fazio, R. H. & Zanna, M. P. (1978a). Attitudinal qualities relating to the strength of the attitude-behavior relationship. *Journal of Experimental Social Psychology, 14*, 398–408.

Fazio, R. H. & Zanna, M. P. (1978b). On the predictive validity of attitudes: The roles of direct experience and confidence. *Journal of Personality, 46*, 228–43.

Fazio, R. H. & Zanna, M. P. (1981). Direct experience and attitude-behavior consistency. *Advances in experimental social psychology, 14*, 161–202.

Feyerabend, P. (1962). Explanation, reduction, and empiricism. In H. Feigl & G. Maxwell (Eds.), *Minnesota studies in the philosophy of science*. Minneapolis: University of Minnesota Press.

Feyerabend, P. (1970). Consolations for the specialist. In I. Lakatos & A. Musgrave (Eds.), *Criticism and the growth of knowledge* (pp. 197–230). Cambridge: Cambridge University Press.

Feyerabend, P. (1975). *Against method*. London: NLB.

Fishbein, M. (1972). The search for attitudinal-behavioral consistency. In J. S. Cohen (Ed.), *Behavioral science foundations of consumer behavior*. New York: Free Press.

Fishbein, M. & Ajzen, I. (1975). *Belief, attitude, intention and behavior*. Reading, MA: Addison-Wesley.

Flanagan, O. (1991). *The science of the mind*. Cambridge, MA: MIT Press.

Fodor, J. A. (1983). *The modularity of mind*. Cambridge, MA: MIT Press.

Fodor, J. A. (2000). *The mind doesn't work that way: The scope and limits of computational psychology*. Cambridge, MA: MIT Press.

Foxall, G. R. (1983). *Consumer choice*. London: Macmillan; New York: St. Martin's Press.

Foxall, G. R. (1990). *Consumer psychology in behavioral perspective*. London and New York: Routledge.

Foxall, G. R. (1994). Behavior analysis and consumer psychology. *Journal of Economic Psychology, 15*, 5–91.

Foxall, G. R. (1995). Science and interpretation in consumer research: a radical behaviourist perspective. *European Journal of Marketing, 29(9)*, 3–99.

Foxall, G. R. (1996). *Consumers in context: The BPM research program*. London and New York: International Thomson.

Foxall, G. R. (1997a). Explaining consumer behaviour: from social cognition to environmental control. In C. L. Cooper & I. T. Robertson (Eds.), *International review of industrial and organizational psychology, 12* (pp. 229–287). Chichester: Wiley.

Foxall, G. R. (1997b). *Marketing psychology: The paradigm in the wings*. London: Macmillan.

Foxall, G. R. (1997c). Affective responses to consumer situations. *International Review of Retail, Distribution and Consumer Research*, 7, 191–225.

Foxall, G. R. (1998). Radical behaviorist interpretation: Generating and Evaluating an account of consumer behavior. *The Behavior Analyst*, 21, 321–354.

Foxall, G. R. (1999). The contextual stance. *Philosophical Psychology*, 12, 25–46.

Foxall, G. R. (2002a). *Consumer behavior analysis: Critical perspectives*. London and New York: Routledge.

Foxall, G. R. (2002b). Marketing's attitude problem – and how to solve it. *Journal of Customer Behaviour*, 1, 19–48.

Foxall, G. R. & Greenley, G. E. (1998). The affective structure of consumer situations. *Environment and Behavior*, 30, 781–798.

Foxall, G. R. & Greenley, G. E. (1999). Consumers' emotional responses to service environments. *Journal of Business Research*, 46, 149–58.

Foxall, G. R. & Greenley, G. E. (2000). Predicting and explaining responses to consumer environments: An empirical test and theoretical extension of the Behavioural Perspective Model. *The Service Industries Journal*, 20, 39–63.

Foxall, G. R. & James, V. K. (2002). Behavior analysis of consumer brand choice: a preliminary analysis. *European Journal of Behavior Analysis*, 2, 209–220.

Foxall, G. R. & James, V. K. (2003). The behavioral ecology of brand choice: how and what do consumers maximize? *Psychology and Marketing*, 20, 811–836.

Foxall, G. R., Oliveira-Castro, J. M., & Schrezenmaier, T. C. (2004). The behavioral economics of consumer brand choice: Patterns of reinforcement and utility maximization. *Behavioural Processes* (in press).

Foxall, G. R. & Schrezenmaier, T. C. (2003). The behavioral economics of consumer brand choice: establishing a methodology. *Journal of Economic Psychology*, 24, 675–695.

Foxall, G. R. & Yani-de-Soriano, M. M. (2004). Situational influences on consumers' attitudes and behavior. *Journal of Business Research*, in press.

Franklin, R. L. (1970). Review of *Content and consciousness* by D. C. Dennett. *Australasian Journal of Philosophy*, 48, 264–73.

Garrett, R. (1996). Skinner's case for radical behaviorism. In W. O'Donohue & R. F. Kitchener (Eds.), *The Philosophy of Psychology* (pp. 141–148). London: Sage.

Gazzaniga, M. S., Ivry, R. B., & Mangun, G. R. (1998). *Cognitive neuroscience: The biology of the mind*. New York: W. W. Norton.

Griffin, D. R. (1976). *The question of animal awareness*. New York: Rockefeller University Press.

Gunderson, K. (1972). *Content and consciousness* and the mind-body problem. *Journal of Philosophy*, 69, 591–604.

Guttenplan, S. (1994). Intensional. In S. Guttenplan (Ed.), *A companion to the philosophy of mind* (pp. 374–375). Oxford: Blackwell.

Harman, G. (1998). Intentionality. In W. Bechtel & G. Graham (Eds.), *A companion to cognitive science* (pp. 602–610). Oxford: Blackwell.

Harzem, P. (2000). Toward a new behaviorism. *European Journal of Behavior Analysis, 1*, 51–60.

Hayes, L. J. & Ghezzi, P. M. (eds) (1997). *Investigations in behavioral epistemology.* Reno, NV: Context Press.

Hayes, S. C. (1986). The case of the silent dog–Verbal reports and the analysis of rules: A review of Ericsson and Simon's *Protocol analysis: Verbal reports as data. Journal of the Experimental Analysis of Behavior, 45*, 351–363.

Hayes, S. C. (Ed.) (1989). *Rule-governed behavior: Cognition, contingencies, and instructional control.* New York: Plenum.

Hayes, S. C. (1992). Verbal relations, time, and suicide. In S. C. Hayes & L. J. Hayes (Eds.), *Understanding verbal relations* (pp. 109–118). Reno, NV: Context Press.

Hayes, S. C. (1994). Relational frame theory: A functional approach to verbal events. In S. C. Hayes & L. J. Hayes (Eds.), *Behavior analysis of language and cognition* (pp. 9–29). Reno, NV. Context Press.

Hayes, S. C. (1997). Behavioral epistemology includes nonverbal knowing. In L. J. Hayes & P. M. Ghezzi (Eds.), *Investigations in behavioral epistemology* (pp. 35–43). Reno, NV: Context Press.

Hayes, S. C. & Brownstein, A. J. (1986). Mentalism, behavior-behavior relationships and the purpose of science. *The Behavior Analyst, 7*, 135–190.

Hayes, S. C. & Hayes, L. J. (1989). The verbal action of the listener as a basic for rule-governance. In S. C. Hayes (Ed.), *Rule-governed behavior: Cognition, contingencies, and instructional control* (pp. 153–190). New York: Plenum.

Hayes, S. C., Strosahl, K. D., & Wilson, K. G. (1999). *Acceptance and commitment therapy: An experiential approach to behavior change.* New York: The Guilford Press.

Hayes, S. C., Brownstein, A. J., Haas, J. R., & Greenway, D. E. (1986). Instructions, multiple schedules, and extinction: Distinguishing rule-governed from schedule controlled behavior. *Journal of the Experimental Analysis of Behavior, 46*, 137–47.

Hayes, S. C., Hayes, L. J., Reese, H. W., & Sarbin, T. R. (Eds.) (1993). *Varieties of scientific contextualism.* Reno, NV: Context Press.

Hayes, S. C., Barnes-Holmes, D., & Roche, B. (Eds.) (2001). *Relational frame theory: A post-Skinnerian account of human language and cognition.* New York: Kluwer Academic/Plenum.

Hayes, S. C., Wilson, K. G., & Gifford, E. V. (1999). Consciousness and private events. In B. A. Thyer (Ed.), *The philosophical legacy of behaviorism* (pp. 153–197). Dordrecht: Kluwer.

Hayes, S. C., Zettle, R. D., & Rosenfarb, I. (1989). Rule-following. In S. C. Hayes (Ed.), *Rule-governed behavior: Cognition, contingencies, and instructional control* (pp. 191–220). New York: Plenum.

Hefferline, R. F. (1962). Learning theory and clinical psychology: An eventual symbiosis? In A. J. Bachrach (Ed.), *Experimental foundations of clinical psychology* (pp. 97–138). New York: Basic Books.

Heil, J. (1998). *Philosophy of mind.* London and New York: Routledge.

Herrnstein, R. J. (1997). *The matching law: Papers in psychology and economics.* (Edited by H. Rachlin & D. I. Laibson) New York: Russell Sage Foundation; Cambridge, MA: Harvard University Press.

Horne, P. J. & Lowe, F. C. (1993). Determinants of human performance on concurrent schedules. *Journal of the Experimental Analysis of Behavior, 59,* 29–60.

Horne, P. J. & Lowe, F. C. (1996). On the origins of naming and other symbolic behavior. *Journal of the Experimental Analysis of Behavior, 65,* 185–241.

Horne, P. J. & Lowe, C. F. (1997). Toward a theory of verbal behavior. *Journal of the Experimental Analysis of Behavior, 68,* 271–296.

Hull, C. L. (1952). *A behavior system.* New Haven, CT: Yale University Press.

Kacelnik, A. (1993). Leaf-cutting ants tease optimal foraging theorists. *Trends in Ecology and Evolution, 8,* 346–348.

Kandel, E. R. (2001). The molecular biology of memory storage: A dialogue between genes and synapses. *Science, 294* (2 November), 1030–1038.

Kane, R. H. (1970). Review of Dennett: *Content and consciousness. Review of Metaphysics, 23,* 740–741.

Keller, F. S. (1958). The phantom plateau. *Journal of the Experimental Analysis of Behavior 1,* 1–13.

Kelley, J. S. (1990). Review of *Content and consciousness* (2nd edition). *Idealistic Studies, 20,* 83–84.

Kitchener, R. F. (1977). Behavior and behaviorism. *Behaviorism, 5,* 11–71.

Kitchener, R. F. (1979). Radical naturalism and radical behaviorism. *Scienta, 114,* 107–116.

Kitchener, R. F. (1996). Skinner's theory of theories. In W. O'Donohue & R. F. Kitchener (Eds.), *The philosophy of psychology* (pp. 108–125). London: Sage Publications.

Köhler, W. (1925). *The mentality of apes.* London: Routledge and Kegan Paul.

Kuhl, J. & Beckman, J. (Eds.) (1985). *Action control: From cognition to behavior.* Berlin: Springer-Verlag.

Lacey, H. M. (1995/1996). Behaviorisms: Theoretical and teleological: A review of John Staddon's *Behaviorism: Mind, mechanism and society,* and Rachlin's *Behavior and mind: The roots of modern psychology. Behavior and Philosophy, 23,* 61–78.

Lacey, H. M. & Schwartz, B. (1987). The explanatory power of radical behaviorism. In S. Modgil & C. Modgil (Eds.), *B. F. Skinner: Consensus and controversy* (pp. 165–176). New York: Falmer.

Leahey, T. H. (1987). *A history of psychology: Main currents in psychological thought.* Englewood Cliffs, NJ: Prentice-Hall.

Lee, V. L. (1988). *Beyond behaviorism.* London: Erlbaum.

MacCorquodale, K. & Meehl, P. R. (1954). Edward C. Tolman. In Estes, W. K., Koch, S., MacCorquodale, K., Meehl, P. E., Mueller, C. G., Schoenfield, W. N., & Verplanck, W. S., *Modern learning theory* (pp. 177–266). New York: Appleton–Century–Crofts.

McFarland, D. & Bösser, T. (1993). *Intelligent behavior in animals and robots.* Cambridge, MA: MIT Press.

MacKay, D. M. (1956). Toward an information flow model of human behavior. *British Journal of Psychology, XLVII,* 30–43.

Mackenzie, B. D. (1977). *Behaviorism and the limits of scientific method.* Atlantic Highlands, NJ: Humanities Press.

Mackenzie, B. (1988). The challenge to Skinner's theory of behavior. In A. C. Catania & S. Harnad (Eds.), *The selection of behavior. The operant behaviorism of B. F. Skinner: Comments and consequences* (pp . 111–113). New York: Cambridge University Press.

McKim, V. R. (1970). Review of *Content and consciousness* by D. C. Dennett. *New Scholasticism, 44,* 272.

Malcolm, N. (1977). Behaviorism as a philosophy of psychology. In N. Malcolm, *Thought and knowledge.* (pp. 85–103.) Ithaca, NY: Cornell University Press. First published in T. W. Wann (Ed.) (1964). *Behaviorism and phenomenology: Contrasting bases for modern psychology* (pp. 141–162). Chicago: University of Chicago Press.

Malott, R. W. (1986). Self-management, rule-governed behavior, and everyday life. In H. W. Reese & L. J. Parrott (Eds.), *Behavior science: Philosophical, methodological and empirical advances* (pp. 207–228). Hillsdale, NJ: Lawrence Erlbaum.

Malott, R. W. (1989). The achievement of evasive goals: control by rules describing contingencies that are not direct acting. In S. C. Hayes (Ed.), *Rule-governed behavior: Cognition, contingencies, and instructional control* (pp. 269–324). New York: Plenum.

Malott, R. W. & Malott, M. E. (1992). Private events and rule-governed behavior. In L. J. Hayes & P. N. Chase (Eds.), *Dialogues on verbal behavior* (pp. 237–254). Reno, NV: Context Press.

Michael, J. (1982). Distinguishing between discriminative and motivational functions of stimuli. *Journal of the Experimental Analysis of Behavior, 37,* 149–155.

Michael, J. (1993). Establishing operations. *The Behavior Analyst, 16,* 191–206.

Midgley, B. D. & Morris, E. K. (1998). Nature-nurture in Skinner's behaviorism. *Mexican Journal of Behavior Analysis, 24,* 111–126.

Mill, J. S. (1859). On liberty. In Mill, J. S. *Utilitarianism, liberty and representative government.* London: Dent.

Moore, J. (1998). On behaviorism, theories, and hypothetical constructs. *The Journal of Mind and Behavior, 19,* 2115–42.

Moore, J. (1999). The basic principles of behaviorism. In B. Thyler (Ed.), *The philosophical legacy of behaviorism* (pp. 41–68). Dordrecht: Kluwer Academic Publishers.

Nagel, T. (1995). Dennett: Content and Consciousness. In T. Nagel, *Other minds: Critical essays 1969–1994* (pp. 82–85). New York: Oxford University Press. First published in *The Journal of Philosophy*, *69*, 1972, 220–224.

Ostrom, Thomas (1994). Foreword. In *Handbook of social cognition. Vol. I: Basic processes* (pp. vii–xii). Hillsdale, NJ and Hove, UK: Lawrence Erlbaum Associates.

Overskeid, G. (1995). Cognitive or behaviourist – Who can tell the difference? *British Journal of Psychology*, *86*, 517–22.

Parrott, L. J. (1986). The role of postulation in the analysis of inapparent events. In H. W. Reese & L. J. Parrott (Eds.), *Behavior science: Philosophical, methodological, and empirical advances* (pp. 35–60). Erlbaum, Hillsdale, NJ.

Pepper, S. C. (1942). *World hypotheses: A study in evidence*. Berkeley: University of California Press.

Perry, J. (1994). Intentionality (2). In S. Guttenplan (Ed.), *A companion to the philosophy of mind* (pp. 386–395). Oxford: Blackwell.

Philosophical Topics (1994). The Philosophy of Daniel Dennett. *Philosophical Topics 22(1&2)*, 1–568.

Pinker, S. (1997). *How the mind works*. London: Allen Lane.

Plotkin, H. (1997). *Evolution in mind*. London: Allen Lane.

Posner, R. A. (1990). *The problems of jurisprudence*. Cambridge, MA: Harvard University Press.

Posner, R. A. (1995). *Overcoming law*. Cambridge, MA: Harvard University Press.

Prelec, D. & Herrnstein, R. J. (1991). Preferences or principles: Alternative guidelines for choice. In R. J. Zeckhausser (Ed.), *Strategy and choice*. Cambridge, MA: MIT press.

Quine, W. V. O. (1960). *Word and object*. Cambridge, MA: MIT Press.

Quine, W. V. O. (1969). *Ontological relativity and other essays*. New York: Columbia University Press.

Rachlin, H. (1974). Self-control. *Behaviorism*, *2*, 94–107.

Rachlin, H. (1989). *Judgment, decision, and choice: A cognitive/behavioral synthesis*. San Francisco, CA: Freeman.

Rachlin, H. (1994). *Behavior and mind: The roots of modern psychology*. New York: Oxford University Press.

Rachlin, H. (2000). Teleological behaviorism. In W. O'Donohue & R. Kitchener (Eds.), *Handbook of behaviorism* (pp. 195–215). San Diego: Academic Press.

Rachlin, H., Battalio, R., Kagel, J., & Green, L. (1981). Maximization theory in behavioral psychology. *The Behavioral and Brain Sciences*, *4*, 371–417.

Rajecki, D. W. (1982). *Attitudes: Themes and advances*. Sunderland, MA: Sinauer Associates.

Reese, H, W. (1986). On the theory and practice of behavior analysis. In H. W. Reese & L. J. Parrott (Eds.), *Behavior science: Philosophical, methodological, and empirical advances* (pp. 1–34). Hillsdale, NJ: Lawrence Erlbaum Associates.

Rice, Z. C. (1971). Review of Dennett: *Content and consciousness*. *Modern Schoolman*, *48*, 177–178.

Ringen, J. (1976). Explanation, teleology, and operant behaviorism: a study of the experimental analysis of purposive behavior. *Philosophy of Science, 43*, 223–253.

Ringen, J. (1999). Radical behaviorism: B. F. Skinner's Philosophy of Science. In W. O'Donohue & R. Kitchener (Eds.), *Handbook of behaviorism* (pp. 159–178). San Diego: Academic Press.

Rosenberg, A. (1988). *Philosophy of social science*. Oxford: Clarendon.

Ross, D., Brook, A., & Thompson, D. (Eds.) (2000). *Dennett's philosophy: A comprehensive assessment*. Cambridge, MA: MIT Press.

Rumbaugh, D. M. (1995). Emergence of relations and the essence of learning: A review of Sidman's *Equivalence relations and behavior: A research story. The Behavior Analyst, 18*, 365–375.

Rumbaugh, D. M. (1997). The psychology of H. F. Harlow: A bridge from radical to rational behaviorism. *Philosophical Psychology, 10*, 197–210.

Russell, B. (1940). *An inquiry into meaning and truth*. London: George Allen and Unwin.

Ryle, G. (1949). *The concept of mind*. London: Hutchinson.

Scheerer, E. (1996). Radical behaviorism: Excerpts from a textbook treatment. In L. D. Smith & W. R. Woodward (Eds.), *B. F. Skinner and behaviorism in American culture* (pp. 151–175). Bethlehem: Lehigh University Press; London: Associated University Presses.

Schnaitter, R. (1988). "Behaviorism at fifty" at twenty. In A. C. Catania & S. Harnad (Eds.), *The selection of behavior. The operant behaviorism of B. F. Skinner: Comments and consequences* (pp. 353–4). New York: Cambridge University Press.

Schnaitter, R. (1999). Some criticisms of behaviorism. In B. A. Thyer (Ed.), *The philosophical legacy of behaviorism* (pp. 209–249). Dordrecht: Kluwer.

Schoenfield, W. N. & Cumming, W. W. (1963). Behavior and perception. In S. Koch (Ed.), *Psychology: The study of a science: Vol. 5. The process areas, the person, and some fields: Their place in psychology and in science* (pp. 213–245). New York: McGraw-Hill.

Schwartz, B. & Lacey, H. (1982). *Behaviorism, science, and human nature*. New York: Norton.

Schwartz, B. & Lacey, H. (1988). What applied studies of human operant conditioning tell us about humans and about operant conditioning. In G. Davey & C. Cullen (Eds.), *Human operant conditioning and behavior modification* (pp. 27–42). Chichester: Wiley.

Searle, J. (1981). Intentionality and method. *Journal of Philosophy, 78*, 720–733.

Searle, J. (1983). *Intentionality: An essay in the philosophy of mind*. Cambridge: Cambridge University Press.

Searle, J. (1994). Intentionality (1). In S. Guttenplan (Ed.), *A companion to the philosophy of mind* (pp. 379–386). Oxford: Blackwell.

Searle, J. (1999). *Mind, language and society: Philosophy in the real world*. London: Weidenfeld and Nicolson.

Seyfarth, R. M. & Cheney, D. L. (2002). Dennett's contribution to research on the animal mind. In A. Brook & D. Ross (Eds.), *Daniel Dennett* (pp. 117–139). Cambridge: Cambridge University Press.

Sheppard, B. H., Hartwick, J., & Warshaw, P. R. (1988). The theory of reasoned action: a meta-analysis of past research with recommendations for modifications and future research. *Journal of Consumer Research, 15,* 325–343.

Shettleworth, S. J. (1998). *Cognition, evolution, and behavior.* Oxford: Oxford University Press.

Shull, R. L. (1995). Interpreting cognitive phenomena: Review of Donahoe and Palmer's *Learning and complex behavior. Journal of the Experimental Analysis of Behavior, 63,* 347–358.

Sidman , M. (1989). *Coercion and its fallout.* Cambridge, MA: Authors Cooperative.

Sidman, M. (1994). *Equivalence relations and behavior: A research story.* Boston, MA: Authors Cooperative.

Skinner, B. F. (1945). The operational analysis of psychological terms. *Psychological Review, 52,* 270–277.

Skinner, B. F. (1948). *Walden two.* New York: Macmillan.

Skinner, B. F. (1950). Are theories of learning necessary? *Psychological Review, 57,* 193–216.

Skinner, B. F. (1953). *Science and human behavior.* New York: Macmillan.

Skinner, B. F. (1956). A case history in scientific method. *American Psychologist, 32,* 221–233.

Skinner, B. F. (1957). *Verbal behavior.* New York: Appleton-Century-Crofts.

Skinner, B. F. (1963). Behaviorism at fifty. *Science, 140,* 951–8.

Skinner, B. F. (1969a). *Contingencies of reinforcement.* New York: Appleton-Century-Crofts.

Skinner, B. F. (1969b). An operant analysis of problem solving. In B. F. Skinner, *Contingencies of reinforcement.* New York: Appleton-Century-Crofts.

Skinner, B. F. (1971). *Beyond freedom and dignity.* New York: Knopf.

Skinner, B. F. (1973). Answers for my critics. In H. Wheeler (Ed.), *Beyond the punitive society* (pp. 256–266). San Francisco, CA: Freeman.

Skinner, B. F. (1974). *About behaviorism.* New York: Knopf.

Skinner, B. F. (1977). Why I am not a cognitive psychologist. *Behaviorism, 5,* 1–10.

Skinner, B. F. (1981). Selection by consequences. *Science, 213* (31 July), 501–504.

Skinner, B. F. (1988a). Reply to Schnaitter. In A. C. Catania & S. Harnad (Eds.), *The selection of behavior. The operant behaviorism of B. F. Skinner: Comments and consequences* (p. 354). New York: Cambridge University Press.

Skinner, B. F. (1988b). Reply to Mackenzie. In A. C. Catania & S. Harnad (Eds.), *The selection of behavior. The operant behaviorism of B. F. Skinner: Comments and consequences* (pp. 113–114). New York: Cambridge University Press.

Skinner, B. F. (1988c). Reply to Stalker and Ziff. In A. C. Catania & S. Harnad (Eds.), *The selection of behavior. The operant behaviorism of B. F. Skinner: Comments and consequences* (pp. 207–8). New York: Cambridge University Press.

Skinner, B. F. (1988d). Reply to Zuriff. In A. C. Catania & S. Harnad (Eds.), *The selection of behavior. The operant behaviorism of B. F. Skinner: Comments and consequences* (p. 217). New York: Cambridge University Press.

Skinner, B. F. (1988e). Reply to Stich. In A. C. Catania & S. Harnad (Eds.), *The selection of behavior. The operant behaviorism of B. F. Skinner: Comments and consequences* (pp. 364–365). New York: Cambridge University Press.

Smart, J. C. (1970). Critical notice: *Content and consciousness. Mind, 79,* 616–623.

Smith, L. D. (1986). *Behaviorism and logical positivism: A reassessment of the alliance.* Stanford, CA: Stanford University Press.

Smith, L. D. & Woodward, W. R. (Eds.) (1996). *B. F. Skinner and behaviorism in American culture.* Bethlehem: Lehigh University Press; London: Associated University Presses.

Smith, T. L. (1994). *Behavior and its causes: Philosophical foundations of operant psychology.* Dordrecht: Kluwer.

Soriano, M. Y. & Foxall, G. R. (2002). Emotional responses to consumers' environments: An empirical examination of the Behavioural Perspective Model in a Latin American context. *Journal of Consumer Behaviour, 2,* 138–154.

Staats, A. W. (1996). *Behavior and personality: Psychological behaviorism.* New York: Springer.

Staddon, J. E. R. (2001a). *Adaptive dynamics: The theoretical analysis of behavior.* Cambridge, MA: MIT Press.

Staddon, J. E. R. (2001b). *The new behaviorism.* Philadelphia, PA: Psychology Press.

Staddon, J. E. R. & Cerutti, D. T. (2003). Operant conditioning. *Annual Review of Psychology, 54,* 115–144.

Stalker, D. & Ziff, P. (1988). Skinner's theorizing. In A. C. Catania & S. Harnad (Eds.), *The selection of behavior. The operant behaviorism of B. F. Skinner: Comments and consequences* (pp. 206–207). New York: Cambridge University Press.

Stich, S. P. (1981). Dennett on intentional systems. *Philosophical Topics, 12,* 39–62.

Stich, S. P. (1983). *From folk psychology to cognitive science.* Cambridge, MA: MIT Press.

Stout, R. (1996). *Things that happen because they should: A teleological approach to action.* Oxford: Clarendon Press.

Symons, J. (2002). *On Dennett.* Belmont, CA: Wadsworth/Thomson Learning.

Thyer, B. (Ed.) (1999). *The philosophical legacy of behaviorism.* Dordrecht: Kluwer Academic Publishers.

Toates, F. (1986). *Motivational systems.* Cambridge: Cambridge University Press.

Tolman, C. (1932). *Purposive behavior in animals and men.* New York: Appleton Century.

Valentine, E. R. (1992). *Conceptual issues in psychology.* London and New York: Routledge.

Van den Putte, B. (1993). *On the theory of reasoned action.* Unpublished doctoral dissertation. University of Amsterdam.

Vaughan, M. (1989). Rule-governed behavior in behavior analysis: A theoretical and experimental history. In S. C. Hayes (Ed.), *Rule-governed behavior: Cognition, contingencies, and instructional control* (pp. 97–118). New York: Plenum Press.

Viger, C. (2000). Where do Dennett's stances stand? Explaining our kind of mind. In D. Ross, A. Brook, & D. Thompson (Eds.), *Dennett's philosophy: A comprehensive assessment* (pp. 131–145). Cambridge, MA and London: MIT Press.

Watson, J. B. (1913). Psychology as the behaviorist views it. *Psychological Review, 20*, 158–177.

Webb, S. (1994). Witnessed behavior and Dennett's intentional stance. *Philosophical Topics, 22*, 457–470.

Wicker, A. W. (1969). Attitudes versus actions: The relationship of verbal and overt behavioral responses to attitude objects. *Social Issues, 25*, 41–78.

Yu, P. and Fuller, G. (1986). A critique of Dennett. *Synthese, 66*, 453–476.

Zettle, R. D. & Hayes, S. C. (1982). Rule-governed behavior: a potential framework for cognitive-behavioral therapy. In P. C. Kendall (Ed.), *Advances in cognitive-behavioral research and therapy* (pp. 73–117). Academic Press, New York.

Zuriff, G. R. (1979). Ten inner causes. *Behaviorism, 7*, 1–8.

Zuriff, G. R. (1985). *Behaviorism: A conceptual reconstruction*. New York: Columbia University Press.